A CONSIDERATION OF
THACKERAY
By GEORGE SAINTSBURY

NEW YORK / RUSSELL & RUSSELL

FIRST PUBLISHED IN 1931

REISSUED, 1968, BY RUSSELL & RUSSELL

A DIVISION OF ATHENEUM HOUSE, INC.

BY ARRANGEMENT WITH THE ESTATE OF GEORGE SAINTSBURY

L. C. CATALOG CARD NO: 68-15158

PRINTED IN THE UNITED STATES OF AMERICA

PREFACE

The text following is composed of the Introductions to the Oxford Edition of Thackeray (1908) with a very few corrections which Time and Chance have made desirable.

As for the Introductions, biographical matter—except in so far as it is mainly connected with individual works—will be mainly found in the first; general critical matter in the first and last. But an attempt was made to connect all—biographically and critically—chapter-fashion, so that the series should not be merely a string of separate essays but a continuous story. Thackeray's many-sidedness is so great that there can hardly be too many such studies of him. In the present case the study had at least one justification—it was of an author who had been, for nearly forty years, more frequently in the hands, and more constantly in the head and heart of the student, than any other in prose and almost than any other in rhyme. I did not neglect those who have written on him already—I owe them much, and I hope that I have not drawn on them too unceremoniously; but I endeavoured to draw chiefly on Thackeray himself.

G. S.

CONTENTS

A CONSIDERATION OF
THACKERAY

I

BIOGRAPHY—THE YELLOWPLUSH PAPERS, &c.

WILLIAM MAKEPEACE THACKERAY was born on July 18, 1811. His birthplace was Calcutta, where his father, Richmond Thackeray (of a Yorkshire family which had been long connected with Cambridge and India), was a civil servant in high position. His mother, Anne Becher, was a beauty and quite young, while his father was but just thirty, when Thackeray was born. He died when the boy was five years old, and next year (in 1817) William Makepeace, like all Indian children of those days, was sent home to be taken care of, in his case by an aunt. His mother did not accompany him; and in the following year married, as her second husband, Major Carmichael-Smyth. But Thackeray was no deserted orphan, and Mrs. Smyth was no unnatural mother. It is an accepted fact that Helen Pendennis owes not a little to her; and though the Major proved in some respects a 'sair step-father' to the boy, it was only because he shared the weaknesses as well as the virtues of Colonel Newcome. There were no children of the second marriage, and Thackeray, his mother (who actually survived him), and his step-father (who lived nearly as long as he did), appear to have been always on the most affectionate terms.

When the Smyths returned from India in 1821, the Major becoming superintendent at Addiscombe, Thackeray went to divers preparatory schools, which he does not seem to have enjoyed. In 1822 he was transferred to Charterhouse, where he stayed till 1828, had his nose broken by George Stovin Venables (afterwards a famous

Parliamentary barrister and *Saturday* reviewer), made
divers friends, began the practice of comic drawing and
novel-writing, but seems to have been made more
unhappy than—from *Pendennis*—one would imagine, by
the pedagogic objurgations of Dr. Russell, the head
master. His holidays were latterly spent at the original
of 'Fairoaks'—that is to say, Larkbeare, a Devonshire
house a mile or so from Ottery (Clavering) St. Mary,
and within easy reach of Sidmouth (Baymouth) and
Exeter (Chatteris). He was entered at Trinity College,
Cambridge, and went up in February, 1829; but his
stay was short, for he took no degree, and went down
at the end of Easter term, 1830, ostensibly on the excuse
that 'the studies would be of no use to him'. He seems
to have spent more money than he should, which is not
unexampled; but he contributed to the *Snob* (the most
certain and notable contribution being his famous mock
prize poem on *Timbuctoo*) and its successor, the *Gownsman*, and he spoke a little at the Union. Also he made,
directly or indirectly (for some of those to be named
he did not know *at* Cambridge), a memorable circle of
friends—Brookfield, FitzGerald, J. H. Kemble, King-
lake, Milnes, and, above all, Tennyson.

He was hardly older when he left Cambridge than
many men are now when they go up, and he was in the
perilous position of possessing a considerable fortune—it
is said some £20,000. In less than four years—by
February, 1834—this was all or nearly all gone, nobody
seems to know exactly how, though there are partial
indications in his works. It is known on indisputable
authority that the Deuceace-Dawkins episode in the
Yellowplush Papers is from life, and that he himself was
Dawkins; but the sum was £1,500, not £5,000. He is
said, on less certain but fair testimony, to have 'given'

or 'paid' Maginn £500 for some probably illusory literary service that 'Captain Shandon' was to render. He certainly, like Pendennis, ran into debt at Cambridge; but as even Pen in three whole years attained to but £700, his creator can hardly have piled up more in half the time. He admits that he lost £200 (which seems very little) on the first year of the *National Standard*, a paper which he bought in 1833, and as it went on rather longer he probably lost more; but if any one will add these various sums together, he will find that they represent but a very small fraction of £20,000. Indeed, a variant of tradition puts his inheritance at '£500 a year', which will at very low interest represent a much smaller original sum. Still, the 'Bundelcund Bank' seems to have reproduced another unfortunate reality. Major Carmichael-Smyth appears to have resembled his great antitype in nothing more than in his tendency to speculate with his own and other people's money; and it would probably be found that the firm of 'Brough and Hoff', the 'Diddlesex Junction', and other sardonic comicalities had, like Rummun Loll's bubble, their representatives on the actual earth. At any rate, by the date mentioned, his money was to be earned.

He had, as it happened, already hit on the right way to earn it, though he was to be long before he was well set in that way, and was to make serious mistakes in it. The way was that of 'Our Own Correspondent', as Warrington puts it to Pendennis—in other words, literature and journalism—with at first a strong bent towards actual 'Foreign Correspondence'. He always had a great liking for foreign travel, and had spent part of his only Cambridge long vacation in Paris. After he had left the University for good, he set out for Germany, in the latter part of 1830, and made a long residence at

Weimar, where he saw Goethe, and dabbled a good deal in art and letters. The visit was fertile in after-results. For the moment, however, he fell in with his family's wish—that he should read for the Bar—returned to England in 1831, and took chambers in the Temple by the autumn of that year.

But Thackeray could never have been a lawyer, and in a year or two (the dates do not seem to be quite certain) he gave up the attempt. He was an associate of Charles Buller, assisting him in his Liskeard election during the Reform campaign, and he made the acquaintance, 'good, but expensive,' of Maginn. In pursuance of the generally fatal idea that a journalist should be his own 'proprietor', he bought from F. W. N. ('Alphabet') Bayley, a typical pressman of his time, the above-mentioned *National Standard* in January, 1833, and went to Paris as its correspondent. When it failed, he made up his mind to continue in Paris and study art. He had drawn—as Mr. Pendennis spoke French—'from his youth up', and somewhat in the same way, though much better. He did not cut himself off from his family; for though his mother and step-father, having left Devonshire, were now living in London, his aunt on his father's, and his grandmother on the mother's side were living in Paris.

Nor while studying art did he give up literature. As early as the beginning of 1835 he appears in Maclise's famous group of convivial *Fraserians*, though no contribution of his to the magazine before that time, save a version of Béranger, is positively known.[1] Next year he made his well-known and authentic application to Dickens to illustrate *Pickwick*, and brought out the curious collections of satire-sketches on the ballet called

[1] As for 'Elizabeth Brownrigge', *v. inf.*

Flore et Zéphyr. For a moment there appeared to be a chance of his being what his French friends would have called *casé.* His enterprising step-father joined some more distinguished Radicals in buying (on the encouragement of the lowering of the newspaper stamp duty) a paper called the *Public Ledger,* rechristened it (with some humour) the *Constitutional,* and got Thackeray appointed Paris correspondent at eight guineas a week. On this salary—in round numbers £400 a year—he married a young Irish lady, Miss Isabella Shawe, on August 20, 1836. But the *Constitutional* had no more luck than the *National Standard,* and failed after little more than six months' run. The loss was heavy—in Thackeray's own case his whole fixed income, in Major Smyth's probably capital as well. The Major went to Paris, changing places with Thackeray, who came to London, established himself in Great Coram Street (a street long since gone to seed, but then a sufficiently well reputed abode for professional men), and wrote hard and widely. A casual piece of evidence in Fitzpatrick's *Life of Lever* shows that even later, and by those who already appreciated his powers, he was thought to 'hack' them too much; but he had as yet no backbone of regular employment on daily or weekly papers, such as is invaluable and almost essential to the journalist. He did some work for *The Times,* including a 'young' but good review of Carlyle's *French Revolution,* which the author received as authors too often do. And he now became—whatever his relations with it had been earlier—a pillar of *Fraser,* contributing reviews of art and letters very largely, as well as some far more important things—ranging from *The Yellowplush Correspondence* of 1838 through *Catherine* (next year and 1840), *The Hoggarty Diamond* (1841), and the 'Fitzboodle' varieties (1842–3), up to *Barry Lyndon* (1844).

But hard, precarious, and not too well paid work was not his only misfortune. His wife and he appear to have been perfectly happy together as far as they were allowed to be, and a reference to her in *The Ballad of Bouillabaisse* is one of the most pathetic things that we have from one of the greatest English masters of pathos. They had three daughters, the first and third of whom lived, while the second died an infant. It was subsequently to the birth of the third (May, 1840), and it may be supposed in consequence of it, that Mrs. Thackeray developed symptoms of mental disorder, which, after some vicissitudes, settled into complete though quiet derangement about two years later. She lived for half a century, surviving her husband nearly thirty years: but she never recovered, and his home was, for the time, completely broken up.

The old superstition, however, about luck in love and other things did not wholly discredit itself. *Punch* was started in 1841, and a year later Thackeray became, first an occasional, and then a regular contributor, both with letterpress and sketches. These contributions include some of his worst and some of his best work—even *The Book of Snobs* containing both. The papers, however, of which this is composed were not begun till 1846, nor published together till the end of the next year.

But meanwhile Thackeray had already put on record collections of his earlier work. In 1840, besides a separate reprint of the *Westminster Review* essay on Cruikshank, appeared *The Paris Sketch Book*; in 1841 *Comic Tales and Sketches* (representing especially the trio Titmarsh, Gahagan, Yellowplush), and *The Second Funeral of Napoleon*. A journey to Ireland, which he made in 1842, was recorded in *The Irish Sketch Book* next year;

while a longer one to the East in 1844 received a similar chronicle in *From Cornhill to Cairo* two years later.

For three years (1843-6) he had no fixed abode—at least, house. But in the last-mentioned year he once more established himself, with his daughters, and at first with his own grandmother, at 13 Young Street, Kensington, a house with a double 'waistcoat', or bow-windowed front, which became known as his to all dwellers round Kensington Gardens in the early fifties. Here he finished *Vanity Fair*, which had been begun, it is said, five years earlier, but dropped; and here, at last, luck came to him. As far as mere immediate popularity went, it was not brought so much by the great novel itself as by the *Snob Papers*, which were running contemporaneously, and by the delightful Christmas book of *Mrs. Perkins's Ball*—the first of a series with which he met the current taste for these things. Indeed, it is said that, by an irony of quite his own kind, it was the *Ball* which really made his position. He took care, however, to maintain it, and but two or three months passed between the last monthly number of *Vanity Fair* in the summer, and the first of *Pendennis* in the autumn, of 1848. He had always been socially given, and was a man of many friends: so that he was neither specially bored nor 'turned in the head' by lionizing. In this same year he was called to the Bar, and may have looked for some appointment. He expresses himself in more than one place (though with something of his usual inconsistency) on the contrast between English habits and those of other countries in this matter. But no 'place with a pinsion' came to him, and it may be permitted to his very greatest admirers to think that this was really best, both for him and for the 'place' (unless it had been a complete sinecure), as well as for literature. For he was not very methodical; he was, though a hard, an irregular and intermittent worker; he was somewhat crotchety, and he was very nervous and sensitive. As a police magistrate especially—the position usually mentioned—he would probably have worried himself into a fever in a fortnight, and half his decisions would have had to be, in some way or other, reversed.

Despite his gigantic frame, he was never a strong man, and *Pendennis*, as its dedication and, in fact, its text records, was interrupted by a very serious illness late in 1849. Indeed, this has been thought to have been the beginning of the end, though others date the final inroad on his constitution from his attack of Roman fever in the winter of 1853–4. Physical weakness, however ('all things are double, one against another'), was tempered by pecuniary prosperity, and he was able, and probably not sorry, to give up regular contribution to *Punch*.

Among the profitable fashions for literary men of the first half of the century was lecturing. It had been already justified, by more than profit, in divers cases, from Coleridge to Carlyle; but it found an additional justification in Thackeray's *English Humourists*, a course of six, which was first delivered in the early summer of 1851. Still, for 'details' (as Anthony Trollope, with humour worthy of his editor, has styled the pecuniary part of the matter), America has always been the Eldorado of the lecturer: and next year he sought it with this cargo, having in the interval written and published *Esmond*—to some, perhaps, his very greatest book. He spent the winter and early spring of 1852–3 in the States —Southern as well as Northern—with excellent results both in 'details', and in friendships, and in new atmosphere and materials. Later in 1853, he went to Switzerland, conceived *The Newcomes* 'in a wood near Berne',

published it in numbers from the autumn of the year
to the summer of 1855, and made £4,000 by it. The
Christmas visit of 1853 to Rome had resulted (compensation again!), besides the fit of fever above referred to,
in *The Rose and the Ring*—another 'furthest' of his in one
direction. It was published in 1854, during which year
he moved from Young Street to Onslow Square. After
finishing *The Newcomes* he once more went to the United
States, taking with him, as lectures, *The Four Georges*,
which were subsequently given at home, and therefore
not published till they appeared in the *Cornhill* during
1860, and as a volume next year. When he returned to
England in the spring of 1856 'there was no [longer any]
mistake about [this] fellow', to adopt one of his phrases
which sticks fastest in the minds of his lovers.

But a master of irony always exhibits it in his own
person, and it was *after* Thackeray had depicted Colonel
Newcome's Parliamentary adventure that he actually
imitated it. The reminiscences of personal experience in
his work are unmistakable, though they may be, and
have been, exaggerated. Here was an anticipation of it.
He stood for Oxford, with a very Colonel Newcome-like
programme, in the summer of 1857, and was but
narrowly beaten by Mr. Cardwell. Then he settled to
The Virginians, and covered the usual two years with its
appearances in numbers. When it was half-way through
there occurred an incident which has had rather disproportionate attention in accounts of Thackeray's life,
but which, for that very reason, cannot be entirely
neglected. The late Mr. Edmund Yates, in his character
of pioneer (or rather reviver) of personal journalism,
wrote in 1858 an account of Thackeray which its subject keenly resented. Both were members of the Garrick
Club, before which Thackeray brought the matter, with

the result that Yates had to leave it. Unfortunately, Dickens, who had previously been on friendly terms with Thackeray, and had presided at a dinner given to him when he left for America the second time, was a friend of Yates's, acted as a sort of second to him, and so brought about an estrangement which only ceased just before Thackeray's death. He had better not have meddled with the matter, for Yates was quite inexcusable. But Thackeray's own conduct was not wholly wise. It is fair to say that Yates, in his *Autobiography*, made some amends, especially by telling a delightful and characteristic story of Thackeray. They were, it seems, before the rupture, walking together, and saw two tubs of oysters marked one shilling and fifteen-pence respectively. '*How* they must hate the others!'[1] said Thackeray, pointing clearly to the twelvepenny group.

His days, after the conclusion of *The Virginians*, towards the end of 1859, were few; but they were far from evil. At the beginning of the next year the *Cornhill Magazine* appeared under his editorship, and at once attained enormous success. He only edited it for rather more than two years, heartily disliking that employment or vocation; but he contributed steadily till the day of his death. The novels thus contributed—at least, the first two, *Lovel the Widower* and *Philip*, for the third and unfinished *Denis Duval* promised greatly—did not *raise* his reputation, though no one else could have written them; but the *Roundabout Papers* were once more, and for the last time, the consummate and unique work of a unique and consummate genius. Once more he changed abodes, building himself a Queen Anne house at the bottom of Kensington Palace Gardens. It was finished early in 1862: but Death did not 'come in at the

[1] Yates says 'each other', which is inept.

window', as the grim proverb has it, till the end of the next year. On the morning of Christmas Eve, 1863, he was found dead from effusion on the brain. He was buried, not in Westminster Abbey, but in Kensal Green Cemetery. A 'monumental bust', however, represents him among his peers.

Any remarks that may seem desirable about the higher and more general traits of his character, personal and literary, will probably be better kept for the last chapter; but a few of the lighter may be given here. Although Thackeray seems to have had no fancy for any kind of sport, he was particularly fond of riding, and even when he was pretty badly off succeeded in proving to his own satisfaction, and (inasmuch as the proofs which exist in his letters are characteristic and diverting) to ours, that it was the truest economy to keep a horse. He was also one of those men—not by any means always, and certainly not in his case, examples of selfish extravagance—who are miserable without a manservant: and here also his epistolary self-justifications are extremely amusing. This was one of his numerous links with the eighteenth century, when no gentleman—even of the most modest means or in the most disastrous circumstances—seems to have been able to dispense with a 'follower'. He liked to live well, and here, again, and in greater measure, the liking is justified in its literary expression. His 'gormandizing' papers are among the very best of his second-best things; and, indeed, he and Walker of *The Original* (who was, perhaps, to some extent his teacher) may be said to have revolutionized the theory of English dinners —not by any means in the silly direction of merely Frenchifying them. His opinions on wine were singularly just and accomplished. There are, it is to be hoped, more persons than one who never drank a glass of '58 claret ('while it was day') without remembering how he asked, 'Boirai-je de ton vin, ô comète?' feeling perhaps, in himself that the answer must be negative. Probably he had enough, and more than enough, of card-playing in his Dawkins period—indeed, there is almost an expression to that effect in *Mr. Brown's Letters*; at any rate, he certainly did not, like at least one younger novelist, lay down the pen only to take up the pack. Nor does he seem to have been always an excessive, though he certainly was a pretty constant, smoker.

But to what, in the heated imaginations of domestic persons during his time, were the horrid head-quarters of smoking and card-playing—to clubs—he was as strongly attached as (*mutatis mutandis* in the acceptation of the word) his beloved eighteenth-century men were. That this was partly due to the heavy fate which for some five years embittered his home or made him practically homeless is more than probable; but it cannot well have been wholly so. He does not seem, like some men, to have hated being alone—quite the contrary; but his fits of solitude alternated with fits of gregariousness.[1] His fondness for travel has been noticed, and it was probably due to much the same combination of nature and circumstances as his liking for society. For a good many years Brighton seems to have been a kind of occasional home to him, and he was never long happy out of Paris.

All these variations of scene and taste and circumstance reflect themselves in his work after a fashion to which we shall have to draw very frequent attention, for

[1] It was, however, gregariousness of a peculiar kind; he seems to have liked to be 'solitary in company' at his clubs. And though a great diner-out, and a most frequent and hospitable entertainer, he was never a great talker in public.

in it consists one of the main elements of his idiosyncrasy. Even in the earliest work Cambridge, London, Paris, travel, ill-luck (self-invited and other), press-work, and many other things have left their mark. The Cambridge colour may be mainly, but not wholly, left till we reach *Pendennis*, and the Paris touches postponed likewise, though merely to the next chapter. But much of this earliest work shows, if not exactly by the actual dates of composition, the *youngest* Thackeray of literature—a prematurely liberated undergraduate, or a novice-Templar, haunting the rooms of his Cambridge friends in town as he had, and more than he had, in Cambridge itself, exploring London and its suburbs. For some time, indeed, he seems to have actually continued that kind of undergraduate life in which 'walking and talking' are the main ingredients, and very healthy ones too, even though the talking (not undiversified by 'Haunts' and 'Back-kitchens' and other relaxations of Mr. Pendennis and Mr. Newcome and Mr. Firmin) may interfere considerably with obedience to the doctrine of the ancients as to 'early to bed and early to rise'.

In those days, when even the nearer suburbs of London retained something of the village about them, and the further ones much—when, too, there were no soul-destroying motors or cycles or even railways—country walks were quite common with Londoners. And the very parks themselves almost gave room for them. When we read of Thackeray and Paget spending half the day in Kensington Gardens and 'lunching at the Black Lion', we must think of a very different state of things from that of to-day. Even twenty years later—in the early fifties, from which the present writer's acquaintance with the Gardens dates—they were as different as possible from the trim, bepathed, bedizened, and bedevilled Gardens as I last saw them. Except the Broad Walk and those by the railings, there were very few paths at all. Along the north side, by the Bayswater Road, and opposite the Black Lion itself, were the magnificent Scotch firs that Matthew Arnold has celebrated. Along the west, looking to Palace Gardens, was a great open gravel-pit surrounded with a 'yew-wood black as night', which must have given many a boy-reader of Tennyson the scene for *Oriana*. To the east, by the Serpentine, was a curious little ranger's cottage or farmstead in miniature, surrounded by piles of cut wood, in which you could very well hide a heroine or engineer a murder if necessary. The rangers and park-keepers never interfered with mild picnics, but I doubt whether they would have permitted a tramp of the villainous modern kind to enter the gates. Indeed, except in and close to the Broad and Flower Walks, the place was very little frequented, and you might lounge and dream and wander for hours without being unpleasantly reminded of your fellow-creatures. And if this was so in 1851—the Exhibition of that year, though not actually in the Gardens, did something towards their vulgarization, but not much at first—how much more must it have been so in 1831? It may have been in these walks, which were favourite things with all the set (compare Brookfield's with Lord Lyttelton), that Thackeray first felt the attractions of Kensington, that singular place which, like Oxford and the West Country, contrives somehow or other to make those who were once free of it its slaves in a manner for ever. But this, if not quite an irrelevance, is something of a digression.

One characteristic of this 'Cambridge-in-London' atmosphere is very prominent in all his earlier work, and, in fact, continues, though much mellowed and matured, to the end. There have, naturally enough, been no greater nurseries of the wilder and more extravagant humour which is specially English than the two great Universities, but it has 'migrated' from the one to the other rather curiously. In the generation before Thackeray—the generation of Wilson, De Quincey, Hook, Barham—Oxford had had nearly the monopoly of it; and without hanging up unnecessary gloves it may be suggested that 'the native has returned' since. But whether it was owing to the beginning of the Tractarian absorption in another direction or not, this most excellent difference, one may regretfully but frankly admit, appears to have been more observable at 'the other shop' about 1830. Brookfield was saturated with it; it took quaint, restrained, elfish form in FitzGerald; even those who only knew Mr. Venables in his later days, if they had the gift, could perceive plenty of it behind and beneath his apparently rather saturnine dignity. The most esoteric and (again to those who have the gift) delectable, though probably to others most infuriating, exposition of it, is that *Library of Useless Knowledge* by Athanasius Gasker (otherwise E. W. Clarke) of which FitzGerald observed to the late Sir Frederick Pollock: 'Perhaps only you and I *and Thackeray* understand it.' Let us hope that comprehension is not quite so limited now. But it is fair to warn aspirants that there are probably still many more people in the world against this Athanasius than for him. Out of all this atmosphere— or rather, this fermenting mixture—of irony and punning, of parody and *charge*, came the things that are dealt with in this chapter—things a little unformed and unlicked at first—indeed, at the actual first more or less schoolboyish—but with infinite possibilities of strength and 'race' in them, and certain with time and good-luck to develop into marvellous accomplishment.

This characteristic lent itself well enough—perhaps even too well—to the fancy for parody and imitation which most clever boys have, and which Thackeray had already displayed at school. It also lent itself—again with a dangerous complaisance—to some literary peculiarities, though luckily not to all, of the forms and styles of the day. At the period when he started—the years about 1830—the two kings which were to dominate nineteenth-century literature, the newspaper and the novel, had really ascended the throne of their Brentford. But they were not acknowledged monarchs, and neither of them, *at the moment*, was in a particularly healthy condition. Of the two great authors of the new romance and novel, Miss Austen was dead, and though Scott was alive, the wand was dropping from his hands, and the kind was falling into those of second-rate practitioners. The higher newspaper of the review and magazine order had, with the *Edinburgh*, the *Quarterly*, *Blackwood*, and the *London*, not merely opened, as it were, a new profession to men of letters, but had served as usher, or *accoucheur*, to a great deal of work, sometimes of the highest merit. It had, however, as a rule, two great defects, sometimes separate, sometimes combined. On the one hand, there was the love of pseudo-Rhadamanthine, 'high sniffing' arrogance, which laid down the law, *ex cathedra*, on all subjects: on the other, that of extravagant horseplay and high jinks. While, unluckily, the practitioners of both styles, but especially of the second, abused personalities disgracefully, Thackeray had too much humour—and that humour was too early developed—for him to be much tempted in the direction of the pedagogic-oracular; but this very gift inclined him to the other pitfall, and though he never (or very seldom) becomes absolutely engulfed in this, he is, in his early work, constantly slipping in and struggling out again. In particular there was (derived from the famous eighteenth-century periodicals to some extent, but exaggerated, and in fact caricatured by men like Wilson and Maginn) a fancy for constructing a kind of half-imaginary, half real framework of editorial and contributorial personality, the most famous example of which is the machinery of the *Noctes Ambrosianae*, while the last remaining (one greatly modulated and attenuated) is the *eidolon* of 'Mr. Punch'. In the early days of the latter, when Thackeray contributed, there was much more of it there; and in the still earlier, when he was already a regular 'Fraserian', there was very much more in 'Regina'. This *prosopo-poeia* has become rather tiresome now; while the personalities on Lardner,[1] Bulwer, and others, though sometimes extremely amusing, are by no means always so, and are often in more than doubtful taste. And everywhere both the witticisms and the criticisms are singularly *uncertain*. The most excellent jests serve as plums in more or less dubious pudding; the soundest observations on art and literature alternate with opinions which, from prejudice or ignorance as to their subjects, are mere rubbish.

In the other department of tale-telling there is very much less mere imitation, save in the form of direct parody, and the vital signs are more unmistakable. But here also there is great immaturity. Even in such an extremely early thing as *The Devil's Wager* there is no

---

[1] These are repeated in the curious *History of Dionysius Diddler*, not published till after Thackeray's death, but apparently designed in 1838–9, and therefore given here. I do not remember any explanation of his dislike to Lardner.

small faculty of tale-*telling*; but, on the other hand, even much later, there is less of the faculty of making the story interesting. For a long time, too, the author, partly led by his natural ironical bent, and partly, perhaps, exacerbated by his pecuniary ill-luck, his domestic misfortune, and the inadequate success of his work, refused too much to 'come out of the shadow', and brought down upon himself the rather foolish accusation of 'cynicism' (whereon much more later) in dwelling, to all appearance by predilection, on folly, knavery, and positive crime. Yet in this department, as in the other, he showed, almost from the first and in ever-increasing measure and with less alloy, qualities of the very rarest kind. The most unmistakable—or what ought to have been the most unmistakable—of these was the omnipresence of a peculiar humour, or wit and humour mingled, unlike that of any previous writer as a whole, but bearing most resemblance to Fielding and Shakespeare—a humour casual, unpremeditated, or at least never laboriously led up to, *parenthetic* as one may almost call it—rising, like bubbles in sparkling wine, independently of the substance of the narrative or discussion, but giving life to it. The second, more slowly developed, and perhaps hidden from careless or obtuse observers by the caricature and the dialect of such things as *The Yellowplush Papers*, was an especially remarkable command of character, sometimes revealed by only a very few strokes, but those of such a vivifying character as we must once more go to Shakespeare to equal. The third was a quite marvellous style. It is only recently that it has become accepted or acceptable to praise Thackeray's style, though there are some persons who have never made any mistake about it, while there are still obstinate dissenters. Indeed, it was very usual to regard him as a careless and rather slovenly writer who stumbled over 'and which' and similar stones of offence. This he certainly sometimes did, and was not impeccable from other points of view of the composition-books; but it matters little or nothing. His style proper—visible quite early, indeed almost at once—may again owe something to Fielding, but it is in its essence almost wholly original. It is more like the result of thinking aloud than the style of any other writer. But it is also more than this. The writer thinks for himself *and* for 'the other fellow'—for an imaginary interlocutor who makes objections, spies the ludicrous side of what has been said, and so forth. Thus, the body of his critical and miscellaneous writings, and the framework of his novels, consists of a sort of fused dialogue or conversation, lighted up constantly by the humour and wit above mentioned, and vignetting the character-sketches, the descriptions, and the rest. This sort of thing could not be perfected at once, but it may be discovered in pieces which he wrote when he was not more than six-and-twenty, such as *The Professor*.

In the very earliest preserved examples it would be unreasonable to expect it: and, with the exception of *Timbuctoo*, the pieces reprinted from the *Snob*, the *Gownsman*, and even from the *National Standard* (the best things in which he saved for *The Paris Sketch Book*), are only curiosities. *Timbuctoo* itself is rather more, because of the singular felicity of its burlesque of the manner of the eighteenth-century heroic couplet. But the 'Ramsbottom' compositions, with their malapropisms resuggested from Hook, are not very exhilarating. Even three years later, the *National Standard* contributions are not much further advanced. The drawings have already a good deal of the curious irregular Thackerayan charm, and the verses much of his future ease, though little either of the humour or the pathos that were to accompany it. But the Thackeray of only a very few years later would certainly not have failed to see—*did*, we may feel certain, not fail to see—that in the reference to the paper's former owner—'We have got free of the Old Bailey and changed the Governor'—the goodness of the jest is scarcely sufficient to cover the badness of the manners. Still, there is interest in the Montgomery review. That *infelix Robertus* seems to have been an expert, if not in producing good work himself, yet in extracting it from others to his own despite. It is still 'young'; but, as in another case, to which we shall come later, any editor who knew his business, had it been sent to him, would have jumped at it. In particular, the trick of reversing the last quotation, with its practical justification, is quite Thackerayan, and almost a stroke of genius. So, too, the 'Foreign Correspondence', being couched in burlesque and hardly at all political, is positively better than that some years later in the *Constitutional* (*v. infra*). Nor perhaps should the so-called 'Originals' (really adaptations from Hoffmann, Uhland, and others) wholly escape mention, though they are hardly worth giving here, because they are valuable early proofs of that Heinesque combination, of romance with satire of romance, in which Thackeray is Heine's only rival, and in consequence of which the strangest mistakes have been made about both, by critics as well as by the public. While, lastly, the *Étude sur Mirabeau* article on Victor Hugo is the first example of Thackeray's curious fashion of criticism—one-sided, hasty, altogether unduly conditioned by prejudice and 'nervous impression', but still admirably acute in its grasp of the absurd, curiously fresh and vivid, justified (in a half-inexplicable

fashion) of its very injustice. It is because of this ger-
minal value that these *Standard* articles deserve to be
given, as some other later things do not: and even in
their case selection would have to be exercised, not in
order to conceal defects, but simply in order to give only
a fair sample of tentative—fair both to author and to
reader.

Between the decease of the *National Standard* early in
1834 and the beginning of Thackeray's miscellaneous
literary activity in the autumn of 1837, there is rather
a dearth of authenticated work of his, except the *Constitutional* articles, on which we shall speak further.
Indeed, save that he spent most of his time in Paris, and
frequented the studios there, we know little or nothing of
him between the first date just mentioned and his marriage three years later. And save the imitation of 'Le
Roi d'Yvetot' in 1834 (on which again *v. infra*) nothing
certainly stands to his name in the bibliographies until
the curious skit on the ballet (wholly pictorial except
for brief underlinings) of *Flore et Zéphyr* in 1836, signed
'Théophile Wagstaff'—a pseudonym, like others, to be
resumed and slightly varied later. The main point of
this is the satire on the elderly male dancer, a personage
of the time on whom Thackeray was always severe; but
Flore herself does not escape, and the whole, though by
no means an artistic masterpiece, is a really important
'document'. With other things of the same kind it has
proved rather a touchstone for critics. That he, an enthusiastic theatre-goer almost throughout his life, should
not only here, but elsewhere, mercilessly satirize theatrical sham and convention, would seem to be incompre-
hensible, and rather horrible to some; while even greater
surprise and indignation seems to have been aroused by
his very similar attitude to things French in general. We

are not infrequently told that this attitude is a proof of his hopeless John Bullishness; of his 'early Victorian' shortcomings; of his sentiment, his moral heresies, and so forth. It is impossible not to smile at this. No doubt there are some folk who cannot see the faults and absurdities of things and persons for which and for whom they, notwithstanding, have a strong fancy. But, fortunately, there are others who can, and the ability is rather commoner, perhaps, among Englishmen of wits than in other nations. Thackeray had it in almost the highest degree, though he was not always equally provided with the complementary and even higher faculty of seeing the merits of the things he did *not* like. And it may be said, with no desire to provoke, but with unruffled calm and maintaining a strong sympathy with the extravagances of *mil-huit-cent-trente*, that most of the absurdities which he detected and exposed in Frenchmen and French literature *were* absurdities, *are* so, and will be so whenever they recur 'a hundred years hence' or a thousand. That he took the moral line too strongly, from the *National Standard* critique on Pétrus Borel and others onward, is perhaps true; but have we not more recently had at least equally flagrant examples of taking the non-moral line—not, perhaps, excused by quite so much talent (we need not call it as yet genius) as his?[1]

When this period—if not exactly of halcyon ease, at any rate of little history and not little happiness—came to an end, in consequence, first, of the responsibilities of his marriage and then of the downfall of the *Constitu-*

[1] It is difficult, when one reads impatient complaints of Thackeray's 'sermons', not to think of the pleasant American story of the negro preacher who declined to preach upon chicken-stealing (much prevalent in the neighbourhood) because it would 'cast a cold on de congregation'. These complainants seem to have felt a similar 'cold'—to be of 'the congregation'.

tional, Thackeray, like other people, had to knock at various literary doors, and did not always find them at once or continuously open to him. In 1837, and at intervals later, he did a certain amount of work for *The Times*, and several of his reviews were recently identified and reprinted. Of most of them there is little to say; indeed, the paste-and-scissors habit which he had acquired on the *Constitutional* itself, and which, curiously enough, has always been not unpopular with newspaper editors, is obvious in them. The 'Carlyle' and the 'Southey', however, deserve a little comment. Carlyle was not effusively grateful to the 'Cornish giant', as he called him—the perpetual epithet being perhaps specially connected with knowledge of his Liskeard expedition with Buller. But this review of the *French Revolution* is a remarkable one for a young man, and not the less important that Thackeray really knew France when survivors of the Revolutionary times were fairly plentiful. Much is again quotation, and Carlyle was probably (author-fashion) annoyed by Thackeray's 'playing down' at the beginning to the popular complaints of uncouthness of style, &c. But this is really only a crafty concession and conciliation, and the total estimate is surprisingly near the truth—things, times, and persons considered. He may have thought of it a dozen years later when he imagined a grave historian's feelings at being knocked off in one of Pen's reviews; but he need not have been ashamed of it. Nor is the brief review of Southey (who has proved one of the most difficult of all writers for critics—especially critics Radical, as Thackeray then was—to deal justly with) unworthy of the same commendations.

Still, for reasons which will be better exposed later, Thackeray could never have been an ideal reviewer; and

for political articles—about the only other kind of work
that *The Times* could have offered him—he had no
aptitude at all. A much more suitable place for him was
the miscellaneous review-magazine which had established itself in virtue of the brilliant success of *Blackwood*.
With 'Maga' herself, though he was later intimate with
Mr. John Blackwood and many 'Ebonites', Thackeray
never established literary relations—whether for political reasons or not I do not know. But *Fraser*, which
was at first almost an 'overflow' *Blackwood*, with Maginn
and Lockhart among its pillars, must have been opened
to him, by his costly friendship with Maginn himself,
almost from the first; and it is certain that from 1837
onwards it was almost his chief refuge and resort when
he had 'copy' to deposit, until *Punch* took its place—and,
indeed, for some considerable time after he had taken
Mr. Punch's shilling. Confident assertions have been
made that the ironic and Bulwer-parodying story of
Elizabeth Brownrigge, which appeared as early as 1832 in
the magazine, was his; and a certain number of other
articles during the next five years have been less confidently attributed to him. To this point we must
devote a little attention.

With respect to *Elizabeth Brownrigge*, particularly careful examination, both of external and internal evidence,
is no doubt necessary. That Mr. R. H. Shepherd attributed it to Thackeray need not trouble us much; for
Mr. Shepherd, a bibliographer of unwearied and un-
discourageable industry, and an editor (as in Blake's
case) of rather unduly undervalued accuracy, never,
that I know of, showed any great power as a literary
critic, and his opinion, bibliographically, is balanced by
that of Mr. C. P. Johnson—in that respect at least his
equal. But Dr. John Brown, who knew Thackeray

intimately, seems to have thought the thing his, and
Mr. Swinburne, whose opinions on literature are never
negligible, is said to have followed on the same side.
Outside opinion, and the excessively weak point that
two and a half years later Thackeray figures, on no
other positive account save a scrap of verse, among the
'Fraserians', there appears to be no evidence in favour
of his authorship.

The piece has been called 'ghastly' and 'gruesome',
but this is an exaggeration. The facts were so, doubtless;
but the handling of them is much less ghastly and gruesome than that of the end of *Catherine*, so that this is
neither for nor against. It is a parody of, and an attack
upon, the author of *Eugene Aram*; but plenty of people
besides Thackeray parodied and attacked Bulwer, and
this is neither against nor for. We are driven, therefore,
to the consideration of the piece itself, and of Thackeray's
known work up to or about its date.

Putting these most carefully together, with the assistance of a not inconsiderable knowledge of the magazine
work of the time, especially in *Blackwood* and *Fraser*, I can
only say that, while I certainly shall never be so rash
as to say that Thackeray did not write it, I can see not
the slightest evidence that he did. The general style is
certainly unlike his at any time; and it is much more
sober and correct than anything that he wrote for long
afterwards. Not till we come to *Barry Lyndon* is there
such abstinence from 'kicks over the traces', from verbal
horse-play of any kind. It is—or seems to me—the
work of a much older hand than the Thackeray of
twenty-one. It might be Maginn himself; it might even
be Lockhart; I do not think it could be Thackeray. If
it was—and I hold that pure criticism can sometimes
say, 'This *must* be So-and-so's,' but never 'This *cannot*

be'—then it is one of the instances—not, I admit, un-known—of a man doing something quite out of his ordinary line, and quite irreconcilable with the ordinary laws of development. I should not be in the least chagrined if some old *Fraser* ledger turned up (as such things have done) and proved it to be his. I should not be very much surprised. But, meanwhile, I do not see how it can safely be attributed to him. The other guessed-at articles in *Fraser* are of much less importance, and for the most part they seem to me to have been fixed upon, rather because of some fancied connexion in subject with Thackeray's other work, or with places and persons actually connected with him, than for any real resemblance in style. The undoubtedly genuine translation from Béranger was corrected and collected later, and the first actual *Fraser* article to be chronicled here is the remarkable *Half-crown's Worth of Cheap Knowledge*, in which the subject is more than the form, though there are some distinctively Thackerayan touches. Not till after this did he give *Fraser* a creation— Mr. Charles James Yellowplush.

But before the *Half-crown's Worth*, and in *Bentley's Miscellany*, not in *Fraser*, there came something of value, which has had little attention from most of Thackeray's commentators. *The Professor* was to all appearance the first of his original and characteristic contributions to prose fiction. For, though it is attributed in the reprint of 1886, where it first took rank with the collected works, only to the *Comic Tales and Sketches* of 1841, it actually appeared in *Bentley's Miscellany* for 1837. The class to which it belongs—a reversion to the old prose *fabliau* or satirical tale of real life—had grown up slowly in Eng-land, but had recently received a very great stimulus from the popularity of Theodore Hook. Few people

read poor 'Mr. Wagg' now, but without reading him
it is practically impossible to estimate rightly either how
much Thackeray and Dickens owed to him, or how immensely they improved upon him. And this estimate, as
far as Thackeray is concerned, wants further comparative study of persons from Leigh Hunt to Douglas Jerrold
before his unique greatness can be clearly perceived.
The subject of *The Professor* is 'low' (it is curious how one
perceives the survival of that immemorial objection in
the most advanced disciples of realism and naturalism
when they talk of Thackeray), and the attitude to it is
burlesque-grotesque. A dull person may lose himself in
the maze before discovering (what he does not in the
least need to discover) whether the main object is pure
farce or satire of Byronism and Bulwerism. But there is
a quite extraordinary 'keeping' in the thing: the writer
never lets any of his horses—sentiment, satire, grotesque-
burlesque—break pace or kick over the traces; he speeds,
but never hurries, to the event; the whole is smooth and
round. I forget who edited the *Miscellany* in those days,
but if he had known his business he would have said,
'More! more! and as much more as ever you can write!'
Evidently he did not, and Mr. Yellowplush entered the
service of another establishment.

It may be asked—I have no doubt that it has been
asked frequently—why Thackeray so often adopted the
plan of burlesque attitude, including misspelling, for
these early attempts. The example of Swift—there is
nothing of importance and hardly anything at all earlier,
except a few dramatic instances, chiefly in dialect—and
of Smollett is only a very partial answer, nor is the
'Ramsbottom' practice much more sufficient, though
it adds a little. I believe myself that there is a much
better and subtler explanation. He was evidently dis-

gusted from the first—his schoolboy parodies of 'L. E. L.',
&c., show it—with the 'high-falutin'' lingo and tone of
much early Romantic poetry and fiction. He was
evidently straining after the pure domestic novel, relying
on no unusual incident and discarding all factitious
style, which only Miss Austen had ventured as regards
incident, and which even Miss Austen had not wholly
ventured as regards style. But he was not as yet sufficiently advanced to dare this without some aid of mask
and domino. Burlesque of fact supplied the domino, and
contortions of orthography and lexicography supplied
the mask.

Moreover, it is of the first interest and importance to
notice how, in spite of this motley, and sometimes
almost through its means, his general style is already
distinguished by that unforced adequacy and nature
which are its greatest glory. To take the three chief of
his own immediate, or almost immediate, contemporaries in prose fiction for comparison, how curiously
contrasted is the fantastic, accumulative manner of
Dickens, heaping simile on simile, suggestion on suggestion, turning sentence into paragraph, and paragraph
into page of phantasmagoric commentary or imagination! And the gaudy writing of Bulwer, though more
ostentatiously shunned and satirized, is not more strik-
ingly absent than the laborious epigrams and 'sentences'
(as ancient criticism called them) of Disraeli—the
patched-on afterthoughts which the reader is expected
to cherish as fine things. Of what the French call *apparat*
—a word which includes our 'apparatus', our 'preparation', and a good deal besides—there is nothing in
Thackeray; and yet his simple phrases have the subtlest
suggestion and appropriateness even in their motleyest
motley and their wildest burlesque. At the very begin-

ning of this, when Mr. Yellowplush's ma 'wrapped his buth in a mistry', the two misspellings automatically gibbet a silly stock phrase, do their duty and pass on.

The fact of the double existence of Mr. Yellowplush, and of his near but not exact, homonym, Mr. de la Pluche, is one of the best illustrations of the importance of observing Thackerayan chronology, and of the inconvenience of not observing it. The two gentlemen are, as has been said, nearly of the same name, quite of the same class, and addicted to the same peculiar '*au*thography'. But they are quite different *persons*, and it is a pity to lose the opportunity of remarking, in their respective cases, the extraordinary creative power of their creator in the great English art of character, individualized, not typified. With the not unamiable husband of Mary Hann we shall deal when we come to him; but the orphan of Miss Montmorency is our present business. He is a very much shrewder person than his seven or eight years' younger brother (whose blood-relations, by the way, appear to have been quite respectable), and his shrewdness takes most of the meaning of that by no means unambiguous term. From beginning to end he is, as he modestly acknowledges to Mr. Altamont, 'tolerably downy'—a very distinct and capable critic of life. In fact, if his next master's unfortunate victim, 'pore Dawkins', is Thackeray himself in his weaker moments, much more is Charles James the stronger Thackeray himself in a somewhat immature and crude state—'too savage', as he said himself, too extravagant in various ways, unchastened in taste, degraded in condition, but with observation almost fully developed, and with power of satiric expression developed almost more fully still, not merely in spite, but by the help, of the burlesque dialect. If, once more,

anybody who reads this will compare the smaller
novels and tales of Theodore Hook with the histories
of Mr. Altamont and Mr. Deuceace, he will be struck,
as Lockhart was, by the astounding difference in genus
and genius. If anybody will compare Mr. Yellowplush's
critical efforts with *their* chief forerunners—certain parts
of the *Noctes Ambrosianae*, and Wilson's other writings,
together with those of Maginn—though the gap is not so
great, the difference will be found almost as striking.
Extravagant as is the motley—more *apparently* extravagant than in either of the others—the wit and wisdom
beneath it far exceed theirs in truth and force.

With regard to the contents of the *Correspondence*, it
is easy enough to understand Thackeray's motive for
suppressing *Fashnable Fax* and the *Letter to 'Oliver Yorke'*,
which keys the rest of the matter on to it, as well as some
reasons for separating narrative and critical parts. But
the *Fax* are amusing enough in themselves, and the
piece has long taken its place among acknowledged
work; while the *Letter* is even better, and really necessary
as a tie. For the rest, no 'sign-post' is needful to direct
the reader to its thick-coming fancies and its wealth of
natural incident and phrase. Those who cannot be content without tragedy and a certain amount of 'grime'
will, of course, prefer the later history of Mr. Deuceace;
and the Earl of Crabs is certainly great. But the battle of
kite and crow over the body of the luckless Dawkins,
and *Mr. Yellowplush's Ajew*—one of the most perfect
things in the broader burlesque, not without the finest
traits of satire under the breadth—are perhaps the
apices of the whole. If *Major Gahagan*, to which we next
come, is the 'maddest' burlesque (as, I think, Mr.
Whibley has observed), *Yellowplush* is the most Puckish
and the most inexhaustibly diverting. Take away the

critical part of it and you mutilate the individuality.
Mr. Yellowplush is never, as Mr. James de la Pluche is,
an authentic flunkey. He is 'criticism of life'—criticism
of life and letters below stairs, in motley of speech as well
as in many-coloured coat and breeches. He is very far
from being the whole Thackeray; but there is something
of the whole Thackeray diffused through him, and it
shows best when the papers are taken in the order of
their composition.

The invincible Major (whose *Tremendous Adventures*
originally, in their magazine appearances, bore the
milder titles, *Some Passages in the Life*, *Historical Recol-
lections*, and *Historical Reminiscences* of Major G.) had been
a floating and phantasmagoric eidolon in Thackeray's
mind for some time—a fact to which there is reference in
the opening paragraph. Years before, in the *National
Standard*, there had been the 'annygoat' of 'Father'
Gahagan; only a twelvemonth earlier 'Goliah Gahagan'
himself, without his commission and orders, and showing
nothing of his autobiographical peculiarities, had signed
the record of the wickedness of Roderick Ferdinand,
thirty-eighth Count of Dandolo, and the cruel fate of
Adeliza Grampus. Nay, much later, in the long un-
collected *Wagstaff Papers*, 'General Sir Goliah Gahagan'
reappears with a new wife (for though virtuous he is
terribly polygamic), with a more polished and less
extravagant style, but with undiminished vivacity and
veracity of his own peculiar kind.

One says 'vivacity and veracity' jestingly; yet there
is an astonishing amount of sober truth in the phrase.
In all Thackeray's better burlesque (and he rarely did
anything better than the tremendous Major and the
simpering flunkey who, in the frontispiece of their collection, accompany poor little Mr. M. A. Titmarsh to the

'brink of Immortality') there is a characteristic which it possesses, if not quite to itself, at any rate in common only with a few examples of the greatest kind in prose. It carries 'suspension of disbelief' with it like a fairy-tale. You know, of course, all the time, not merely that the Tremendous Adventures never happened, but (which is not quite the case with Mr. Yellowplush's) that they never could have happened. But this doesn't matter. They are quite real *ex hypothesi*; they carry the atmosphere of their own universe with them, and they blandly permeate and intoxicate you with it, as if it were so much laughing-gas—as indeed it is.

Perhaps there is something less of this mysterious reality in *The Fatal Boots*. The reason is not that Bob Stubbs is a detestable little brute: he is not much more detestable than Barnes Newcome, and not at all more than the later—not the earlier—Barry Lyndon, whom indeed he much resembles. Nor is it the poetic justice— poetic justice will no more 'bite' than allegory will, unless people are afraid of it. But the victim of Mr. Stiffelkind's revenge is not quite humanly possible. His mother might very probably be as infatuated with him as she is represented—that is common enough; his sister not impossibly. But why should beauties and heiresses have fallen in love with a hideous, cowardly, awkward, bad-blooded, not affluent little cad? It is no answer to say that such things do occur in life; for fiction is more philosophical than life, and more bound to observe system. Nor is Mr. Stubb's own conduct quite intelli-gible, for he is too much of a fool to be quite as shrewd as Thackeray sometimes makes him, and vice versa. The book is full of good things, of course, and the illustra-tions endear it to some, no doubt. But it will not quite *wash*.

On the other hand, the delicious trifle of *The Bedford Row Conspiracy* may be warranted not to shrink however often you wash it, and in whatever critical water. It is a borrowed—and quite openly borrowed—trifle. It is 'transposed' with an amount of ingenuity quite miraculous from the *Pied d'Argile* of Charles de Bernard—an author whom official French criticism rather belittles, and whom those who cannot judge for themselves accordingly belittle likewise, but who may be quite confidently styled one of the very best of French novelists of the second class. Thackeray had a great fancy for Charles de Bernard, who, like himself, was both a wit and a gentleman, and who had humour of a kind very uncommon in Frenchmen. I do not know anything quite resembling this pair of stories as an example of the 'transposition' referred to.

In all these works or worklets—*Yellowplush* and *Gahagan*, the *Boots* and the *Conspiracy*, as well as in the *Professor*—Thackeray had entered his proper kingdom—that of the novel—though he had made no extensive conquests in it, and had confined his incursion mostly to the comic or even the farcical provinces and departments. The *Character Sketches*,[1] the last pieces to be considered in this first chapter, are not nominally or ostensibly tales: but they are more or less elaborate studies for tales, and the results of the observation and experiment which they show had been partly, and were to be more fully, embodied in actual fiction. 'Captain Rook' is Mr. Deuceace, and 'Mr. Pigeon' is Mr. Dawkins, who has abandoned the harmless solace of the flute for the much more dangerous blandishments of 'Maria'. The

[1] The second and third (1841) are somewhat later than the first, and than anything else in this chapter. But Thackeray himself joined them together, and they shall not be put asunder here.

Captain's earlier university career is quite familiar to readers of the later Thackeray, and not to such readers only. Lady Fanny Flummery is more or less *criblée* in most of the novels and tales, though Thackeray was afterwards one of the few faithful friends of poor Lady Blessington—princess of the Lady Fanny tribe. *The Artists* is devoted to a subject of which he was unceasingly fond, and which will have to be treated more fully. And let it be observed that in these *Sketches* the style, as a rule, with a few dialogue-exceptions, is perfectly serious, without misspelling or mountebankery of any kind—a style nearly as composed and full-dress as any that Thackeray ever attained or attempted; that there is almost his full knowledge of the world and of men even in the earliest; that in the history of Captain Rook and Mr. Pigeon, Thackeray has not merely depicted and satirized his own calamity and folly, as he did in *Yellowplush*, but has generalized it out of all mere personality.

In short, in all the matter of this volume he is 'making himself': in some he is already made.

But during these years he tried one way in which he never did anything good. Those who have paid a little attention, by accident or purpose, to the bibliography of Thackeray may look for something to be said here concerning his *Constitutional* work—the letters of 'Our Own Correspondent' from Paris during the short life of that paper. The exclusion of any detailed survey is the result of mature deliberation, and can be supported by many reasons. In the first place, the articles are of the kind which among all the ephemera of journalism is the most ephemeral—summaries and comments dealing with political matters from week to week and day to day. To make them even intelligible to any but special students of the time, they would need annotation. But there is much more than this. They are not good; they are hardly even as good as those from the *National Standard*, which have been given here on the ground of their earliness. Everywhere else Thackeray improved immensely: here he did not. The greater part of the matter is mere translated paste-and-scissors work; the comments show neither grasp, nor political acuteness, nor power of putting the writer's own views forcibly and pungently. In fact, anybody who is familiar with *Philip* can see that Thackeray, not with the sham humility of the fool, but with the ironic humility of the wise man, had himself apprized the value of his political work perfectly well. It would be an unjust justice in hanging out afresh these *chaînes de l'esclavage* (his own name for them in the case of George Esmond Warrington), which the wearer wore gallantly and unflinchingly while it was necessary, but which have neither interest nor beauty of their own, and which he himself did not choose to expose to public gaze as his. In everything else of the time there is either intrinsic goodness, or interest of promise, or interest at least of experiment. There is nothing of any of these kinds in the *Constitutional* letters, and so I do not discuss them.

II

THE PARIS SKETCH BOOK, AND ART CRITICISMS

DUE warning has been given in the Preface, that though the main principle of arrangement would be chronological, a merely rigid consistency would not be allowed to prevail in this respect. In these earlier chapters especially, though each is planned to present a more advanced stage than the one preceding, the structure must, necessarily and otherwise, be 'clinker-built'—overlapping, that is to say, in such a sense that some work in each will be earlier than some in its fore-runner. Necessarily, for it would be preposterous to disturb Thackeray's own arrangement of much early work, and some almost of his very earliest, in *The Paris Sketch Book*. Otherwise than necessarily—in order (for reasons to be presently set forth) to get together the rather frequent expressions of the author's criticism in Art-matters which key on to much of the *Sketch Book*. I had at first preferred as an alternative the grouping of the Parisian matter such as the *Second Funeral of Napoleon* and the other Parisian *Corsair* and *Britannia* articles together; but on the whole the present arrangement seemed more convenient.

The interest of *The Paris Sketch Book*, as Thackeray's first advance in force, and by way of a real book, on the public, can hardly be exaggerated. And it has other claims—its variety of subject, the unity given to that variety by the presence (to use Nestor Roqueplan's ingenious term) of the element of 'Parisine' throughout, and the known and lifelong attraction which that element had for the author. It is impossible, however, that any reader with even a slight tincture of criticism in him, if not fully acquainted with the circumstances of the case, should not be a little puzzled by it. I remember being very decidedly so myself. A more 'accidented' book, as the language with which it has so much to do would put it—a book with more curious and startling ups and downs of goodness, there hardly exists in literature: and there are not many which present such a positive jumble of subjects, atmospheres, tempers, attitudes, styles. The Dedication, eccentric as its substance may seem, is in Thackeray's most individual and nearly in his very best manner. He could hardly have improved on it in the days of the 'Roundabouts' themselves. The introductory 'Invasion of France' though only one of the essay-sketches which had been more and more practised from Leigh Hunt to 'Boz', is an excellent specimen of them, with not a little idiosyncrasy. Its successor, the history of the delusion and downfall of Pogson, is of the best early Thackeray—a wonderfully fresh variation on the companion tragedies of Mr. Dawkins and Mr. Pigeon. Quite different, but as good or better still, is the long letter on the Fêtes of July. It is dated July 3, 1839, but most, if not all of it, might have been written in 1859 as far as the manner goes.

And so with others. But with yet others it is different, and with some of these one wonders a little why they were ever written; with some why they were not written better. When their *provenance* is known and sufficiently considered, this wonder vanishes. In the first place their actual composition covered no small space of time. One article, and by no means the worst—the already more than once glanced at 'Devil's Wager'—represents almost the earliest period of Thackeray's work, having been

contributed to the *National Standard* nearly seven years
before the collection appeared. Most, though not most
of the best, were collected from various newspapers and
magazines to which they had been contributed 'at the
hazard of the pen'—some of the best having gone to
the American *Corsair*, edited by N. P. Willis. It may
be remembered that Philip contributed to an American
magazine and did not get paid for his contributions,
and it is certain that Thackeray does not later exhibit
any great affection for the author of *Hurrygraphs* and
Dashes at Life. Fraser, the *New Monthly*, and other
periodicals were also drawn upon. The book was in
fact a pure miscellany—even the 'Paris' of its title is
a very loose and questionable bond of union.

It need have been none the worse for this. The
Roundabout Papers themselves are the very miscellany
of all miscellanies: and they are inferior in their own
way to hardly anything in literature. But by their time,
Thackeray had attained the faculty of surrounding
everything he treated with the amber of style—of
making everything interesting and everything original.
Here he had not. Much of the matter is quite openly
translated or adapted from Charles de Bernard and
others. More is curiously 'retold': sometimes for reasons
not now very apparent—as in the case of the histories
of 'Cartouche', 'Poinsinet', 'Mary Ancel', 'Beatrice
Merger'. Only special amateurs in crime-mysteries can
now get up the slightest concern in the Peytel matter—
even though the particular case interested Balzac (on
the opposite side) as well as Thackeray. It is, however,
pretty certain, to some who have read what both these
great novelists and critics of life have to say, that
Thackeray was right and Balzac wrong. 'Napoleon and
his System' is almost entirely one with the other political

articles contributed to the *Constitutional*, though it will give readers rather a favourable notion of Thackeray's political style. In particular it is saved by his correct and salutary affirmation of the undying dislike of France for England. But much of it is translation, and the rest not over brilliant comment. 'The Painter's Bargain' and 'The Devil's Wager' itself are romantic-grotesque stories of a Hoffmannish kind, and still more, perhaps, resembling prose Ingoldsby Legends, very good reading, but not consummate. 'A Gambler's Death' is much more in the author's own special way, and has some most vivid and characteristic touches; but he would have done it much better only a very little later. Of the various criticisms on Art and Letters it would not be true to say this, for they are very much what his criticism of *contemporary* art and letters always was—a queer impulsive mixture of shrewdness and prejudice, of knowledge and ignorance. Altogether a singular *olla podrida* or *pot-pourri*; but with the relish of the one, the fragrance of the other, only partially achieved.

Yet if one reads this unequal collection carefully, and remembers what other things the readers of 1840 had to read, it seems strange that more of them should not have detected and enjoyed (to use a later phrase of its author's about a character whom he never identified with himself), 'the sense, the satire, and' if not exactly 'the scholarship', the literary savour of it, so different from anything elsewhere offered them. In that opening descriptive sketch—a thing already hackneyed—what a curious freshness and variety there is! what vividness, and at the same time what quaint originality! above all, what a unique abstinence from thumping the same note in order to force people to attend to it; from splashing and blobbing the same line by way of emphasis! The boat, the quay, the coast, the harbour, the hotel—most writers (and some very famous ones) would have given you a paragraph at least, if not a page, to each. Thackeray touches each off in two or three strokes, quite suggestive enough to alert 'uptakers'. The personages are extremely numerous; each one of them is made as alive as he need be, and much more alive than almost anybody else could make him; but, in the same way, with the least expense of line and colour. They rise, do their part in the procession and panorama, and pass: they are not dragged back with clumsy and absurd bobbings up and down of the curtain to beg for applause. How complete, again, is the story of that second Dawkins, Pogson, not quite so innocent as his more luckless predecessor in one way, equally so in another, favoured by fortune and Mr. Titmarsh (who himself was *haud ignarus mali*) very much more. There is stuff in it for a far longer story: but Thackeray neither compresses it unduly, nor spins it out; neither squeezes it down, nor lets it run over. It is just 'good measure'— the best; and he gives to you of his abundance freely.

Even in the more miscellaneous articles, miscellaneous in both senses, as just explained, and belonging less to their author's proper vocation, the same and other proofs of genius exist. There is hardly anywhere else such a piece of interpretation—of showman's work, with an artist of the first class for the showman—as the passages on Robert Macaire in 'Caricatures and Lithography'. In this same paper, read the admirable and consummate remarks—Thackeray in a nutshell—on Smollett's sketch of literature in the reign of George II. It was historically wrong to call Mrs. Lennox a 'figment': figments do not eat magnificent apple-pies, as Johnson made this lady do at the all-night sitting recorded by Hawkins. But it was critically and creatively right.

In 'Meditations at Versailles' we come across one of those papers which give handles both to the attackers and to the defenders. Undoubtedly the former have something to say, as they have in reference to all Thackeray's polemic against 'snobs', of which this is in reality an early specimen—a 'first state', as it were, of *The Book of Snobs* itself. Undoubtedly the famous 'Historical Study' of 'Rex—Ludovicus—Ludovicus Rex' is unfair—and goes perilously near, as unfair satire inevitably does, to being ignoble. Ludovicus could not help being 'bald and paunchy' when he was old: many most estimable people undergo these inevitable outrages of time—and there is excellent testimony to the fact that he was a really handsome cavalier when he was young. The satirist himself has to admit that in his unlucky old age the 'Magnificent' king was really magnanimous as well. There are plenty of things to be said against him, but Thackeray has not said the right things. He has made the same mistake (but, as being more of a novice, more clumsily) that he made in *The Four Georges* a decade and a half later: and he has not equally redeemed it. But the adaptation of the 'Prophecy of Cazotte' (Thackeray has evidently said 'Cagliostro' by mistake) has a scornful melancholy magic of style that atones for much, and the whole article is full of wonderful broken lights of phrase and portraiture.

On the whole, perhaps, the critical parts of the *Sketch Book* are those which have drawn the heaviest fire: and as nearly the whole of the rest of the volume will be occupied with critical matter, it is necessary to say something about this part of Thackeray's work. Indeed, as far as his art-criticism goes, we shall hardly have, save for glances, to return to it. The literary criticism will occupy us often; and we may deal with it first here.

Of course it is no use arguing with those who say 'Here are great writers and great books—Hugo, Heine, Dumas, George Sand, this and that work of theirs— and Thackeray dares to make fun of them or condemn them!' But even this, manifestly absurd as it is, is not quite so strange as the objection, which I think I have seen, that the French consider *Kean* a very clever if not a very great play, and yet Thackeray makes fun of it. To which, of course, it can only be replied that if all Europe thought *Kean* a fine play, and only one person perceived the absurdities that Thackeray points out, all Europe would be wrong and the one person right. For these are absurdities, sometimes in themselves, sometimes as exhibiting ignorance of his subject, which the author had no business to commit if he took that subject at all.

But there is another class of objections which do not answer and upset themselves quite so definitely; and which were referred to in the first chapter. Thackeray, it is said, is hopelessly John Bullish; he insists on applying English ideas to French ways and work, and the result is inadequacy and unfairness. Now this is not an objection which can be met by simple negation. Undoubtedly if a man says, as in the famous instance, that it is very silly of the French infantry to wear blue uniforms, he says a very silly thing. But it may be at least questioned whether Thackeray does do this— whether he is not entitled to urge that the indictments he brings against French books are brought under codes and before courts where no nation can plead lack of jurisdiction. One may not wholly admit this plea; one may think that he takes the moral line too much. But, after all, does any one, however much he may admire the men of 1830, deny that they talked a good deal of nonsense, and unhealthy nonsense too? The present writer has borne the Romantic banner as high and as steadily as he could for a good many years; but *he* could not deny this.

No; the faults of Thackeray's literary criticism— which we may touch again and again till we reach *The English Humourists*, the best example of it with some of the most striking illustrations of its faults themselves— are not by any means due to too rigid Anglicism, for he sees English faults quite as clearly as French. They do not even lie in a too great adherence to the 'moral heresy' or to orthodox standards of any kind: for no one ever was less of a Pharisee than he was, and his standpoint was, to say the least, not uncompromisingly ecclesiastical. They were due rather to the absence of fixed codes and creeds than to the presence of them; to a curious impulsiveness and inconsistency which has something to do with the unequalled truth to nature and the wonderful fresh variety of his style and thought, but which is not exactly suitable to the pure critical *ethos*.

Of his art-criticism, the present writer speaks with more diffidence, having had no technical education in that matter, but only a great love of it for a great many years, and a steady endeavour not to 'like grossly', but to feel, as far as possible, *why* he likes. It is impossible, of course, not to see at once that Thackeray himself had this education; that whereas in literature he was an almost peerless creator but at the same time almost an untaught or self-taught one, he was in Art, though curiously hampered in his creation, by no means an amateur, but, if not a master, an apprentice who had duly and far from negligently served his time. Exactly why his execution was so hampered it is not easy to understand; at least no expert has ever succeeded in explaining it to my inexpertness. One is driven to the rather obvious supposition that his fingers simply would not do what his brain told them to do, and what his eyes told him they ought to have done. He never made the slightest mistake about his own performances: indeed I think that somewhere in the wandering isles of his letters there is a sentence not unlike that which I have just written. And there is the very amplest evidence, in the pages that follow, that he knew technical faults and merits quite well and, what is more, was perfectly well acquainted with the technical means by which they were produced and avoided. Nay more, he has, I think, the very great credit of being the first person who distinctly pointed out, in *The Paris Sketch Book* itself, and in that same remarkable article on 'Caricatures and Lithography', not merely the much greater practice of Art in France, and the much greater rewards for it, not merely the more general enjoyment of it and the like, but the radical difference between the French and the English attitude to it. 'For abstract art', he says, 'we have no appreciation,' thereby not merely laying down but almost originating the very objection which 'warm young men' now urge against himself.

Nor did he fail to practise what he preached, to a very large extent. Nothing could be better, from any point of view, than his criticism of the dismal French Classical school of the Empire in his first article, 'The French School of Painting'. His remarks on its Romantic rival are perfectly sane, and those (here not extensive) on Delacroix and Delaroche respectively have quite the root of the matter in them, while he can appreciate the middle style of Ingres. But then we come to the flaw. 'The absurd humbug called Christian or Catholic art' draws down a philippic from Thackeray. It is true that this early (chiefly German) pre-Raphaelitism was rather weak—that it was not till years after this, and in England, that masterpieces were produced in it. But one sees at once that this is not the ground of Thackeray's objection. He has seen nothing like it before; he does not like the 'Catholic' suggestion in it. He ridicules the gold-leaf haloes just as 'Zeluco' Moore's famous character ridicules the blue uniforms. It is 'absurd': it is 'silly'. I have sometimes thought that there are no two words in the whole vocabulary of criticism which a critic should use with more gingerly and self-suspicious reluctance than those two words 'silly' and 'absurd'. They too often mean simply this, 'I dislike the thing; but I can't tell you why, and I won't inquire.' Now this attitude is absolutely fatal to criticism; it is at once the critic's besetting and his unpardonable sin. I do not think that, till quite late days, Thackeray can be cleared of it.

If this drawback is visible in his comments on French Art it is certainly more visible still when he comes to English; and we must admit that Dr. John Brown set something like a *pretium affectionis* on this criticism when he called Thackeray 'one of the best of art critics'. He is so, when he happens himself to have an affection for his subject, not quite so otherwise; and I fear that we must demand something more from a 'best' critic. Moreover, his very affection often induces him to overpraise. Nothing can be better than the famous, or should be famous, paragraph on 'The Fighting Téméraire'; it is worthy of the picture itself. But how, in an adjacent article, did he come to salute Mulready as 'King' of British Art? He seems constantly to be going to do more justice to Etty than has been done by almost any one to that most remarkable failure of a Titian or a Rubens; yet he is as constantly 'put off' from doing it, not because of the failure, but because Etty seems to him to have forgotten a sufficient provision of fig-leaves. That the artists were angry with him (as we know from FitzGerald and could have known without any information whatsoever), matters very little. But, perhaps, in no case does that apparatus of forced high jinks which was referred to in the opening Introduction, interfere so much as here. One may not in the least sympathize with Edgar Poe's indignation at the 'devilled kidneys' in *Charles O'Malley*. Devilled kidneys are good; so is toasted cheese; so are beer, porter, gin and water, brandy and water, and other such things—in their proper places, and supplied neither in excess nor in defect. In these very papers Thackeray's fancy of a complete *menu* of the Fatted Calf is quite admissible and amusing. But it is very difficult to feel a proper exhilaration over Mr. Titmarsh's indulgences at various public-houses, and the manner in which the trusting caterers are indemnified by Mr. Oliver Yorke. They are not 'in a concatenation accordingly'; we feel that they were put in to suit a passing fashion, and that they have nothing in common with the admirable 'gor-mandizing' articles to which we shall come later.

We go, here, much beyond the stage of Thackeray's actual production to which we confined ourselves in the preceding chapter and shall confine ourselves in the next, and even the next after that. For here the liberty is justified, first, by the fact that all the work really belongs to the earlier stage, though some of it was written quite towards the end of that stage, and secondly by the solidarity of subject, and even to a great extent of manner, though towards the latest the mere 'high jinks' business fortunately drops out. A great deal of the criticism is admirable, and a great deal more of it very noticeable. It is on the whole the very best example that we have in English of the kind of art-criticism which Diderot introduced in his *Salons*; though there the technical knowledge was less at first-hand than Thackeray's. The point, however, in both cases is that the pure technical judgement, and what artists disdainfully call the 'literary' point of view, are inextricably blended.

The result of this blend is shown at its best, at least at its most sustained, in the famous *Essay on Cruikshank* which, if not quite a 'first early' is early enough. Gratitude for old childish enjoyment, and that hearty goodwill which was one of Thackeray's rarest and most amiable moral qualifications as a man of genius, may pitch the tone a very little too high. For, inexhaustible as was Cruikshank's artistic imagination, and marvellous as was his technical command of method and effect, one cannot quite forget that, in a very large proportion, perhaps the majority, of cases his figures are not human creatures at all, but arabesques and grotesques of humanity. Still, nobody, with the actual examples given in the paper, is likely to forget this: and the great, the rare, the astonishingly bountiful merits of the master are brought out in a way which it would be difficult to better. On one side of modern art-criticism we should no doubt get more 'studio jargon'; more allusion at first or second-hand to the actual processes of the draughtsman and the engraver; while on another (or perhaps the same) we should get more tricks of style, more attempts at arabesque, if not grotesque, with the pen. But we should hardly get such a happy example of the blend of technical knowledge and hearty unconnoisseured liking on the one hand, or of that of technical knowledge and literary appreciation on the other. And as much may be said of the best passages in almost every article.

Yet one must recur to the 'allowance'—to the admissions. Although not to such a great extent as in the case of the purely literary criticism—his greater technical knowledge in a matter where technicalities are not merely sports of opinion, saved him to some extent—there is no doubt that Thackeray does show, in these very art-criticisms, the uncertainty and undependableness that makes it impossible generally to put him in the first rank as a critic, though few people have left finer isolated examples of criticism. This uncertainty of touch is due of course to a large number of individual causes, in the separate instances; rarely to mere ignorance; not seldom to a neglect to equate and compare the pieces of his knowledge; often to the moral excess; sometimes to casual outbursts of political, social, or even personal feeling; but always, I think, in greater or lesser part to that peculiar impulsiveness in which Thackeray stands alone among the greatest prose men of letters. To regret this impulsiveness would itself be hopelessly uncritical; for it is beyond all doubt the source, in part if not in whole, of that extraordinary freshness and naturalness which we shall never be tired of noticing in him. But of course it has its dangers, even in creative work; and for the critic it is perhaps the very greatest danger of all. Even for him, it is an inspiring and driving power; a critic who has not some impulsiveness makes very dry and insipid work of it.

But it requires brake and throttle-valve to be in the best order and kept constantly at work; and this is what Thackeray, at any rate till late in his life, could not, or would not do.

Add the excessive discursiveness to which this impulsiveness leads—which is indeed only the same thing in another form—and the defects of this criticism are sufficiently confessed. But the discursiveness also has its charms: and without it, as without the other, Thackeray would not be Thackeray.

III

CATHERINE—A SHABBY GENTEEL STORY—
THE SECOND FUNERAL OF NAPOLEON—
MISCELLANIES, 1840-1

THE matter (or most of it) indicated above has communities of interest in more respects than one. In the first place it is very mainly occupied with attempts in the author's real vocation, that of a writer of prose fiction: and in the second place most of it was composed under the influence of the great affliction of his life—the gradual breaking-down of his wife's mental health. This trouble was of long duration, and it was of a somewhat peculiar character—of a character likely to influence, most specially, the production of literary work. It was not one of the common cases of a sudden and more or less violent alienation, requiring complete seclusion and professional treatment. It came on after the birth of their third child in 1840; but it was not declared absolutely hopeless for two or even three years after that; and it was not till the third year, or in fact the fourth (1843), that the house in Coram Street was given up. During this time Thackeray did everything for her that personal care could effect. He took her to Ireland; he took her to Paris; he took her to German baths. When it was thought necessary that she should be under direct medical surveillance before the final separation, he lived in the neighbourhood and saw her constantly. Now all this necessarily involved not a little expenditure: and, as has been previously said, all his private means had disappeared long ago. While perhaps only those who have tried it know what a serious tale of scattered articles at five, and ten, and even twenty guineas each[1] it takes to build up a respectable income, even with no extra calls on it.

From another point of view the wind was partly tempered to him, partly blowing at its sharpest. To some writers the constant moving about, and the absence of the accustomed study, books, &c., would have been a most serious trial, if not an insurmountable difficulty: but Thackeray was not of them. Whether from idiosyncrasy, from a habit acquired in his more Bohemian days, or from some other cause, he seems always to have preferred writing, as an Irishman might say, 'somewhere else'. He would, when there was nothing to induce him to do so but his own fancy, leave home to write at the club, the club to write at Brighton, Brighton to write at Paris. On the other hand, few men were more influenced by their affections: and the positive testimony which he has left as to the writing of the *Shabby Genteel Story*, which comes into this chapter, and the *Hoggarty Diamond*, which comes into the next, no doubt applies to almost everything from the *Shabby Genteel Story* itself to *The Irish Sketch Book*.

Catherine, however, with which we open, was finished before, though not long before, this period of gloom, during which it is improbable that it would have been begun, and during which also it would probably have been irksome to the author to finish it. It is a very odd book—the oddest in all Thackeray's work, and the most difficult to 'place' satisfactorily. It was highly prized by a few good judges at the time, but not generally

---

[1] We know that for *The Times* article on Fielding he received only five guineas: from a later saying about his lectures it would seem that five-and-twenty was more than he ever received from *Fraser*, even for long articles of nearly his best kind and time.

liked: and there have been few thorough-going partisans of it since. For myself I prefer it to *Barry Lyndon*, though it is more immature: but I have never been able exactly to understand the precise point of view from which it was written. Indeed, the author (who very seldom went wrong about his own work when he came to look at it completed and in perspective) frankly informed his mother that it was 'a mistake all through'. 'It was,' he says, with still greater accuracy, 'a disgusting subject, but not made disgusting enough.' However, this does not quite exhaust the difficulty. 'Disgusting enough' *for what*? It could hardly have been made more disgusting (in fact a good deal of repulsive detail was actually removed in the reprint) without becoming a mere study of horror and grime in itself and for its own sake—the sort of thing which he had long ago fulminated against in the tales of Pétrus Borel. But this was certainly not his object. On the other hand, if the object was what it holds itself out to be— the satire by parody of books like *Jack Sheppard*, with something more than a glance backward at *Eugene Aram*, and something of a glance sideways at *Oliver Twist*, then one may question, first, whether it is not a little too disgusting as it is, and secondly, whether in any true sense it 'gets at' any of the originals. It is neither melodramatic enough, nor romantic enough, nor senti- mental enough to do this: nor does it caricature any of these features sufficiently. On the other hand, as a piece of *Jonathan Wild* irony, though quite admirable in parts, it is not sustained enough: the author either cannot or will not keep on the grimace and gesture of the half-Mephistophelian, half-angelic mentor; and is constantly telling a plain tale, by no means disagree- able except for the unusual sordidness of the characters.

In fact we have another admission from him, which might also be anticipated by a tolerably keen critic, that he had 'a sneaking kindness' for his heroine. We know he has, and so have we: and therefore we are not pleased when poor Mrs. Cat comes to such an extremely painful end. In short the author never knows quite what hare he is hunting: and the reader is perpetually puzzled and vexed at the way in which the dogs change scent and course.

Resist this puzzlement, however—or better still, recognize the fact once for all, in virtue of and in duty to your critical faculties, and then let it 'lie on the table' —make up your mind not to an orderly *menu* of three courses and a dessert, but to picnic and pot-luck—and you will find that you get this, and a good deal more. In the first place, *Catherine* is Thackeray's first considerable and substantial *story*. Most of the things he had done in this kind had been slight sketches; the *Yellow-plush Papers* were only connected by the personage (a very minor one) of their narrator: while the great, the really gigantic, Goliah, though entire and perfect in his delightful self, had merely a bundle of yarns to give us. *Catherine* is a complete novel; there is beginning, middle, and end; not yet perfect but very well advanced character, sustained in different cases and personages throughout the book; good conversation and description; as well as no small manifestation of the author's peculiar fashion of showmanship; still more of his idiosyncrasy of style; and not a little of his predilection for a special subject and period—the manners, customs, speech, and folk of the eighteenth century. No wonder Carlyle thought it 'wonderful': for it begins with one of the vivid, slightly garrulous, half-historical, half-picturesque settings which he had done more than anybody else to teach Thackeray, but which Thackeray had, almost before Carlyle taught him, struck out and adjusted to his own idiosyncrasy. And this is well followed up. The opening chapters of *Catherine*, despite the company to which we are introduced, are absolutely of the best novel-romance kind—as good as Scott or Fielding, with a very remarkable *difference*. The difference is that which, in the middle of the sixteenth century, Alfonso Garcia Matamoros, most wonderful of forgotten pedants, anticipated M. de Buffon by laying down as *habitus orationis a cujusque hominis natura fluens*. 'The habit of the expression flowed from the nature' of Thackeray: it was the special 'cut of *his* jib'. To define it is as impossible as not to recognize it; to describe it or part of it piece by piece is not difficult; to exemplify it would take more space than here can be given, and would be both dull and unnecessary when the pieces themselves are to hand. There is a curious saturation with history and literature which betrays itself, not in digression or padding, but by constant allusion and suggestion; a light, current, apparently facile, sketching of scene and character which suddenly plunges (as a great phrase of Walt Whitman's has it) to 'the accepted hells beneath', but recovers itself at once and goes placidly on; above all, a shower of original and memorable phrases, never paraded, never dwelt upon too long, but more absolutely startling in its unique felicity than the most laboured conceits of mere phrasemongers.

It is of course true that before long, the want of thorough *digestion* in the scheme begins to betray itself; and the rather worse than picaresque degradation of the characters begins to be irksome. 'A hero' (under which term a heroine may be included) 'ought to be good,' said the neo-classics—foolishly, no doubt. But somehow *Catherine* shows us a not quite so foolish side in the saying. 'A hero ought to be successful'; foolish again, but once more with a certain justification from this singular story. Moreover, Thackeray—partly following the picaresque tradition; partly perhaps half weary of his task; partly under the generous delusion which makes the neophyte of genius give too much—has overloaded his story with incident in proportion to its length, and has made leaps and bounds of omission which, possible in a chronicle-drama, are dangerous in a novel. There is stuff here enough for a three-volume novel and the actual story is a short one-volume tale. Ensign Macshane is admirable, but somehow he seems to belong to another story. The triumph of 'Captain Wood', alias Corporal Brock, at Court, &c., though not absolutely impossible, is one of the fatal 'improbable possibilities': and Thackeray, though he is quite right in his doctrine that a villain is not a villain pure and simple, somehow makes Captain Wood too much of two gentlemen at once—or rather two blackguards— one a quite tolerable rascal and the other an atrocious ruffian. Galgenstein, the best sustained character throughout, has little individuality: and it must be a very singular taste that can enjoy Tom Billings in any way. While as for 'Cat' herself, she is, like her history, that most dangerous thing, a failure of a masterpiece. And so it happens that though the excellences of the thing are plentifully provided up to the very close, ghastly as it is, the faulty disposition of these excellences and the company in which they find themselves make the book almost impossible to *enjoy*. 'There are too many cinders in this mashed potato', as an acute though unprofessional critic once put it—

not of *Catherine* indeed, but in terms thoroughly ap-
plicable thereto.[1]

The current of thought which produced *Catherine* is
unmistakable in the article *Going to See a Man Hanged*,
which appeared a little later in the year and before the
breakdown of Mrs. Thackeray's health; but here the
ironic handling is purposely made to pass into that
indignant sentiment which is so often its next door
neighbour in Thackeray Street. The anti-capital-
punishment fad was one of the special crochets of mid-
century Liberalism, and he kept to it for some time:
but in his later and wiser days admitted that he was
wrong. The leader of the party on the occasion was
the late Lord Houghton.

The favourite English contrast of the tragic and the
farcical appears well enough in *Cox's Diary*, which,
under the infinitely inferior title of *Barber Cox and the
Cutting of his Comb*, appeared in Cruikshank's *Comic
Almanac* for 1840, before the completion of *Catherine*,
though after the appearance of most of it, and months
before the beginning of disaster. It ranks, naturally
and in more than place of appearance, with *The Fatal
Boots*. Both are intimately and specifically connected
with their illustrations: and both are deliberate ex-
travaganzas. But the *Diary* seems to me to be not
merely far the pleasanter, but also much the better of
the two. Grant the *oncle d'Amérique* and the missing

[1] No account of *Catherine* would be complete without some reference
to the curious and unlucky fact that soon afterwards appeared a *second*
Catherine Hayes (b. 1825), an Irish lady of unblemished reputation and
a singer of considerable repute, actually known later to Thackeray himself. She seems to have taken the matter quite sensibly; but the Irish
papers raised an absurd fuss, perhaps partly due to Ensign Macshane,
though he is a very good fellow for a rascal. But the disturbance and its
ultra-farcical and almost inconceivable further result belong to the
Pendennis time.

will (and if you will *not* grant these things what becomes of half the novels and half the dramas in the world?) and there remains no great improbability in any incident or character—only a permissible farce-distortion. No very original figures are wanted to work the puppet show, and none appear: while most of them, if not all, in Thackeray's own favourite metaphor 'go back to their box' to be used again. But the whole goes trippingly off: the dialogue is mostly admirable; the dinner and ball to the nobility (no new thing of course) is very light and good; and as for the billiard chapter (appropriately assigned to the month of April) it could not be better:—'these dabels is goot' indeed! I have sometimes thought that the piece has an added interest as being probably not unlike what was wanted of Dickens when he was asked to carry on Seymour's idea of the book that he called *Pickwick*; while it no doubt owes something to the great Mr. Jorrocks, who had appeared a very little earlier. Nobody, of course, would dream of putting it in competition or comparison with Thackeray's best work, or even his second best. But still it shows how he could give idiosyncrasy and 'turn' to things almost quite in common form, how perennial and perdurable his humour was. You might get parallels in story for almost every chapter of *Cox* from Theodore Hook. You might read them, *once*. I have read *Cox's Diary* at least a score of times.

A Shabby Genteel Story, unlike *Catherine*, was written, as Thackeray himself says in the pathetic note prefixed to it when it appeared in the *Miscellanies*, at the 'sad period of his life'; it was indeed actually interrupted by his misfortunes and never finished. For *Philip*, which, since its composition twenty years later, has usually had the *Story* prefixed to it as at once *lever de rideau* and

Introduction, is in no sense the finish of this, but only a sort of long distant sequel, almost less really connected than *The Virginians* is with *Esmond*. Except for the *saudades*—the remembrances of things old and sad and sweet—there was very little reason why Thackeray should have made such connexion as there is at all: and he has taken liberties unusual even with him in the process. George Brandon (or George Brand Firmin) and Mr. Tufton Hunt are transferred from Oxford to Cambridge (a migration at which no member of the former University will raise one note of protest), and the process by which Brandon 'went out in medicine' will give considerable thread to untwist, chronologically and otherwise, to any literal and painstaking commentator: not to mention that from having been, though a *roué*, a rather exceptionally good scholar, he becomes a mere quoter of the Latin grammar. One cannot say that Caroline would *not* have developed into the Little Sister: but there is no essential community between them, as there is between Beatrix Esmond and the Baroness Bernstein. For this and other reasons it seems unnecessary to apologize for separating the *Story* once more from its afterthought, and putting it in its proper place.

It is not much wonder that it remained unfinished. It was actually during its composition that the author first noticed the symptoms of his wife's malady. It does not seem to have been liked, for, referring to it in prosperous *Cornhill* days to his mother, he speaks of his straits for money, and of the publisher having 'refused him £15' apparently on this very account. Yet it is on the whole extraordinarily good. Among that peculiar class of creations which may almost be called romantic farce—and as you have romantic tragedy and romantic comedy, why not?—Andrea Fitch deserves one of the very highest places. He is hardly even exaggerated; there is no occasion to suspend disbelief about him; he is simply a well-natured, not ungifted, but weak-brained British snob, who is sincerely aping a French *buveur d'eau*, and has all his good points and none of his bad ones. This is the way in which 'Missafis' played his little part; there is no doubt of it: there is nothing to say but 'Pass! artist with the romantic properties: and all's well!'

Perhaps there is a very little more exaggeration in his amorous Marianne, but not much: and the same may be said, with even more emphasis on the 'not much', of the Gann family (barring Caroline for the moment) and their domestic, and their friends from the infatuated Swigsby downwards, and almost everybody. Of Caroline herself it may perhaps be hinted that we see rather too little to judge how much of a success she would have been. The Little Sister gives us little help: we ought to have seen the Caroline of the sham honeymoon and the not sham desertion more fully than in the mere retrospect. Certainly there is no fault in her here, nor is there in Cinqbars or Hunt, though they are more of types than Thackeray usually allows himself to draw. The most questionable figure is beyond all doubt the hero Brandon: and here once more we may trace the remains of the novitiate. It was always necessary (I do not say that it was a merit) for Thackeray either to like or to dislike his principal characters. He had not been able to make up his mind whether he liked or disliked 'Cat', and so he could never quite bring her off. He had nearly made up his mind that he disliked Brandon (there is no doubt that he did by the time that he resuscitated him as Dr.

Firmin), but he had not quite: and once more there is wavering in the touch. The story is such a torso that from some points of view it is unfair to judge it at all. But for those who are not shocked by its 'shabby gentility' (of which more later), it ought always to have very considerable charm. It is not the least of the innumerable *bienfaits de la lune* to her children that she inspired 'Pallid horb!' and the context thereof.

Even more closely connected with the disaster, though not actually cut short by it, was the article on Fielding, which accordingly I put next. It was written (he told Mrs. Brookfield) at Margate, the scene of *A Shabby Genteel Story*, the author, after his odd fashion, walking out every day to a 'little bowling-green with an arbour', writing there, and coming back to wonder what was the matter with his wife. He speaks of it elsewhere, apparently, to his mother, as 'nearly a week's work' (showing that he cannot have been long absent on each occasion), and he naturally did not consider five guineas a lavish payment. Indeed, it represents about a guinea a thousand words, which (though better than Southey's 'ten shillings for a morning's work' in *his* novitiate fifty years earlier) is not precisely munificent.

The article must be read with interest because it is the most considerable purely literary study of a single author that Thackeray had yet done; because that author is *the* author of all others whom he most resembles, and to whom he is most indebted; and because it is a distinct anticipation of *The English Humourists*. But it cannot be called a very good article: and it is impossible not to think that the circumstances explain some of its special lacks of goodness. Thackeray, it has been said, was always an unequal and incalculable critic, and a certain desultoriness was of the essence of his writing. But he generally manages to convey a curious unity in diversity into his compositions—a unity which is here quite wanting. Though by no means pinched for room, he not only does not cover his subject but does not attempt to cover it, and deals with hardly anything but the plays and *Amelia*, his attention to which is itself a sign. For we know that the later 'Amelia' of *Vanity Fair*, while she got her name from Fielding, got at least part of her nature from poor Mrs. Thackeray herself. The disproportionate amount of space devoted to Fielding's morality is, of course, in character with Thackeray's criticism generally: and the not disproportionate but rather exclusive stress on Fielding's tenderness likewise. But the first has a quite evident special connexion with the Jack Sheppard and Dick Turpin business, which had recently been filling his mind, as the second has with his actual trouble. One bold but perfectly true saying may be quoted, because of his constant generosity both to Cruikshank and to Dickens. 'Fielding's men and Hogarth's are Dickens's and Cruikshank's drawn with ten times more skill and force.' *And it was so.*

After Mrs. Thackeray's illness declared itself, the whole family were, for a certain time, more established in Paris than anywhere else—the children with their grandparents, Thackeray himself either with his wife, or, when she was moved to a *maison de santé*, in lodgings near her. It was natural, therefore, that much of the production of the end of 1840 and the greater part of 1841 should have more or less reference to the French capital, and this is the case with nearly the whole remaining matter of this chapter, *The Second Funeral of Napoleon*, the *Corsair* paper, two of the *Britannia* articles (the third, 'Reading a Poem', connects itself rather with the 'Yellowplush' series, but is inferior), and the memorable *Memorials of Gormandizing*.

Although almost any one of the more considerable pieces which Thackeray produced during his nearly ten years of struggle would have done for a text, there was reason in the selection of *The Second Funeral* for reprint in the *Cornhill Magazine* three years after his death, unusual as such a proceeding would have been in any case. For Thackeray himself had never reprinted it: and though it did not miss the admiration of some good wits at the time of its appearance (with the admirable *Chronicle of the Drum* affixed), it was quite a failure in point of sale. Very few of the royalties—sevenpence halfpenny out of half-a-crown—on which both he himself and FitzGerald characteristically dwelt in letters, ever found their way into his pocket. It was, moreover, the first substantial text (though murmurs of the kind had been heard before) for that parrot chorus of 'Cynic!' which has never entirely ceased, though it has of late years become *amoebean*—the other parrots answering with 'Sentimentalist!' Of this curious duet-contest of silliness one can only say 'et *vitulâ* tu dignus et hic', which is appropriate enough, though *ansere* would be better still if it would only scan. We shall have to do with it often. But the present occasion was certainly exemplary of that peculiar combination of cant and folly which is specially English and which Thackeray was born to scourge: as well as of the other combination of folly not exactly with cant, but with *blague*, which is as specially French, and to which he was the equally predestined boatswain's mate. There were certainly sincere and ardent admirers of Napoleon in France then, but the government and the official people generally would (to use the old story), if a hatch-

ment had been put up to him with *Resurgam,* have taken
good care to have it changed into *Requiescat in pace*:
while all the business of Joinville's homecoming was in
the lowest vein of Bobadilian swagger and theatrical
sham. But the English objection to Thackeray's treatment of this, though not so ignoble, was sillier. We had
fought Napoleon fairly, and though, after one magnanimous attempt, it had been found impossible to treat
him with absolute generosity after he was beaten, we
had not, except in the view of very sentimental people,
treated him *un*fairly then. We had, in the actual business of the 'translation', behaved with a correctness
which neither Lancelot not Amadis could surpass.
Further, Napoleon, though of marvellous genius in war
and politics, had no other good quality that the most
amiable and resourceful recording angel could manage
to discover in, or extemporaneously add to, the list
of human virtues. Yet Thackeray is not hard on him;
he is never rude to him; except slightly touching on
his creation of a sham aristocracy he hardly says anything unfavourable of him. It is the 'Vanity of Vanities',
—the humbug in part, the hollowness in all but whole,
of the performance—that he touches with a satire, now
light, now grave, but never heavy, an irony thrown up
by humour of gayer kind that is irresistible and unsurpassable. He had never perhaps done a faultless
thing before: he did one here. The alternations but
never discords of mood and tone; the admirable descriptions, of the peculiar Thackerayan kind, using
utmost economy of words to produce the fullest largeness
of effect; the manners- and character-painting; the
absolute idiosyncrasy of style—all these are marvellous.
They had nobody among rising English men of letters
in that winter of 1840–1 who had done—there were not

more than three or four other men living who were to do—anything so perfect in any style as this is in its own.

The other articles must be passed over briefly, though not one is negligible, and all (save perhaps 'Reading a Poem') are admirable. The additional Paris Sketches from the *Corsair* and the *Britannia* are better than the *average* of *The Sketch Book* itself. 'Men and Coats' [1] (not unsuggested perhaps by *Sartor* and by Diderot) is very pleasant. But *Memorials of Gormandizing* rises to a higher strain. It appears to have been intended to form part of a book, '*Dinner Reminiscences, or The Young Gormandizer's Guide*' which was actually advertised in *The Second Funeral*, but which never appeared: though there are some 'condolences and vails' for it in other articles which will come later. The 'Memorials' as they stand could not be better. The only blot on them—the drinking of Sauterne after Beaune—appears to have been due to Gustavus, not to Michael Angelo; the actual bills and menus will be priceless for posterity: and the whole article is itself a 'made dish', as the honest simple old English phrase goes, of the most superlative quality.

In fact, from this volume (let us remember, though we postpone, *The Chronicle of the Drum*, and that 'Dear Lucy' appeared in the 'Memorials') it is evident to any competent judgement what an amazingly accomplished and versatile genius England had in the Thackeray who was but just thirty years old. The accomplishment is in parts still a little behind the variety and the quality, but only a little: and in parts again it is almost if not

---

[1] This was a very little later in composition than some pieces to be mentioned in the next chapter. But it combines and contrasts with its companion in *Fraser* very happily.

quite up to them. The best of *Catherine*; the best of
A Shabby Genteel Story; the best of *Cox's Diary*; all *The
Second Funeral*; the handful of lighter articles; the verse
—where else shall we find a twelve or eighteen months'
work of such volume, such vigour, such variety?

IV

THE HOGGARTY DIAMOND, ETC.

THE Great Hoggarty Diamond, like most of the work dealt with in the previous chapter, belongs to the period when the shadow was most over Thackeray: and perhaps in a way it helped, all guiltlessly, to make that shadow darker. It was actually refused by *Blackwood*—one of the rare instances of utter and unaccountable mistake on the part of the usually keen-sighted conductors of that periodical. Although received and published by *Fraser*, it does not seem to have been liked by the public (a justification, some may say, of the *Blackwood* refusal), and it is said that the author was asked to cut it short. This is not at all improbable, for the latter part is certainly huddled up: and not a few things in it would have borne, and actually invited, expansion in Thackeray's best manner. Nay, its ill-luck seems not to have entirely abandoned it yet: for the preface of the 'Biographical Edition' volume in which it occurs says little or nothing about it, and one careful commentator on Thackeray has pronounced it 'dull'.

Its author, on the other hand, thought it the best thing he had written before *Vanity Fair*, and as usual he was right, even if, as in the case of *A Shabby Genteel Story*, he might have been in danger of a 'pathetic fallacy'. For, as he also says himself, his heart was very soft when he was writing it, with thoughts that, on Lord Chesterfield's maxim, might have made it hard.[1] Not merely his wife's actual illness, but the loss of their second child a year or two earlier, as well as the pressure

[1] *Le mal moral endurcit le cœur autant que le mal physique l'attendrit.*

of want of money, have left their marks on it: there are
not a few tears in the ink with which it is written. Yet
these tears have made the record in no way thin or
pale or washy; in fact the present writer's judgement
of it was formed when he had little or no knowledge
of the circumstances of its composition. If it is not so
perfect as *The Second Funeral*, it must be remembered that
it is creation and not merely criticism: if it has less
power than parts of *Catherine*, it is far less unequal; if
it has not the wilder humour of *Yellowplush* and *Gahagan*,
it tries more difficult strings and does not fail in the
trial. And that extraordinary fullness and variety of
living presentation which was to be—which was already
—Thackeray's great and almost unique attribute appears here marvellously to those who have eyes. The
story is but a little one still—still only, as it were, a
one-decker beside the regulation three. But in the crew
of the average three-decker itself, during the three
generations or thereabouts during which that noble
craft swept the seas, men thought themselves lucky if
they found one or two, extremely lucky if they found
half a dozen, really live characters, neither hopelessly
wooden nor merely replicas of something antecedent.
Everybody in *The Great Hoggarty Diamond* is alive from
forecastle to cabin. The captain (to clench and drop
the metaphor) is not the best of all, but that can hardly
be helped. A hero who is also the narrator takes upon
himself almost impossible difficulties: it is well if he gets
out of them no worse than does Samuel Titmarsh. Mrs.
Titmarsh, though she is hardly the heroine, and though
of course the contemners of Amelia and Helen cannot
be expected to admire her, plays her part well enough.
The pathos of it and of the whole need not annoy any
sensible person: it is not dashed and brewed to mawkish-

ness in the fashion of some writers, and it certainly sets off the comic and satiric parts legitimately enough. The richness and variety of these and of the characters that work them out are quite astonishing; Lady Drum of herself would almost carry the thing off. If you take her as a mere *menteuse*, half the fun is lost. It is quite clear that she did know something about the Hoggarties, though she romanced it up with a mere tissue of fiction. And all the other 'noble' characters, Lady Fanny and Lady Jane, Tiptoff and Preston (though the latter is slight and almost conventional), fit very well. On the other hand, the contrast of the Roundhands, Gus Hoskins, and the rest, supplies the foil in Thackeray's own special way, and they again clamour for comparison with such originals as they had in Hook and others.

But the author has not contented himself with a mere contrast of almost promiscuous manner-sketches. He has knit it all with another study of 'diddling', not now mere gambling, but commercial fraud of the kind which, never unknown, was becoming commoner than ever in consequence of the mania for companies. And all the studies here, from that extremely human swindler Mr. Brough downwards, are again admirable. Compare, for instance, the advance in Captain Fizgig on Captain Tagrag in *Cox's Diary*. They are very close, but the later figure is far less of a caricature, and, little as he has to do, more finished and 'signed'. As for Mrs. Hoggarty, the gallery of Thackeray's intolerable female creations—aunts, mothers-in-law, and so forth—a chamber of horrors in a fashion, but of most attractive and irresistible horrors to those who do not suffer from them in the flesh—a gallery effecting purgation by pity and terror like few—could most certainly not spare her.

And over all there is the perpetual soft 'snowing of meat and drink' in the shape of delectable and memorable phrase and situation. From the rosolio and the history of the miniature onward the situations are inexhaustible and the language always more than matches the situations, while never drumming them in and bawling for attention to them. It was the absence of this latter practice, I suppose, which made people so slow to recognize Thackeray; they had not sharpness of eye or fineness of ear enough to detect, and therefore they did not enjoy, the constant *doubleness* of speech and suggestion and allusion. Even for those who are more fortunate or better trained the supply is so plentiful and so unostentatious that there is no getting to an end of it. You may read Thackeray fifty times and find something fresh at the fiftieth. But with a certain class of readers the enjoyment never begins: and it is not surprising that they feel themselves defrauded. The adventures of a mere clerk in a swindling company, who is himself not even a swindler! 'Go to,' they say, 'this is milk and water!'

At the same time it would be distinctly uncritical not to recognize that there were some excuses for the readers of 1840 and thereabouts. In the first place, say what we may, there is no doubt that the two generations since (taking the usual intervals of thirty years at 1870 and 1900), nay, that even readers a decade later, had a great and illegitimate advantage—that of looking back at this early work through the later and greater. It is certainly easier to detect the virtues of Yellowplush and Titmarsh after they have been emphasized, isolated, magnified in *Vanity Fair* and *Pendennis* than to anticipate *Pendennis* and *Vanity Fair* from *Miss Shum's Husband* and *The Hoggarty Diamond*. Not only were the actual qualities lesser in themselves for the most part, and more mixed with defects; but they were presented in a manner perhaps not wilfully but inevitably suited to disgust or at any rate not to attract the public. Yet these readers cannot be wholly acquitted, and they undoubtedly represented an ebb-tide in appreciation. They were ill-served by their professional Mentors— general English criticism in the second quarter of the century is, with some great exceptions, far inferior to that of the first and third. Nor did they do much for themselves. They had left Tennyson to 'ripen his wine', as the French say, for ten long years, without caring in the least whether he ripened it or not. They had turned an obstinately deaf ear to Browning. They mostly still thought Carlyle a crackbrained jargonist. They had welcomed Dickens, much less for his real genius than because everybody, from pit to gallery, could see that he was 'funny', and because he both harrowed and edified the gallery in the way they liked. Thackeray, on the other hand, was a puzzle: and the age, which was at least honest, was not one of those which feel that it is creditable to like puzzles. It did not care whether this was creditable or not: it knew that it did not like them.

Yet he went on undauntedly accumulating his proofs for the Order of the Spirit. That he would have done so without the pressure of necessity there is, perhaps, little reason to believe. He must in any case have drawn —it seems to have been as necessary for him to draw as to breathe; and he must have furnished some of these drawings with the quaint letterpress which we know so well. He might, for his own or others' amusement, have expanded these things now and then into pieces like *The Rose and the Ring*. He was a great letter-writer as it was: when it becomes possible to collect all his extant letters they will form no mean body in bulk and an extraordinary one in merit. But as an independent gentleman or a place-holder, he would probably have rivalled Horace Walpole in epistolary quantity. Otherwise we should probably have lost him—a fact which may be pointed out but certainly need not be moralled on.

Some little pieces which followed *The Hoggarty Diamond*, and one or two that slightly preceded it, are mostly trifles. *Rolandseck* and *Little Spitz* owe their origin no doubt to Thackeray's older Weimar experiences, refreshed by those of his recent visits to German baths in hopes of benefit to his wife. The better *Sultan Stork* is a fresh plume in the mighty helmet of the invincible Major Gahagan. *Dickens in France* partly does the justice which Thackeray always liked to do to his successful rival, partly takes up that old theme of the 'Kean' article in the *Sketch Book*—the extraordinary fancy of the French for travestying English life, and taking the travesty quite seriously. The *compte rendu* of the play and its intervals is quite admirable: and if the 'thonging' of Jules Janin which follows, itself treats the matter with rather too much seriousness, there was some excuse for it. 'Honest Janin' (for Thackeray in his usual way became reconciled to him directly he knew him) is not the only French critic—nor the only French critic of the name of Jules—who has criticized English literature without being able to read it: and the practice is certainly not one to be encouraged.

But these things are little more than, in the excellent Carlylean phrase, 'honest journeywork in default of better'. Thackeray did not himself reprint any of them, though no doubt many poor people would have been

glad to do so had they been theirs: and I at least should
have been sorry not to possess *Sultan Stork* and *Dickens
in France*. With *The Fitz-Boodle Papers* and *Men's Wives*
it is different. These he took care to reprint (not quite
completely, but nearly so) in the *Miscellanies* of 1857;
they contain some of his best and most characteristic
work; and it may be thought surprising that he did not
publish them separately very much earlier. But he had
probably been disgusted by the comparative failure of
The Paris Sketch Book, the *Comic Sketches*, and *The
Second Funeral*: it is to be observed that *The Hoggarty
Diamond* itself never appeared as a book till eight years
after its magazine date and when *Vanity Fair* had turned
the tide. As for these groups themselves, they are both
due ostensibly to the new *eidolon* George Fitz-Boodle:
and 'Confessions', 'Professions', and *Men's Wives* are in
fact mere sub-titles. Nor is it quite superfluous to point
out that the new *nom de guerre* and the personage attached
to it have a certain connexion with reality. Thackeray
does not want to confine himself to burlesque of any
kind such as Yellowplush and Gahagan could appropriately father. He is flying at higher game than the
lower middle-class society, for which the Titmarshes
were suitable till Michael Angelo left his Paris and
London Bohemianism and established himself at Mrs.
Clapperclaw's lodgings. Fitz-Boodle is of the clubs
clubby, as Thackeray, not merely or mainly of his own
choice, had been forced to be now for years. There is
never so much of Thackeray in him as there is in Titmarsh the greater: but he has Thackerayan touches.
Indeed, the people who go wrong in trying to identify
certain of Thackeray's characters stock and block with
real persons, might take a lesson from these various *eidola*.
They always have something Thackerayan; they never by

any chance contain anything like the whole Thackeray. As he dealt with himself so did he with others.

Yet I am much mistaken if, in these Fitz-Boodle Papers, there is not something of a Thackeray more developed, more 'grown-up' than any that we have yet seen. In all that has gone before, even in *The Hoggarty Diamond*, even in *The Second Funeral*, there has been a certain youthfulness. The writer enters into his characters and their life with marvellous completeness and accuracy, but he does not yet quite dominate them. Here he begins to do so, and even in a way to dominate life itself, in that singular fashion which was to distinguish him later, and in which only Tourguénieff among still later novelists approaches him. To a certain extent this may of course be set down to the advance of years: for nothing in these two groups is earlier (as far as appearance goes) than the end of 1842, and some things in them are as late as the end of 1843. Nor was the Greek comic poet quite right when he said that 'number of years brings nothing but old age itself'. Still, eighteen months, merely as eighteen months, is not much. It is impossible not to assign some influence to the sorrow and to the hardship through which he had passed, among the influences which made him know the earthly as well as the heavenly powers better. He has not, of course, deserted the comic, even the farcical: but farce and comedy are shot and shadowed throughout with a deeper tissue and atmosphere of 'criticism of life'. At first Fitz-Boodle is almost a conventional 'plunger': and his contempt of 'littery gents' and awkward exception of 'Oliver Yorke' form part of that rather clumsy *prosopopoeia* or *eidolopoeia* which has been more than once referred to. Even the 'Professions', though full of clever things, and in the 'gormandizing' case almost of the best class, may be dismissed if any one likes (though I should not like) as merely very excellent fooling.

But the 'Confessions' are much more. When he republished the group, Thackeray left out 'Minna Löwe', perhaps because of too close a personal touch (for there certainly does seem to be something of the kind), perhaps because he thought it over-farcical. But it was rightly restored, forty years ago, for more than completeness' sake, inasmuch as Dorothea and Ottilia need that Ebrew Jewess to set off themselves and the tale of George Fitz-Boodle's misfortunes in love. Compare these things with the five or six years earlier *Professor*, good as that is, and the advance will be seen at once. Here, too, as for obvious and numerous reasons was fitting, does that 'Heinesque' character which has also been noticed come out more powerfully than ever— the cynical sentimentalism, the satiric romance, which seems to puzzle some folk so hopelessly in these two masters and which is so delectable in its amaritude to others. Nor should we miss one of those quaint infusions, if not of actual experience of actual conditions and surroundings, which go for so much in Thackeray— the episode of the polyonymous Mr. Blake and the Mediterranean heath and Connemara. Thackeray had just been in Connemara when it was written: and, though only a German commentator will take the rest of the anecdote as autobiographical, it knits the old times of travel and of many other things to the new with that magic touch of association which only such knittings possess.

Another point, though of a different nature, must be noticed, because of its great curiosity. When the late Dr. Garnett republished Shelley's long lost *Victor and Cazire* I observed at once the extraordinary resemblance

between the contrasted 'Willow-songs' of 'Ottilia' and
one of the poems thus disinterred. Dr. Garnett, when
I told him of it, acknowledged the resemblance, but
thought it impossible that Thackeray could have seen
the poem. I cannot in the least see the impossibility.
We know that at Cambridge he was much interested in
Shelley, when Shelley had only been dead less than
ten years. There must have been copies of the book
about: for we are told that something like a hundred
escaped destruction, and that at least two reviews of it
appeared. Why should not Thackeray have seen one,
or seen the piece copied somewhere? As not everybody
who has a Shelley certainly possesses *Victor and Cazire*,
it may be as well to print the piece. As will be seen,
there is no question of plagiarism whatsoever, but only
of reminiscent parody. The likeness of rhythm and
spirit is unmistakable.

> Fierce roars the midnight storm
>   O'er the wild mountain,
> Dark clouds the night deform,
>   Swift rolls the fountain—
>
> See o'er yon rocky height
>   Dim mists are flying—
> See, by the moon's pale light,
>   Poor Laura's dying.
>
> Shame and remorse shall howl
>   By her false pillow—
> Fiercer than storms that roll
>   O'er the white billow;
>
> No hand her eyes to close,
>   When life is flying,
> But she will find repose,
>   For Laura's dying!

Then will I seek my love,
Then will I cheer her.
Then my esteem will prove,
When no friend is near her.

On her grave I will lie
When life is parted,
On her grave I will die,
For the false-hearted.

Dr. Garnett, though he had not noticed the 'Ottilia' song, thought this piece might be the plagiarism from 'Monk' Lewis which actually caused the withdrawal of the book. It is more Della Cruscan than Lewisian, I should say; while everybody will, of course, notice the resemblance of the whole group to Fitz-Eustace's song in *Marmion*.

Men's Wives are more unequal: and it is not, I think, difficult to discover the reason. The first, 'Mr. and Mrs. Frank Berry,' is a mixture of some of Thackeray's most favourite motives, handled in nearly his happiest manner. The 'Slaughter House' reminiscences—still a little revengeful, but far from wholly so—and the fight are beyond praise: the dinner, the partial revolt of Frank, and his submission to his Angelica are not unworthy of their overture. And the whole has the right and harmonious tone which can hardly be given except by a man who is applying universal knowledge of humanity to a part of humanity which he knows *intus et in cute*.

But in the much longer and more important 'Ravenswing' this is not quite the case. It also is full of good things:—the ejaculation of Mr. Hooker Walker that the eyes of his beloved are as 'big as b-b-billiard balls, by Jove!' and the return from Richmond are only the chief among a hundred touches admirable in phrase and situation. But without sharing in the least the objection to 'lowness' one cannot but remark, not wholly with satisfaction, that the author has dropped back to his shady, his 'shabby genteel' surroundings, and that in doing so he has rather forgotten his present mouth-piece. Was George Fitz-Boodle exactly the sort of man to know all about 'The Bootjack' and the loves and quarrels of tradesmen? He might have known the Ravenswing as a *diva*; he might have heard a great deal of gossip about her; but this intimate chroniclership is not endowed with verisimilitude. The character-interest, too, of the piece is rather too much in the sense of a theatrical 'character-part'. Nobody is other than human: it was as impossible by this time for anybody of Thackeray's making not to live as for a coat of Mr. Woolsey's not to fit. But the humanity is more typical than individual: more conventional and superficial than deep and ingrained; more French than English. And the result is that, though Morgiana is a good creature, one feels that her adventures are perhaps rather unduly prolonged, and does not care to see her through them quite as much as usual. In hardly any case, I think, often as I have read everything of Thackeray's, can I take up a piece of his, small or great, without reading it through. I have read 'The Ravenswing' through more than once or half a dozen times; but I have also *not* read it through sometimes. A scene amuses; but you can lay it down.

Now I believe the explanation of this to be furnished by the actual postcript, which declared that the body of the piece was 'written a long time since'. Without internal evidence it would of course be extremely innocent to take this as evidence: but it happens to confirm the internal evidence and be confirmed by it re-markably. 'The Ravenswing' bears all the appearance

of a piece written at least as early as *A Shabby
Genteel Story* in the main, but doctored with some more
modern touches—the passage about 'Members deceased' in Clubs is only one of a dozen—and put by
the author under the cloak of Fitz-Boodle when it had
been proved that the magazine public did not dislike
the cut of that jib.

On the other hand 'Dennis Haggarty's Wife' is certi-
fied as not much earlier than the date of its appearance
by evidence of two different kinds. On the face of it
it could not have been written before Thackeray's Irish
tour of 1842—the description of the Irish part is too
fresh and vivid. But the manner of it would give bail
for its maturity if there were no such circumstantial
corroboration. It is, of course, not long—a trifle some
would call it. But where has even Thackeray exhibited
better that dreadful irony of fate of which his delineation
is always so much more effective than the plasterings
with gloom and grime in which our later pessimists
have indulged? He never did a maturer thing: though
he has dashed the strokes with something of passion.
Indeed, none of his numerous pictures of connexions
by marriage has a more vivid quality—goes more 'to
the blood', as the good old phrase went, than this.
If we had that story which has never yet been told
but which he says[1] he told to the lady at dinner 'between the entreés and the roast', we should know all
about it; but as it is we can only guess.

As to the fourth, 'The ——'s Wife' (which he did not
himself reprint, though it was reprinted in America
during his lifetime, and which has only recently been
added to his works in England), it does not seem to
me at all unworthy of its company. It has the German

[1] In the *Roundabout* on 'Two Children in Black'.

stamp which is on so much of the Fitz-Boodle division: it is effectively told: and Angelica Diabolica has already something of Beatrix in her. Probably he thought that there was too much romance in it and not quite enough: while on the other hand there was not enough satire of romance. Perhaps he had—I do not know—gone closer to some German or French original than he cared to do in a piece not burlesqued. But though the thing is no wonder, it is quite good enough to resume its original place in the quartette, which it indeed completes rather artistically. For 'Mr. and Mrs. Frank Berry' is comedy with the mildest tragic touch, and some farce to compensate for this; 'The Ravenswing' is ungenteel comedy, farcical too; 'Dennis Haggarty' is pure tragedy with only the permissible lighter overture; and 'The ——'s Wife' comes in well to these with its romantic tragedy only blended with a satiric grimness. Altogether Mr. George Fitz-Boodle served his creator well: and one is rather sorry that that creator's pencil was less busy with him than his pen. For some reason, or none, there is hardly any part of Thackeray's writings so destitute of light from 'the author's own candles' as that written under Fitz-Boodle's name: and unless I am deceived we do not even know what he was like in the flesh.

V

THE IRISH SKETCH BOOK—CONTRIBU-
TIONS TO THE 'FOREIGN QUARTERLY
REVIEW', 1842–4

THE extraordinary versatility which has been noted as characterizing Thackeray's decade of probation is illustrated once more in *The Irish Sketch Book*. Nor need we pause to inquire whether this versatility was the restlessness of unsuccessful tentative, the unquiet persistence which tries all doors before it finds one that gives access to the whole house. The two volumes differed from any of their predecessors in more ways than one. They gave much more extensive handling to a single subject than he had before attempted. They were much the most serious: for though there is plenty of Thackeray's lightest touch there is no mere burlesque. Indeed, the resemblance of *The Paris Sketch Book* and *The Irish Sketch Book* is merely verbal and titular. For the first time, and necessarily, the author was bound to unity of subject in a work of very considerable substance.

The tour which provided this subject occupied the summer and autumn of 1842: and the record of it was published next year. By the time that it was begun, Mrs. Thackeray's case, if not quite pronounced hopeless, was nearly so, and Thackeray's mind must have been settling towards that hardest of all makings-up.

Ut quod vides perisse perditum ducas.

Even without the confirmatory letters which have recently been published, it was always easy to perceive in the book the alternation of depression, attempt to bid dull care begone, and approaching cicatrization—to some extent—of the wound. But these are not too prominent: and they should not be made so artificially in reading it.

Neither need any one be over careful or troubled about its political colour. It is said, though with some discrepancies of detail, and as far as I know, not by any one who professes to have seen the document, that Thackeray wrote, either for the first or the second edition, a preface strongly condemning English government in Ireland, which was suppressed at the publisher's desire. And Sir Leslie Stephen expressed the opinion that Thackeray, had he lived, would have been a Home Ruler. Sir Leslie did not personally know his future father-in-law. It is quite likely that the preface was written, and of the tenor mentioned. But what Thackeray wrote on politics was never of the smallest importance. He had not 'the political head': if he had been even wiser than he was he would have said like Mr. Midshipman Easy of things ecclesiastical, 'Well! I don't understand these things'. And his opinion, on whatever side of politics it might have been given, could have been nothing but a curiosity. What is certain is that Irish 'patriotism' was not inclined to take the book as a manifesto on its side; that there was no political party so often under the lash of Thackeray's sharpest satire as these same Irish patriots; and that the lesson of the book certainly has not seemed to all readers to spell what Sir Leslie thought it spelt. Indeed, a person not unacquainted with the subject once recommended to all who would understand the Irish question three books— Spenser's *State of Ireland*, Wolfe Tone's *Autobiography*, and *The Irish Sketch Book*.

But the importance, for us, of the different constructions put upon it is that there is not really in it *any* political colour so strongly daubed that it interferes with the harmonious composition of the thing from the artistic point of view, or with the comfortable reading of it from the humbler point of pastime. From both it seems to me a very remarkable thing: and there is hardly a book of Thackeray's that I have read oftener. As has been suggested above, that necessary unity of subject— or at least of canvas—is a very great gain for him. No one, speaking critically at all, could say that he was by nature overprovided with a tendency towards the architectonic: in fact, this was notoriously his weakest point, if it be not slightly absurd to apply the term weakness to a source of the greatest possible strength. Without his *tangential* quality, the greatest and most delectable part of Thackeray would not and could not exist. But he had not merely an excuse for the display of it now: he had a positive call. It was his business to survey Ireland in zigzag from Dublin to Bantry and from Waterford to the Giant's Causeway; his duty to take the miscellany of sport and business, scenery and manners, high and low, rich and poor, as the stuffing of his book. The only danger was that he should not be content with the variety of his subject and should indulge too much in arabesque and grotesque of treatment. He might have been tempted to do this earlier: but he saved himself completely from doing it here. No opportunity for really comic handling, within limits, is lost, but none is forcibly made; and none is 'improved' out of keeping and decorum. It is curious, and it shows what a master he was, that he who has undoubtedly worked the burlesque capacities of Irish character to almost their utmost elsewhere, is quite sober and faithful in his record of them here: and that the light comedy is as successful as the merely farcical. From the astonish-

ing fertility of the Dublin schools in prizemen to the
innocent pride of the gentleman from 'Tchume' in his
infallible judgement of the weight of a quarter of mutton
it is all reported in 'the grave and chaste manner'. He
does not 'Theodore Hook it' or 'Dickens it' even with
matter so tempting as that of the behaviour of the college cook at Glengariff. That, on the other hand, there
are some of those 'serious' or 'obvious' outbursts of his
which make some of his critics so angry cannot be denied.
He will flare out at capital punishment, having elsewhere in the book shown how absolutely necessary it
is; he will (shocking to relate!) commiserate a widow
who has a ne'er-do-well son; he will use exceedingly
violent and inconvenient language about convents and
Roman Catholicism generally. In fact, he will be the
Thackeray whom we know—the Thackeray who is
Thackeray—and not somebody else. Now we cannot
do without Thackeray: with the somebody else it is
but too probable that we could, and should be
happy to, do.

The idiosyncrasy of the book thus consists in a blended
and double unity—that of subject and that of handling.
It is at once a panorama of Ireland and a *poly-*, if not
quite a *pan*-orama of Thackeray. It is a book of travels
and one of the best: but it is also a kind of novel, or at
least biography, with its author for hero. We have a
view of Irish places and manners in 1842, if not as extensive, at any rate almost as varied as that of Little Billee
during his respite at the masthead. But we are also personally conducted over Thackerayania in that year and
1843: and the two experiences, while not in the least
clashing, support and supplement each other marvellously.

Of course this particular application of literature was

not absolutely new: nothing ever is. Not to make a
History of Literature out of a commentary of this kind,
it exists before Montaigne and in Montaigne eminently
after a fashion; it is evident enough in Addison; Sterne
adapts it to this very purpose of travel-writing. It had
been obvious to those who could see, in the earlier
Thackeray, almost from the very first. But in himself,
hitherto, there had been veils and disguises of burlesque
and grotesque as well as adaptations and adulterations
to suit the various personages assumed—Yellowplush,
Gahagan, the Titmarshes, Fitz-Boodle. And in his predecessors just mentioned, and others (with the exception of Fielding, who has much less of the personal
element), there had been more or less *pose*, and much
more than less determination (at least in Montaigne and
Sterne) to make the delineation of themselves the first
consideration, the subject the second. It is in this last
point that Thackeray differs from all other writers. If
any one thinks that there is in him any pose—any deliberate self-showmanship, let that person know once for
all that he has utterly failed to comprehend his author.
The subjects of most, in fact of all, other egotistic writers
are, as it were, apropos of themselves; secondary; mere
stalking-horses or arquebuss-rests, or spring-boards.
Thackeray's egotism is always apropos of his subject;
subsidiary to it, caused by it. He can, whenever it is
necessary, lay it aside altogether, as Montaigne and
Sterne never can. Of the two absolute summits of his
work and of prose fiction—the home-coming of Rawdon
Crawley in *Vanity Fair*, and the mock duel which really
closes *Esmond*—the first contains absolutely nothing of
his personality, and the second so little, that only
the most punctilious criticism need acknowledge it.
Thackeray would probably have behaved as the

Marquis of Esmond behaved in the situation: but that
is all.

Here, of course, the conditions are different from those
of a novel: but not so very different. The Thackerayan
camera has to accept its scenes, personages, conversations, incidents, from the outside: they are not invented
inside it. But none the less it gives its own peculiar
presentation—its 'Thackeray-type'—of each word, and
thing, and place, and person. A mere catalogue of the
gallery would be out of place here, fondly as one thinks
of its individual pictures. The wonderful sketch of the
Kingstown-Dublin road—so vivid and so free from
exaggeration and repetition—with the characteristic
self-satire on it; the Feast of the Lobster; the coach-drive
through the South-Eastern counties—but the catalogue
is insinuating itself already. And the excursions—such
as that remarkable one into Irish chapbooks which had
no little effect on Thackeray's future writing—are more
than worthy of the main journey. I used, by the way, to
think that Thackeray must have invented the apparently burlesque verse of the *Battle of Aughrim*, which
is much like his own actual burlesques. But I found out
that it was genuine, though I have mislaid the author's
highly respectable name.

Besides the connexion, not merely with 'Dennis Haggarty's Wife' (see last chapter), but with *Barry Lyndon*
(see next) and other things, as well as with his almost
assured homelessness, *The Irish Sketch Book* has other
interesting links with Thackeray's biography. The tour,
as planned originally, was to have been taken in Fitz-
Gerald's company: and letters to him in its earlier part
at least have been published. But the close of the journey, the second visit to Dublin, in which he saw much
of Lever, and enjoyed 'wax candles and some of the best

wine in Europe' in such hospitable profusion, was the
occasion of one of the few outside accounts of him that
we have for this earlier period —the reminiscences contributed to Fitzpatrick's *Life of Lever* by a certain
'Major D.' This excellent officer seems to have behaved
to Thackeray with the usual kindness of his country, and
to have admired him; but to have been rather puzzled
and suspicious; to have feared that the guest was trying
to make fun of Ireland and things Irish; to have thought
him censorious and acid. We know well enough, from
even more authentic sources, that Thackeray's temper
at the time was pretty variable—and no wonder.
But Lever himself seems to have made no mistake
about him. The most interesting part of the information derived from this source is the opinion, generally
it would seem entertained in Dublin circles, that
Thackeray was a sort of 'Swiss of literature'—hiring
himself out to any periodical that would pay him.
Although this was scarcely the case, we know, again,
that he had had to 'stand in the market' from dire
necessity. But the fact is, that the prejudice against
miscellaneous literary work for pay was still strong and
deep. More than thirty years later than this, and more
than a dozen after Thackeray's own death, an excellent
lady expressed her disgust and astonishment that persons educated at Oxford and reckoned among gentlemen should write 'for penny papers'. Stamps and paper
duties were in the way of penny papers in 1842: but
there can be no doubt that the cost *ne faisait rien à l'affaire*.

Thackeray's dedications were always graceful, but the
actual one of this book, to Lever, as originally written,
was even prettier than that which appears, though a little
more controversial. And the book had the good fortune
not merely to be godfathered by 'Harry Lorrequer,'

but to be the subject of a letter of compliments from 'Boz'. The 'pink covers' to which Thackeray made characteristic reference, and the 'green' for once rallied round the future 'yellow'.

Of the articles from the *Foreign Quarterly Review* which follow *The Irish Sketch Book*, in 'The Oxford Thackeray', only *one*, 'Dumas on the Rhine', had already been printed (and that only by Mr. Lewis Melville) with Thackeray's Works. But all the others, and some which I did not think worth giving, appeared in a volume entitled *The New Sketch Book* (London, 1906), having been unearthed from the *Foreign Quarterly Review* by Mr. Robert S. Garnett. There is, so far as I know, no direct external evidence of their authorship. But there is some, and that not weak, of an indirect kind, such as the fact that the *Review* had just passed into the hands of Chapman and Hall, Thackeray's publishers for the Sketch Book at the time when those articles began to appear, and that he definitely mentions in a letter to FitzGerald his having read Hugo's *Le Rhin*, adding that he was actually writing about it. This is pretty strong, though after all not decisive: for just after a book appears a considerable number of gentlemen of the press are usually reading it, and writing about it, and making references to it in letters to their friends.

One is driven, therefore, to internal evidence: and it is by this that I have been guided both as to admission to and exclusion from the Thackeray canon. About this article on *Le Rhin*, and about the last of the group, that on Michiel's *L'Angleterre*, there can be no doubt whatever. They are as certainly Thackeray's as if he had included them in the Miscellanies of 1857. The Michiels article in particular connects itself with passages in the acknowledged works from *The Paris Sketch Book* to *Philip*.

That the book was an impudent *supercherie* is of course certain: and it is possible, though not necessary, that the author never was in England at all. But the curious thing is that Michiels was by no means a mere gutter-journalist. Not only does he seem to have had the best of it in an encounter with Arsène Houssaye for buccaneering on a great history of Flemish and Dutch Painting which he wrote: but he did some other fairly solid work in art and letters, and edited what is still, I think, the only modern edition of that interesting Pléiade, pluralist, plagiarist, and victim of Malherbe, Desportes. On this occasion, however, he seems to have been tempted of the devil that so frequently besets French writers on England. I remember a very amusing article, I think in *Household Words*, summarizing some further efforts of the same imaginative kind in reference to the Exhibition of 1851, where (I think again) M. Edmond Texier was the chief performer on the long bow. 'The German in England' is also fairly well 'signed.' The abstract of *The Mysteries of Paris* is either by Thackeray or by some one who has caught his style thoroughly—a thing at this time unlikely for any one even to try to do. 'French Romancers on England' and 'New Accounts of Paris' are exceedingly probable. These, therefore, with 'Dumas on the Rhine' and another to be mentioned presently, are given.

On the other hand, Mr. Garnett has printed five other articles, of which four at least seem to me either not Thackeray's or Thackeray very much 'edited', cut about and padded with alien matter. The doubtful one is that on Herwegh: those on Dumas' *Crimes Célèbres*, on Gutzkow's *Letters from Paris*, 'Balzac on the Paris News-papers', and 'English History and Character on the French Stage', are, to me, more than doubtful. Several

of these of course read, *from their titles*, very much as if
they might be Thackeray's: but this, it must be remembered, is an additional reason for care in considering
them. And the result of that consideration has been, in
my case, unfavourable. The 'Celebrated Crimes',
though we know that Thackeray did read the book, is
absolutely unlike his style in almost every way. And
there are hardly any quotations: whereas there was
nothing that he liked better than to quote, translate, and
(it must be admitted) in some cases ingeniously travesty.
The Gutzkow article is also very unlike him, or like
nothing of his but the political papers in the *Constitutional*, and not *very* like them. The Balzac piece and the
general one on 'English Character' are less certainly impossible: but I am not satisfied with them. The Herwegh essay seems worth excepting from the doom on
the chance chiefly of the translations being his.

There is some special interest in these pieces because
of their date. In part slightly earlier than the Irish tour,
in part contemporary with the writing of *The Irish
Sketch Book*, and only in very small part later than 1843,
they represent much of Thackeray's energy as *homme de
peine* in that year and 1842. With *The Fitz-Boodle Papers*,
and the more miscellaneous contributions to *Punch* and
Fraser which will follow, they present an extraordinary
combination of quantity and quality for a couple of
twelvemonths and less. Of course many journalists and
novelists in regular work could beat the quantity easily:
but perhaps not quite so the quality. It also happens
that there is, on the whole, in these reviews, a much
greater unity of subject than in most of Thackeray's
batches of miscellaneous articles: for the series, though
not purely literary, is very mainly so.

It shows the author, from this point of view, at an

interesting stage. He has not got rid wholly—he never, as has been said, got rid wholly, though he did so to a much greater extent—of the inequality and flightiness of his literary judgements. He is not yet reconciled to Dumas—indeed Dumas had not yet written the great romances that were to atone for so much. He still feels the absurdities in Victor Hugo first and most; but, then, in the same way, the marvellous second crop, which began with the *Châtiments*, and did not cease with the *Légende*, was yet far in the future: and *Le Rhin*, full of beauties, is also full of absurdities and worse. It is evident, as Mr. Garnett has rightly pointed out, that he has already conceived that one-sided view of Swift, about which we shall have something to say when we come to its full development in *The English Humourists*. He lets his little crotchets about 'rails being better than swords' and the like interfere somewhat with his criticisms. And of course those who choose to do so may say that he is still too uncompromisingly English in his standpoint.

On the other hand, the acuteness is here in even greater measure than ever, and the expression in measure now and then as great at least as we have ever yet seen, though there are undoubted traces of 'collar-work'. The amazing grandiosity of Hugo, and the more amazing seriousness with which his admirers received it, are a commonplace now:—not the stanchest defenders of the poet who possess the slightest tincture of humour or of common sense dream of denying them. But they were not quite such commonplaces then: and Thackeray exposes them with admirable humour and even with considerable leniency. The wonderful Hugonian catalogues of names—so effective in poetry, so superfluous in prose—are capitally treated. And the critic is perfectly

sensible of his author's merits. The great description of
a storm which occurs early in *Le Rhin* is given in the
original language, with a single critical remark which,
in its different way, is worthy of it. 'We have not ventured to translate the above noble description into
English, for it would be a shame, we fancy, to alter a
single word in it; so complete does it seem to be. *It
bursts into the narrative and is over in a page, like the event it
describes.*' There have been critics (and not bad ones
either) who, if they had been lucky enough to conceive
the parallel given in those sixteen words, would have
cockered and cosseted them, have watered them down
and rolled them out, into sixteen sentences.

The work therefore is honestly and well done; it is
even done better than similar work has been done before.
And yet one feels that it is not the work that the writer
was born to do. He does it too conscientiously to make
the subjects of his articles mere 'pegs'; indeed the theory
of the *Foreign Quarterly*, I believe, was more or less
opposed to that common practice. Almost all of those
which are given here would have supplied him with
such pegs: and he does sometimes hang a tiny digression,
in his own vein, upon them. But for the most part he
sticks to the business which is not his business, and
struggles manfully through the book. The best *review*,
beyond all question, is the *éreintement* of M. Michiels, who
most thoroughly deserved it: the next best perhaps is the
Herwegh article, which is even a little un-Thackerayan
in its direct grip of the matter. It suggests that if it is
his (and there are some things both in the verse and in
the prose which do not look like anybody else's) he
would have made a better reviewer of German generally
than of French.

And so these pieces, though as yet not to be admitted

to more than a sort of provincial franchise, do, when used with proper care, add something to our general knowledge of Thackeray, and in more than a very few passages to our enjoyment of him. That is the reason of their discussion here: but it is not necessary to say anything more about them, except to acknowledge with all due thanks Mr. Garnett's labour as pioneer in their recovery.

VI

BARRY LYNDON, AND MISCELLANEOUS
PAPERS, 1843-7

THE LUCK OF BARRY LYNDON, as it was at first called, is itself a most curious instance of *heur et malheur*. Its author wrote it against the grain: and its production was spread over a long period, beginning soon after the conclusion of that Irish tour which, of course, suggested it, and extending into the Eastern one, where it had happier companions and a larger air. It did not please during its appearance in *Fraser*: and though the author reprinted it as a whole (with some omissions), it was not till a dozen years later, and then not by itself, but among the *Miscellanies*. Now, there is no book of his which it is so safe to praise. The praiser, indeed, is completely 'on velvet': for stanch Thackerayans will not gainsay him because it is Thackeray's, nor will the adversary, because he thinks it freer from Thackeray's faults than any other of his books, less sentimental, less English, more profitably provided with gloom and grime.

It may possibly be owing to natural perversity; but I confess that I like *Barry Lyndon* less than any other book of Thackeray's, less even than *Catherine*, which is much inferior in art, and very much less than *Philip*, which may be said to be inferior in art likewise. That I like *Catherine* better should I think relieve me from the mere charge of preferring 'rose-pink and sky-blue'. Moreover, I happen to think Thackeray's great exemplar, *Jonathan Wild*, one of the capital books of literature, and almost faultless except for its one virtuous character: consequently, I am at least not to be ruled out of court as a confessed and incorrigible sentimentalist. So I may perhaps claim permission to say why, *among Thackeray's books* (which is an always-to-be-remembered proviso), I am not specially fond of *Barry Lyndon*.

Among anybody else's, though I should have exactly the same faults to find with it, I should consider them, no doubt, at least compensated by its merits. Parts of it are equal to almost anything that even he ever did. The opening Irish chapters are quite admirable; they show his marvellous powers of improving experience capitally; and it is most curious to compare them with contemporary work by actual Irish novelists, though they probably owe something in the literary way to Maginn's short Irish stories. The campaign of the two Chevaliers—de Balibari *et d'industrie*—is again super-excellent. In fact, if this had stood alone as a Fitz-Boodle paper (the great George was, it seems, supposed to have had to do with *Barry Lyndon*) it would have been classable as A 1 for many a hundred years. Lady Lyndon's first husband and the elder Chevalier de Balibari—but especially the former—are creations of the author's best; no other living man could have drawn, with such few and such powerful strokes, a character, if only a minor character, so complete and so original as Sir Charles. Her Ladyship, though not quite so good as she would have been a few years later, is still excellent. Of the seasonings of eighteenth-century manners and so on the same may be said; while everywhere and all over the book there is abundance of the incomparable Thackerayan incident, situation, phrase, insinuation, suggestion, aside—as well as direct narrative and exposition. I do not myself care very much for the tragical History of the Princess of X.: but it is beyond all question a finely told story of its kind. Barry's mother should not be forgotten, of course: nor the ingenuity (which however seems to me a trifle

overdone) of Barry's own glosses on his later rascalities.
To conclude this part of the matter, it may be more than
conceded—cheerfully and vigorously asserted—that the
general style shows to the very full that advance in
dignity, success without trick, flexibility, general artistic
achievement, which has been noted in the Fitz-Boodle
Papers. All these things a good critic should never have
had at the time, and at all times should never have, the
slightest difficulty in recognizing. And yet——!

To begin the devil's advocate part, Thackeray does
not seem to me either to have conceived clearly, or to
have maintained steadily, his own attitude towards the
story. There can be no doubt—in fact it is agreed—that
he took *Jonathan Wild* in no slavish sense as a model. But
in doing this he hampered himself enormously by
making it an autobiography. You *can* make a man
represent himself as a scoundrel or a fool or both:—
the authors of the *Satyre Menippée* had done it, Butler had
done it, Thackeray himself has done it here with great
success in parts. But it is a frightful strain: and it is a
great question whether it can possibly be done on a very
large scale without 'incompossibility'. Whether the
actual Barry of the story *sibi constat* is a point upon
which, I suppose, opinions may differ. As, according
to the celebrated dictum, fine healthy Eton boys will
grow into frivolous members of Parliament—or did so
grow at one time—so the far from ungenerous scape-
grace of the early chapters, and the not altogether hate-
ful *picaro* of the middle, *might* grow into the unmitigated
and even cowardly scoundrel of the end. *Facilis descensus*
and many other tags will warrant it. But has not
Thackeray forgotten that he is Barry rather too often?
Fielding is never 'out': he keeps his cue of sardonic
showman infallibly and impartially towards every

puppet on the stage—the great Jonathan, the divine Letitia, Mr. Bagshot, Miss Straddle, everybody. He never confuses himself with them: and you never confuse them with him. I do not find this always to be the case with Thackeray here. The History of the Princess is not, of course, a case in point—that is merely an 'inset' tale, according to the well-recognized eighteenth-century fashion. But was Mr. Barry Lyndon, either as Redmond Barry, as the Chevalier, or in his glory, exactly the person to moralize on the Seven Year's War, as he or his creator does in chapter iv? I have no objection to moralizing if 'de morals is goot'. Thackeray's sermons never bore me when they are his, or Mr. Pendennis's, or those of anybody *congruous*. But that Barry should preach me I own surprises me.

There is, moreover, another point in which the autobiographical scheme, not necessarily of course, but as a matter of fact and by likelihood beforehand, had hampered and clogged the narrative and exposition. We get too many things recounted and too few acted, with the effect of something like the *récits* in conventional French tragedy. Barry's experiences with Dr. Johnson, for instance, would have made a famous scene of the same kind as those actually furnished by the Doctor in *The Virginians*, where the scheme is also in a way autobiographical, but more loosely managed and less concentrated on the display of a single character.

In short, to make a clean breast of it, *Barry Lyndon* fails—to me—in interest: it does not carry me along with it in either of the two ways in which a story can perform that office. That I am really very indifferent on the point of what happens to the characters (except the two above mentioned) is not in itself fatal. I do not care in the least whether Jonathan Wild escapes or does not

escape the gallows which he so richly deserves: nor what
becomes of the divine Letitia. But then I take the very
keenest interest in the way in which the fortunes of these
two very disagreeable persons are recounted by their
most agreeable historian. Thackeray generally gives me
both sources of interest and almost always the latter;
here he does not. Very likely it is my fault. But I perceive no evidence that he himself took much delight in
the book or 'got it with a nobler gust'. That he told his
daughter *she* would not like it is no evidence on this head,
because he doubtless only meant that it was 'unpleasant'
in subject. But he seems to have been constantly putting
it off, and to have worked at it, not merely in his usual
fits-and-starts manner and disliking the work as work,
but generally 'against the grain'.[1] Still it has had
plenty of worthy admiration, and it can very well do
without my liking. That it could not have been written
by any one but a consummate genius I am quite sure;
but I think that genius did better work elsewhere.

The miscellaneous articles which Thackeray wrote for
Fraser and other periodicals (with the exception of
Punch) during the middle and later forties, may con-
veniently be dealt with here, leaving the very few which
he produced subsequently for a niche at the end of a still
later chapter. They are extremely various in subject:
but they all display, more or less, that ripening or fully
ripened power, the development of which we have been
watching. On the other hand, they are almost all
articles de commande:—the free spirit is hurried through
a torment and difficulty of not wholly divine obligation.

---

[1] He appears to have read a great deal for it: and had perhaps not
digested his reading as well as he did later. It will be observed that his
omissions are almost always improvements: but they might have gone
further.

In some of them, such as *Grant in Paris*, there is a touch of the earlier and confessed 'savagery' which we could spare. Who was Grant, and what was his father's house, that he should be broken on such a wheel as this? In others, as in no small part of the *Punch* miscellanies, which were contemporaneous with them, and which will be given together, there is a certain triviality. The things do not really 'blemish his composure' as the cold spite of Octavius has it of Antony, but they cannot be said exactly to add to its distinction. Others again are free from any blemish, or from all but insignificant blemishes. And the whole batch once more illustrates that magnificent *variety* of Thackeray's genius which had hardly been anticipated by any one else. Something in the total reminds us of Hazlitt, whom he has praised so splendidly in the curious review of Horne's *New Spirit of the Age*—the *gusto*, the variety itself, the strange and rare mixture of relish for the things of the street and the things of the study. No one perhaps was ever so literary as Thackeray while being so little bookish merely, no one could so share the interests of men of the world while transcending them. And as this is the last of such batches (till we come to the supreme *Roundabouts*) that we shall have together, it may not be improper to say something about a good many of these essays and sketches, which make a bundle only inferior to the *Roundabouts* themselves, though their author left most of them to take their original chance.

Only one of this batch, I think, was, until the supplementary collection of 1886, united to the standard body of Thackeray's Works; and that was *Little Travels*. The 1886 collection[1] itself gave most of the rest, but not all:

[1] I refer to it as such because it appeared in that year as *one* volume. In the larger 'Library' edition it formed *two*, the first of which is dated 1885.

and the recovery of the remainder is due to the exertions of various inquirers from Mr. Shepherd to Mr. Melville. Among the latter division are most of the works of a new eidolon, Lancelot Wagstaff, almost (outside *Punch*) the last of many. The Wagstaffs 'had it by kind': they are of a house as ancient in this service as the *Tatler*: they came over literally with Richard Conqueror, who, established this dispensation in England. 'Théophile' Wagstaff had fathered or godfathered *Flore et Zéphyr* years before: and Lancelot no doubt stood to him as Samuel Titmarsh did to Michael Angelo. Except Titmarsh himself all these agreeable persons appear to have died early, and we may henceforward almost neglect them. In Arthur's bosom they no doubt forgather with the Bickerstaff clan itself, and Jedediah Cleishbotham, and Captain Clutterbuck, and a great deal of other good company.

The two little *Pictorial Times* reviews on Macaulay and Disraeli seem to be worth noticing, because they are probably samples of a much larger body of work of the kind and because of the interest of their subjects. Thackeray had earlier first joined in and then protested against the rather inept though natural laughter at Macaulay's famous 'Windsor Castle' letter, and he was always a little disposed to rally his great senior at Trinity. One of the most amusing things in his letters is his description of Macaulay's horror at the suggestion that he and Thackeray should be 'changed over' in introductions to a lion-hunting American lady. But his admiration for the historian was as generous and as genuine as it was for most of the great men of letters of his time: and it is here heartily expressed. Nor need any one quarrel with the political touch given to it: for everybody may, and should, back his own side. It is not, however, to be so generally laid down that everybody may *black* the other side: and it is to be feared that there is a little political rancour in the *Coningsby* notice. Certainly, though there is extremely high praise in it, it is not likely, if Disraeli knew the authorship, to have been without its influence on the famous but not particularly damaging sketch of 'St. Barbe' in *Endymion*. But it must be remembered that nobody, on his own or any side, took Mr. Disraeli seriously for years after this: and that his eccentricities (in more than one sense of the word) were recent and flagrant.

Two larger things of different kinds, which follow the Macaulay piece in time of composition, require no extrinsic considerations to recommend them. *Jérôme Paturot* is a delightful book in itself, and those who cannot enjoy it are deeply to be commiserated. For it is perhaps the best of a curious class of books— M. Laboulaye's *Paris en Amérique* is another, but less good—where the letters of knowledge suddenly and for but once transform themselves into letters of power. But Thackeray has made a rehash of it which is even better than the original. As for *Bluebeard's Ghost*, it is absolutely the most delectable example—next to 'The Notch in the Axe', and with a noteworthy difference from that—of its author's unequalled faculty of satiric transformation of story on the smaller scale. *Rebecca and Rowena* is of course more considerable in bulk and less uniformly satiric in appeal: 'The Notch' itself is more good-natured. But as a middle passage from the roaring burlesque of the Yellowplush and Gahagan stage toward these later and more thoroughly mellowed examples, *Bluebeard's Ghost* cannot be surpassed. A little broad farce remains, but not more than enlivens and brightens the thing: and perhaps nowhere earlier is 'my Amontillado manner' better reached than in some of the rest. The touch about the bits of string collected by the lamented Bluebeard, and Sister Anne's remark, 'Dolly Coddlins is the matter', as she goes down the middle in Sir Roger de Coverley, are things unforgettable.

Something has been said already of *Grant in Paris* which is put in the mouth of Mr. George Fitz-Boodle in his most 'haw-haw' mood. There is plenty of amusement—of a kind—in it. And it is fair to say that Mr. James Grant, who seems to have been for some reason a special *bête noire* to *Fraser*, was a sufficiently absurd and irritating specimen of a certain kind of journalist. The only book of his that I ever read (he must be carefully distinguished from his namesake and contemporary the respectable author of *The Romance of War* and scores of other red- and yellow-backed volumes of our youth), his *History of the Newspaper Press*, published nearly thirty years later than this and long after Thackeray's death, was a sorry performance enough; and Thackeray's own quotations show that this Paris thing was worse. Still, he was hardly worth so much powder and shot, and perhaps the particular powder and shot were sometimes such as Thackeray had better not have used. I cannot help thinking that something of the sort was in his own mind when he wrote the remarkable *Box of Novels* review which follows, and which actually opens with a *mea culpa* for past savagery. It is one of the best of all his papers of the kind, but it is also one of the most characteristic: and that being so it is very far from being without faults. There was no particular reason for anti-militarist protests in the circumstances, though, by the way, the fashion in which these are made is very difficult to reconcile with Thackeray's alleged Home Rule proclivities. But the faults are very few and the merits are great. In particular the hearty, ungrudging, yet not undiscriminating praise given to his two great forerunners in popularity, Lever and Dickens, does one good to read: and in regard to the latter occurs one of the great examples of the unmatchable Thackerayan phrase —so effortless and simple apparently, so perfect in its simplicity. 'It [*The Christmas Carol*] is the work of the master of all the English humourists now alive—*the young man who came and took his place calmly at the head of the whole tribe, and who has kept it.*'

I remember, when I first read most of these pieces on their resurrection in 1886, being divided between admiration of the magnificent panegyric of Hazlitt, which opens the review of Horne's *New Spirit of the Age*, and wonder whether the attitude to the book (which I had not then read) was just or unjust. It happened, further, that I never filled in the gap till the other day, when Horne's book was reprinted—having a kindness for the author of *Orion* and rather imagining that it would not be increased by familiarity. It certainly is not. How much exactly of the faults of the *New Spirit* is due to Richard 'Hengist' himself is uncertain: for his parts and those of his collaborators are not, I believe, certainly marked off, and one of them—Miss Barrett, soon to be Mrs. Browning, was, for a woman of genius, capable of almost any silliness. Whether the oracular platitude direct of the early Victorians be more or less ridiculous than the epigrammatic platitude reversed of the early Edwardians, may be an interesting question for debating societies: it is sufficient that either of them is enough to amuse a man, if he is in a good temper, for a time, to irritate him, if he is in a bad one, for the same time, and thereafter, in both cases, to bore him to extinction. Anything more hopelessly inept than the denunciation (to which Thackeray refers but not by name) of the *Ingoldsby Legends* in this book I do not myself know, except some contemporary exploits which it is not lawful to mention. And the praise is almost as inept as the blame—that of Dickens being one of the very clumsiest and most extravagant panegyrics ever written. At the same time Thackeray—as we have seen and shall see that, just at this time, he was unusually prone to do— 'takes the great axe to it' rather disproportionately: and it would be no great loss but for the Hazlitt passage, which is a gem. Too many men are ungenerous to their contemporaries; but want of generosity to immediate predecessors is unfortunately rather the rule than the exception. In both respects Thackeray is blameless.

Little Travels varies the collection with a kind of sketch wherein Thackeray was not seldom at his very best: and there is some of that best in the piece. But the papers composing it are to some extent marred by the curious and, for him, most unusual touch of something like bad humour, which has just been mentioned. One cannot say whether this was due to the fact that, as we know from a letter which has been published, he was not only writing *Barry Lyndon* abroad, against the grain, and without the documents he wanted, but trying to achieve a *Life of Talleyrand*, which never got into being, but which would certainly have been a great curiosity if it had. If this batch of sketches of the travel in which he usually so much delighted be compared, not merely with the sunset serenity of the *Roundabout* 'Notes on a Week's Holiday', but with the extremely early overture to *The Paris Sketch Book*, and that (a few years later than *Little Travels*) to *The Kickleburys on the Rhine*, the difference of mood will appear remarkably. He grumbles at the voyage and his fellow-voyagers; he grumbles at that

most harmless and attractive 'second-growth Paris',
Brussels; he grumbles, not without reason but not quite
in the right way, at the absence of pretty faces; he
grumbles at almost everything. The criticisms on
Rubens are 'knowledgeable', and they are not wholly
unjust; but he does not, as he does elsewhere, apportion
the justice as distributively as he should. There may
have been special reasons:—we know in the odd fragmentary way in which we do know things about him,
that he had difficulties in getting payment for some of
his work, difficulties about recovering some of the old
Indian wreckage. Probably he was getting weary of the
pillar-to-post charing and choring which had been his
literary fate for some years now. It was indeed lucky
that the Eastern trip came when it did: for though he
worked hard on it and did not give up the hack-work
when he came back, it 'changed him', as Brighton and
Paris, Southampton (where he often was in these years)
and Chaudefontaine could not do.

The 'Wagstaff' group, with one exception, are not of
the first order, though '*The* Partie Fine' is capital in its
way, and the *Chest of Cigars* interesting from the already
noted resurrection of Gahagan the delectable in that
state of old age which Macbeth recognized as the proper
one, but not his—loved, honoured, with troops of
friends. The 'N. P. Willis' review has not only the circumstantial interest of Macvey Napier's preliminary
inquiries about *a* Mr. Thackeray' (one of the sweetest
little ironies of the History of Literature) but much of its
own. It is surprising that Napier let in what he did; for
many a *perruque*—thick-skulled, ambrosial—must have
been shaken over it: it would be delightful to have what
he left out. The minor reviews help the general estimate
of Thackeray's character as a reviewer; and his inclu-

sion of *Mrs Perkins's Ball* in the last is a humorous and not indecent audacity. But the two most interesting of our last half score of items are additions to the 'gormandizing' series:—one of them, *Greenwich-Whitebait*, belonging to the Wagstaff sketches, the other, *Barmecide Banquets*, a *Fraser* review. The first, interestingly connecting itself with one of the 'Spec' papers in *Punch*, is a *locus classicus*, celebrating in literature an agreeable form of festivity which, long out of fashion, is now, they say, dead. Without disrespect to The Ship (where the present writer has eaten many whitebait) it was never really merry in Greenwich after they shut up The Trafalgar, which had a much better view of the river and was older-fashioned. Some years after this, Thackeray saw, from the windows of one of these hostelries, the *Great Eastern* lying in the stream. I wonder if he had been there earlier, during the actual launch, and heard the queer *scroop*, as she ground from time to time a little farther down the launching ways, urged gingerly and sideways by hydraulic rams, lest she should rush end-on to Greenwich itself, and overleap it and the county of Kent, and plunge into the Channel? One had not been entered in Thackeray then: but it was something to be entered in Greenwich-Whitebait itself.

Barmecide Banquets is a more serious composition: and as such is transferred from the somewhat intangible and shadowy Lancelot to George Fitz-Boodle, himself the discoverer of the Profession of Gormandizing. I do not know whether this work of Joseph Bregion and Anne Miller is actually rare, but I have sought it diligently in second-hand book-catalogues for twenty years without finding, and cookery-books are notoriously perishable. It holds a particularly interesting position as coinciding with and taking note of the actual transition from the times of vast Gargantuan 'courses' of incongruous viands huddled on the table together, and followed up by fresh mobs of food, on the one hand, and mere 'joint and pudding' on the other, to that of no food on the table and of a comparatively limited number of dishes. The authors seem to have been better on general principles than on the composition of particular *menus* (Thackeray has some delicate and wise criticism on this point), but undoubtedly beneficent in intention and 'sound upon the goose'. Their critic is good in both ways. His plea for the mahogany (even then alas! disappearing) and his argument against blocking the centre of the table; his apology for champagne (all the more creditable that we know he rightly preferred the bumper of burgundy or of bordeaux) and for 'a good drink' after dinner; how admirable they all are! And how much surprised he would have been to hear—no, not surprised; he was too wise to be surprised at anything—that, sixty years later, champagne would fetch more than double the price of first-growth claret of the same age, and a good vintage in each case!

And so farewell to this interesting group of miscellaneous essays. It is practically the last of the kind; for Thackeray soon after gave all his miscellaneous work to *Punch*, and then stopped it altogether. Before we come to the novels a few scattered articles of 1848–63, written rather on occasion and 'to oblige' than for his own purposes, shall be noticed collectively; and the wonderful series of the *Roundabouts* will crown the whole edifice. But with those here shown the day of odd jobs is practically over for him. Other times, other odd-jobs-men.

VII

BALLADS, AND CONTRIBUTIONS TO 'PUNCH'

IT has sometimes been held that in no single volume of Thackeray's works can his literary quality be better and more completely discerned than in that which contains his work in verse. Here, as elsewhere, he never made the smallest mistake of over-valuation in respect of his performances; here, almost more than elsewhere, he did, not hypocritically but honestly, undervalue them. The very title which he chose for them generally is an evidence of this: for, though 'ballad' is not out of place for the very highest creations of poetry, it also has, and had still more in his time, a belittling sense—a connotation of 'street'-ballad and the like. Most of the things are avowedly burlesque: some of them are almost (though of course intentionally) doggerel.

Yet neither side of the great combination—'thinking in jest: feeling in earnest'—is ever far away: and the shield turns, or, without turning, shows its other side through, with a magical rapidity and illumination. Perhaps he only once worked the process of his poetry out 'in a popular style that the *reader* could well understand'. This is in the 'Willow Song' already once discussed, where, having executed a quite serious and rather beautiful pastiche of Shelley or of Lewis, he proceeds to parody the parody and make the tragedy farcical for the benefit of the meanest apprehension. But the double development, or rather the inconceivably rapid gyration of mood, in the single picture of subject, is always going on from the *Chronicle of the Drum* to *Vanitas Vanitatum*. The Vanity itself is the centre: but the poetry, as it spins round, builds out of its gyres a picture as varicoloured and gracefully outlined as the spray column of a fountain. For poetry it is, though he would not call it so: poetry not seldom more poetical than you shall find in whole volumes of the demurer and more orthodox Muse—poetry in form and in fact, in thought and colour and sound alike. A certain command of metrical form seems to have been born with Thackeray. This command was a curious heritage of the generation which came after the great Romantic period, and profited by the breaking up of the domination of the couplet. It has been pointed out how masterly is his command of that couplet itself, only slightly burlesqued, in *Timbuctoo*: while he seems to have almost literally lisped in the looser measures which verse-writers of the most diverse genius—Coleridge and Southey, Moore and Monk Lewis, Scott and Shelley— had made familiar. A Life rather than the Works would be the proper place for printing these trifles in full—the ingenious experiment in double and triple rhymes which begins 'In the romantic little town of Highbury, My father kept a circulatin' Library', with the subsequent rhyme of 'Waterloo' and 'immortal who', and the even cleverer one of 'Drogheda' and 'embroider'; the 'Cabbages' parody on 'L. E. L's' 'Violets'; the Penenden Heath piece with its excellent pairing of 'canonical' and 'chronicle'.[1] These are not extraordinary things of course: but they testify at least to the possession of a quick wit, a true ear, and a faculty of doing what is wanted with the pen distinctly superior to that which he could exercise with the pencil. None of them, or of

[1] In a letter to his mother from Cambridge, Thackeray says that he shall put in the *Snob*, altering them a good deal, some verses called 'Genevieve'. He does *not* say that they were his own, but it has been taken

those later and actually published things of which we gave samples in the first volume, is much above 'crambo' level; but they supplied practice. Soon, too, he took to translation, or at least rather free adaptation, and, as has been seen, his first certain contribution to *Fraser*, altered afterwards for *The Paris Sketch Book*, was of this kind. This version of *Le Roi d'Yvetot*, which is given with the variations of the later form, appeared in an 'omnibus' article—one of the series of '*Fraser* Papers' which then came frequently, but not every month. The prose framework of this was probably Maginn's, while the inset verses and translations might be his or anybody's. It will be observed that when Thackeray reprinted it in *The Sketch Book* he altered it largely: in fact he was always a considerable alterer, and a complete edition of the Works with various readings would be a not uninteresting though a very laborious task. In this first instance he changed the arrangement from common

for granted: so they may be given in a note here, though I confess that neither the verse nor the satire strikes me as very brilliant.

TO GENEVIEVE

A DISINTERESTED EPISTLE

SAY do I seek, my Genevieve!
    Thy charms alone to win?
Oh no! for thou art fifty-five,
    And uglier than sin!

Or do I love the flowing verse
    Upon thy syren tongue?
Oh no! those strains of thine are worse
    Than ever screech-owl sung.

Since then I thus refuse my love
    For songs or charms to give,
What could my tardy passion move?
    Thy money, Genevieve!

             A LITERARY SNOB.

measure to fourteeners (compare Browning's similar
variation in *Cristina*). The phrase is sometimes altered
for the better, sometimes not; indeed the idea occurs—
and it certainly would not be unlike him—that, not
having a copy of *Fraser* at hand, he wrote out the *Sketch
Book* version from memory. In either form it runs a
little more easily than the directly translated *King of
Yvetot* which accompanied the second. Of the other
three Béranger versions *Jolly Jack* is, I think, the least
good: while the only perfectly serious piece *O Virgin
Blest* is very good indeed and (except that the final point
is lost) miles above the French as poetry. There is one
loose rhyme in it, but Thackeray was always given to
licence in this way. It is curious to think of him as a
hymn-writer, though *Pendennis* seems clearly to indicate
that as a boy he felt the influence of *The Christian Year*,
which came out when he was sixteen, and is said to have
been partly composed at or near 'Baymouth'. At any
rate, the enormous and astoundingly unequal corpus of
English hymnology contains 'many worse, better few'
than this.

His first considerable piece of verse—in fact the
longest single piece that he ever wrote (unless *Ariadne in
Naxos* was longer)—was not a translation; but it was
certainly an imitation. The *Ingoldsby Legends*, though
not yet collected, had been appearing for some time
with great and just popularity, and *The Legend of St.
Sophia*, originally called 'The Great Cossack Epic of
Demetrius Rigmarolovicz', which appeared in *Fraser*
for December, 1839, is neither more nor less than an
Ingoldsby pastiche. It is much the best of such imita-
tions, but with the originals in possession one does not
quite see the necessity for it. The later Béranger versions
were of 1840; the next year saw two of his *opuscula majora*

in rhyme, the return to Brentford in the *Testament* of its monarch, and the admirable *Chronicle of the Drum*. It is not the least amusing of literary anecdotes that George Cruikshank, for whom *The King of Brentford's Testament* was written on regular literary commission, estimated it, and paid for it, at the rate of one guinea. Perhaps he thought that the omission to rhyme in the odd lines was a mark of carelessness and to be 'considered in the bill'. There is a story, I believe authentic, of a London publisher and editor who, in the days of the popularity of rondeaux, triolets and ballades, insisted on deducting for the refrains. The thing is curiously perfect with a very minimum of apparatus: the sober sarcastic 'under-hum' of the verse being achieved by sheer mastery of style and rhythm exactly suiting the drift. But in range and scale it of course comes short of the *Chronicle*—one of the very greatest things in serio-comic verse-literature, no matter what the age or what the language. It is curious that *here* Thackeray's anti-militarism, while giving the motive of the piece, is so kept in hand by his art that it never becomes obtrusive, and almost offensive, as it does in prose. In fact, the piece is a signal example of the truth that treatment, not subject or sentiment, is the secret of art itself. He is much more lavish of rhyme here than in the *Testament* but cavalierly lavish still, giving or withholding it as it suits him, and with an effect which, though it would not have pleased Dr. Johnson, may please us very much. The fashion in which he has assimilated in his anapaestic metre the lighter and more rapid as well as the slower and more solemn rub-a-dub of the drum itself is really *prestigious* (the adjective was English in the seventeenth century), and the choice of the contrasted stanza for the conclusion could not be bettered. The vividness of the

satirical-historical panorama, the ironical-natural tone
of the whole, the felicity of occasional phrases, and the
solemn beauty of the sudden turn at the end—these are
things that cannot easily be paralleled. Thackeray may
owe suggestions to Praed here and elsewhere, but they
are mere suggestions of the vaguest kind, and he always
makes them his own. Years passed before these two
masterpieces were reinforced, first in 1847 by *The
Mahogany Tree*, then in 1849 by *The Ballad of Bouillabaisse*, and more than a decade after these before what I
should class as the supreme and characteristic quintet
of Thackeray's verse[1] was concluded with *Vanitas
Vanitatum* in the heyday of the *Cornhill* triumph. To
dwell in detail on any were impertinent. They all
illustrated in different ways what it was not quite so impertinent to point out in their forerunners, the extraordinary conjugation of spirit and form, which never
lose touch of each other as they float and flit between
the Houses of Mirth, and (if not exactly of Mourning
yet) of Melancholy. Poet Laureate, Historiographer-
Royal, and Jester at once to the Goddess Melancholia—
that is Thackeray's real station and title as a verseman,
and indeed as a man of letters.

He does not forget his office in the minor pieces, but
Melancholy often lends him to her sister Mirth altogether for a time. It is not mere surplusage to give as
has been usual, separately and together as well as with
their original settings, the various inset verse pieces
which adorn almost all the major and many of the
minor prose works. They are wanted in the earlier
collocation to complete the presentation of the indivi-

---

[1] If any one likes to add *The Age of Wisdom* and the *Cane-bottomed
Chair* or *Piscator and Piscatrix* to make the quintet a septet—a Pleiad—
I agree heartily.

dual work; they are wanted in the later to complete that of Thackeray as a poet. All alike supply something like a microcosm of his moods. The two most considerable divisions or segments of them, *Lyra Hibernica* and the *Ballads of Policeman X*, employ once more the old devices of eccentric spelling—and for obvious reasons. Even as poetry (with all respect to Wordsworth) in its serious modes naturally seeks an ornater and more beautified diction than that of ordinary life, so does it, in these other attitudes of burlesque, affect extravagantly travestied lingo. It must be quite clear to all calmly critical minds that *The Battle of Limerick* and *Jacob Omnium's Hoss* at once necessitate and justify their respective dialects. Their form is 'inevitable' enough to please 'W. W.' himself: their spirit is a Hamadryad which would cease to be without her shrine. And so with many others which we must not, though fain, specify.

But on the other hand these grotesque shroudings and sheathings are even less necessary to their writer in verse than in prose. There is nothing of them in the great quintet above discussed; there is nothing of them in *Piscator and Piscatrix*, a charming thing, nothing in *The Age of Wisdom*, a fine and terrible one, nothing in the graceful *May-Day Ode* and the admirable *King Canute*, nothing in many others. Jargon was easy to Thackeray and he could do wonders with it; but it was not in the very slightest degree indispensable, though it not only did its own duty supremely, but threw up, as nothing else could, the art of the pieces written without it.

On the whole he used his poetical faculty, as he used his pictorial, mainly though not wholly to *illustrate* his prose work. But though he used it less he was far surer with it, and it was of a far higher quality than his actual illustrations. Indeed, in one sense, there are no degrees in poetry, though there may be many mansions in the poetic house. Parnassus is allotted very much on the principles of the Paradise of Dante—divisibly and indivisibly. Thackeray chose often to dwell in the lower courts and perhaps never to ascend to what are commonly considered the highest. But always—in his mere tags and scraps of verse-jest, as well as in such things as that marvellous serious doggerel[1] which cannot be given here but which has 'tears in its voice' almost as magical as those of the *Bouillabaisse* itself—

'Tis one o'clock: the boy from *Punch* is waiting in the
    passage here,

—always, he is a poet.

In time, in miscellaneous character, and in actual community of origin, Thackeray's prose contributions to *Punch* have an overwhelming claim to be preferred as the immediate sequels to his verse. It is to be assumed that, in consequence of Mr. Spielmann's divulgation, we can identify the whole of them—which is certainly not the case in regard to those furnished to *The Times*, to *Fraser*, and to other periodicals: while there are reasons for believing that it is the case with regard to a rather small fraction of his contributions to the *Morning Chronicle* and some others still. No one of these *Punch* papers is very early; he was thirty—the age when you may become a bishop—when he wrote the first; and there is therefore neither the excuse nor the attraction of the novitiate for withholding or for giving any of them. Furthermore, they undoubtedly contain some of his best and most characteristic work. But he himself reprinted but a part of them; and though much was added by the fresh

[1] See *Letters of W. M. Thackeray* (London, 1887), pp. 25, 26.

sifting (conducted by persons unusually well qualified in every respect) of forty years ago, a good deal was even then rejected. Nor is it difficult to understand the reasons of the rejection, which will not soon lose their weight. I do not think that it will be impertinent to set forth a short examination of them here.

They must have been mainly two:—the character of the periodical itself, at the time more particularly, and the relation to it of the writer.

Putting mere customary cubbishness and platitude apart—the banal determination to think that things are 'going off', and the banal dislike of continued prosperity —everybody thinks well of Mr. Punch. No other comic periodical has ever existed for so long a time with so high a record of continuous achievement with pen and pencil. But *Punch* was started at a time when, as has been previously pointed out in these chapters, journalism was not exactly at its zenith; and when one looks over the list of the team thoughts will occur. Except Thackeray himself and Leech (Doyle and Sir John Tenniel did not join till ten years later), there is hardly one of them who can be said, in an admirably eloquent phrase of the slang of yesterday, to be 'quite—' in the way of genius. Mark Lemon appears to have been a good man of business, and therefore in some respects a good editor—though he certainly was not so when he let Thackeray's *May-Day Ode* go to *The Times*—but he could at no time be called a great man of letters. A proportion (varying no doubt in the case of different persons) of the works of Douglas Jerrold, outside the *Caudle* papers, creates mere amazement when one turns to it. The brothers Mayhew *se sauvent de planche en planche* (when the plates are Cruikshank's), to take refuge only in the compilation of *London Labour and the London Poor*, a thing historically not valueless. Tom Taylor does not any longer exist. Gilbert à Beckett the elder is an awful example of the professional-amateur 'funny man': I do not think anything would induce me to read the *Comic History of Rome* again. Percival Leigh is a name; but not as Ulysses was and is. Moreover, the politics of the paper, never quite impartial, did not at that time even pretend to the comparative impartiality of a general *fronde* which it has since usually aimed at, and sometimes achieved. They were, if not uncompromisingly Radical, acridly partisan on the 'popular' side; and so dangerously likely to put fire to those of Thackeray's culverins which were loaded with powder of that sort. Some of the things which he wrote about the Duke of Wellington for instance, I am quite certain that he would never have reprinted, even very shortly after they were written.

But there is something else. It is rather odd that no one has—after a century of voluminous newspaper writing and in the present thoughtful times—written a work on the 'Ethics of the Regular Contributor'. They are curious and complicated: nobody perhaps knows them except one who has both contributed and edited, or helped to edit, very considerably. The 'regular', if he is a gentleman or an honest man of any kind, never 'scamps' his work; and if he is a prudent one he has a much greater interest in not doing so than a casual, because he stands to lose much more. But it is almost impossible that the regularity should not blunt his edge somewhat; and it is not his fault that at the given moment when his work is required he has had no time or means to strop it fresh again. These things are so obvious that newspapers have repeatedly tried to do without regular contributors or with very few—of course finding, for equally obvious reasons, that this is impossible.

Now I am not sure that this *lues contributoria* or 'regular contributor's disease' did not sometimes attack Thackeray in his *Punch* days.

For these reasons, while everything that he himself reprinted has been considered here, and also everything which has the sanction of forty years' companionship with this, I have not thought it desirable to discuss all the rest; but have sifted carefully. The task is not easy: for, as always with him, there are some of the best things in the worst; but it seemed to me that it had to be done. A decision had also to be arrived at as to the classification of the matter. Pure chronological arrangement is here impossible, for it would, for instance, muddle up *The Book of Snobs* with all manner of contemporary *entrefilets* and minor articles. The best plan seemed to be (I can only apologize to those who do not like it) to keep *The Book of Snobs* itself for separate presentation in full in the next chapter but one, but to deal here with some of the more substantive contributions, such as the *Little Dinner at Timmins's*, and to devote the next chapter to the remainder, arranged chronologically as far as may be consistent with leaving connected works and series undisturbed.

Thackeray's *coup d'essai* in *Punch*, the *Legend of Jawbrahim-Heraudee*, might, if merely from the fact that it *is* the first, have been resuscitated rather earlier than it was. The sham Orientalism was, of course, no new thing: it had been done with admirable impertinence in Canning's 'Bauba-Dare-Adul-Foolah' and less admirably elsewhere and oft. And it can be easily overdone—not all Thackeray's own uses of it are worth reprinting. But this is amusing enough. John Abraham

Heraud, who died not so very many years ago—actually as a Poor Brother of the Charterhouse—was a journalist and man of letters at one time in good practice, and a Fraserian. But he was also one of those curious producers of unreadable epic whose line never fails for long, and of whom his contemporary but elder, Edwin Atherstone, was the most stupendous and terrible representative in the nineteenth century. 'Jawbrahim' is by no means ill-naturedly laughed at, and he distinctly scores off Poof-Allee-Shaw: while some more eminent brethren do not escape. I never had the courage to investigate the genuineness of the quotations; and it is hardly necessary for any one to do so. But the graduated memory of the tyrant, of Roolee-Poolee, and of Samboo Beg is quite ingenious. Of course the thing is a trifle; but one could endure much trifling if it were all of this kind.

The more ambitious but still largely farcical *Miss Tickletoby's Lectures on English History* were not the first of Thackeray's productions to be cut short 'by request'; and though they too are amusing—in parts decidedly so—and would be memorable as the first vehicle or frame of the admirable 'King Canute' poem, their kind is not a good kind. It has been noted often how odd it is that both Dickens and Thackeray should have attempted this curious and hopeless task of making history into a party pamphlet and burlesquing it at the same time. But Thackeray had at least the wit and the grace to do the burlesque intentionally, and to draw no such inimitably unintentional self-caricature as Dickens did when he protested that he did not know what he should do if his offspring got hold of 'any Conservative or High Church notions'.

I have known persons of very far from negligible

judgement who were very fond of *The Next French Revolution*, but I cannot say that I quite share their enthusiasm. Thackeray's intimate knowledge of things French (or at least Parisian) and his not altogether unreasonable anti-Orleanism enliven and inspirit it no doubt; and the manifestoes are often capital. But part of it seems to me rather dead; and part of the rest, including the 'Jenkins' matter, rather deadly-lively. This latter part keys on to a certain number of smaller articles in which *Punch* carried on a sort of guerrilla with the *Morning Post*, and which have seemed to me in very few cases worthy of reproduction. Thackeray did not think any of them worthy of his own *Miscellanies* ten years later nor did (I presume) Sir Leslie Stephen when he reprinted the 'further skimming' of 1886. And I think they were both right. Indeed it may be observed that Thackeray himself never reprinted the *Revolution*; but as it has been part of the 'Works' for nearly forty years it must of course stand.

Very different language must be used about two other pieces. *A Little Dinner at Timmins's* has always and justly held a high place among its author's smaller but not smallest things. 'A leg of beef is not a company dish' is as certain a signature as the crossed spectacles themselves, and more inimitable. Of the De la Pluche series (which appeared at intervals till as late as 1850, but which belongs chiefly to 1845-6) something has been said by anticipation as to its connexion and contrast with the *Yellowplush Papers*. Looked at by itself one would suppose that it must delight everybody who is not a fanatic of orthography and high seriousness. The author was now all but fully estated in his powers; and he used them lavishly here. The mis-spelling itself is at its most perfect—never, as it sometimes is earlier,

overdone and always an all but inseparable accompani-
ment to the style and thought. The character-drawing,
the story-telling, the variety, are all worthy of the most
serious work of art, and nowhere has Thackeray been
more prodigal of his most accomplished verse.

Mr. De la Pluche, as previously remarked, is a much
softer person than Mr. Yellowplush. But he lends himself—and his queer lingo lends itself still more—with
facility to the same business of satirizing various aspects
of life under cap and bells. The Railway mania could
not but suggest such satire to Thackeray even if he had
not been (as it seems pretty clear that he was) bitten by
it to a certain degree; but Jeames was too useful a person
to be treated on the principle which Diderot's impudent
victimizer summarized in the phrase *On suce l'orange;
on en jette l'écorce.* The gauge question is railway still,
but railway from quite a different point of view; and
even those who regret the broad gauge in itself extremely
(there certainly has never been such comfortable
travelling since) may acknowledge the nuisance which
it, however guiltlessly on its own part, occasioned. But
the later and minor papers are not out of place, though
it is very interesting to note how much less savage as
a literary and dramatic critic James is than Charles
James was. The 'organ is mellered' as the other great
manipulator of metropolitan dialect has it—though not
in the same circumstances. It was an excellent organ
both in its harsher and its softer tones; but it has here
done its work. Only in mere passages and episodes where
the circumstances demanded it, was it to be heard
again. But its latest sounds, which I take to be the
utterances of Mr. Ridley, senior, in *Philip*, are still delectable. 'Prob'bly 'av 'ad misfortunes: which many 'av 'ad
them' the mild butler said of the Reverend Tufton

Hunt. Thackeray had had misfortunes which (some of them at least) were nearly over; and it had been partly owing to these misfortunes that he had taken the motley. He could leave it off now or soon—only to resume it for special purposes and for the sake of old, not all unhappy days.

VIII

MISCELLANEOUS CONTRIBUTIONS TO 'PUNCH'

THE contributions to *Punch* already dealt with were all—even 'Jeames', which is the most loosely connected of them—more or less integers, though they might be printed in instalments; and they were therefore classed together. Side by side with them, but running farther, is another series of groups which are now to be given in their chronological order, while a selected crowd of purely individual and occasional articles will follow. The *Book of Snobs*, from its magnitude, is reserved for the next chapter. It will be understood that these three chapters—VI, VII, and VIII—run to a certain extent side by side, and present *mainly* the work of 1844–9.

Of the groups which open the present batch the 'Fat Contributor' is the most miscellaneous, in part at least the earliest, and the most representative of moods and manners earlier still. Indeed Thackeray seems to have kept this particular *eidolon* of himself as a sort of safety-valve or safety-mouthpiece for his moods of the more extravagant farce. And while it is exceedingly curious to read the Eastern parts side by side with *Cornhill to Cairo*, which actually deals with the same scenes and incidents, it is more curious still to remember that, at practically the same time, the grim irony of *Barry Lyndon* was forging towards its close, and the delightful light comedy of *Mrs. Perkins's Ball* was being born in the author's mind and taking shape from his fingers. The 'F. C.' begins with a touch of that ill temper, perhaps actually produced by the cause assigned (too many dinners) which we noted in contemporary work such as *Little Travels*; but it soon wears off. The discovery of 'Dolores' forty years ago was a joy which has not staled. 'Punch at the Pyramids,' it is true, was probably better to read at its first appearance than forty or sixty years later: yet how many equally good things had 1845 or 1885 to offer? And the later Brighton papers are among the best of Thackeray's frequent and grateful fees to 'Doctor Brighton'. In particular the 'Brighton Night Entertainment' is one of the Thackeray 'Particulars'. Many people have done more or less burlesque summaries of theatrical performances; it seems somehow to have been irresistible from the earliest days of the modern theatre. Dickens (to come to Thackeray's own contemporaries) did them nobly; but not quite with the extraordinary *quality* of these others. Nobody in fact could confer this quality unless, like Thackeray, he was suspended between the opposite magnets of romance and satire. But, as has been said, the stout victim of Dolores and his own diaphragm was more frequently attracted to the farcical.

There are some, perhaps many, who would call the *Prize Novels* farce too; but here a good deal depends on definition. The series was originally planned to include Dickens and himself. But Mr. Punch refused to admit Dickens: in which that sage probably did not unwisely, for Dickens was very vulnerable in this way, and, though less fiery than Thackeray, was very much less placable. It would have been amusing, perhaps intensely so; but we can easily guess what it would have been like, and so it is the less loss. That of himself, good or bad, would at any rate have been a very great curiosity. For Thackeray, at least in narrative, has never been successfully parodied or indeed imitated at all. If anybody could have done it, he could; for these particular

'Novels' are admittedly by far the best of their often
tried kind. It was, however, as Sir Rowland Hill said
to his enemy Yates of another matter, 'rather a dangerous accomplishment', and it certainly secured him
the posthumous enmity of Mr. Disraeli. Lever's good
nature was proof against 'Phil Fogarty', though in
a sense this might be said to be a more damaging performance than 'Codlingsby'. For this latter, though
it might be a little more galling to vanity, did not 'touch
the ark' by threatening the sale, while 'Phil Fogarty'
certainly reminded the public rather too broadly that
Lever's military novels, delightful as they are, do rather
run in a mould. For my own part, *dulcia refrigeria* as
these are, I should put them below 'George de Barnwell'
and 'Crinoline'. The former is 'really too good'—as a
famous champagne shipper, now deceased, is said to
have observed half mournfully to a customer who was
tasting appreciatively, 'The public really ought not to
have it'. It is quite astounding how fresh it remains,
while most things of the kind wither and stale with the
originals that they satirize. And there are few tales
half-told for the completion of which I would give more
than for that of the history of Jools who sat upon the
counter of the Misses Mordeky in company with the
choicest sprigs of English nobility, and enjoyed with
them 'the flagrant and arheumatic Qby'. My own impression is that here the subject was too great even for
the author; that *nobody* could have finished 'Crinoline'
to sample.

The other three collections, *Sketches and Travels in
London*, *Mr. Brown's Letters* and the *Proser* papers of
Dr. Solomon 'Pacifico' (that remarkable *civis Britan-
nicus* having his name borrowed for no obvious reason
except that it was much in people's mouths at the time),

for the most part discard the wilder trappings of vanity as far as farcical incidents or farcical handling are concerned. Their mouthpieces—'Mr. Spec,' 'Mr. Brown,' 'Dr. Pacifico' himself—are more undisguised disguises of the author than he had ever assumed before; and while the subjects of the first and third are absolutely miscellaneous (there is more unity in the second) all are really modern equivalents of the old Queen Anne essay in the less didactic and more general kind. Their average level is very high: indeed except the *Roundabouts* there is no part of Thackeray's miscellaneous work that shows him better. The Introduction to the Travels takes the liberty of being mainly introductory; 'A Club in an Uproar' is not a masterpiece; and 'A Roundabout Ride' is perhaps as exemplary an example of that 'regular contributor' work of which we have spoken, as could be found. It is not bad; it is not uninteresting; it is even a kind of document for the historian of London manners and topography. But it is quite obvious 'copy'; copy such as any newspaper might be glad enough to get, but which would pretty surely never have come into existence except on the laws of demand and supply. On the other hand 'The Curate's Walk', 'A Dinner in the City', and 'A Night's Pleasure' are wonderful things. They go from strength to strength. I have seen the 'Walk' (it is accepted that Frank Whitestock was William Brookfield) called 'dull'—a verdict which can only be said to illustrate Thackeray's own dictum that 'with us there is no appreciation of art in the abstract'. I suppose it is dull because it deals with little children and missions, and halfpenny-worths of fresh bread, and Faith and Hope and Charity and 'that old-fashioned sort of thing'. All I can say is that if there is anything better done from Balzac to Maupassant, or from Dickens to Mr. Kipling, I do not know that thing. The art makes the subject interesting no matter whether it is interesting beforehand or not. And that is the business of Art.

The other two pieces deal with less perilous subjects and call to their aid large accompaniments of Thackeray's most amusing verse. I do not know that they are better; but their attractions have more volume and variety. The speeches and the dismembered snatches of song in the 'Dinner'; the 'Cave of Harmony' and its actual ditties in 'A Night's Pleasure'; the rather libellous but extraordinarily vivid picture of 'Bardolph of Brasenose': these have always been considered capital stories (as old Mrs. Wardle says), and great part of them has the additional and permanent attraction of preserving vanished manners and customs to frame character that never can vanish. Nor should a word of notice be omitted in regard to the curious, late, and rather isolated 'Waiting at the Station'. Though isolated as I have called it, it is not in the least out of keeping; and it is one of the most genuine of Thackeray's curious 'soliloquy pieces'. This at any rate is not 'copy'. 'Child's [*sic*] Parties' is full of agreeable Thackerayisms; but it is a pity that he did not live to know the authentic fact of a child declining to have a party *unless* there were champagne.

Mr. Brown's Letters to his Nephew begin to criticize life, if not more steadily, rather more as a whole, and in a more definitely serious fashion. To some extent they take up the subject of 'Club Snobs' from the *Book* of that name, and extend the consideration beyond mere snobbery. In the same way the author returns to other favourite themes of his—dress, dinners, marriage. The whole is a very perfect example of the 'middle' Thackeray—almost if not quite passing into the achieved one.

Of clubs, at the time when they had been got into pretty thorough order, and before they had been multiplied and vulgarized, Thackeray is of course *the* historian in the higher sense. Yates, in his desperate efforts at self-excuse, asserted that the author of the *Snob Papers* and *Mr. Brown's Letters* had himself been too personal and had, sometimes by his pen and sometimes by his pencil, identified this member of the 'Garrick' or that of the 'Reform' with his awful examples. There was of course no real parallel between this (had it been the case) and an elaborate and very unfavourable commentatory portrait *by name* of a public character who was also a personal acquaintance. But it may be admitted (all the more readily since he admitted it himself) that Thackeray sometimes sailed a little too near the wind in this respect. He has left amusingly eager apologies on the subject in his letters to Mrs. Brookfield. But in no sense did he commit the unpardonable sin of dragging a person in *by name*, for insult or unfavourable mention, in respect of matters only known or to be known by private acquaintance.

Mr. Brown, too, is a good *persona*. In his character of intelligent fogy (it was a little early for Thackeray to assume it, for he had not yet reached even his own Age of Wisdom) he requires none of the antic dispositions of his predecessors from Yellowplush to Fitz-Boodle; and he can criticize shrewdly and unpedantically, but directly and home. Some of the untoward fashions which he satirizes have passed, and come back again, and passed once more, to come back and pass till the Day of Judgement: for your fashion is your true Flying Dutchman or Wandering Jew, with rigging and build, with words and speech, a little altered from time to time. But the *badauds* who indulged in them have not passed;

and will not. On the more general laws of taste which govern his decisions he is sound as always—as sound now, in the days when it would certainly not pay clubs to stand even rudimentary free lunches to their members, as in those when this hospitable habit was customary. Once more, the passing figures, like Silenus and Nudgit, are more alive than the heroes and heroines of most elaborate novels or plays: once more, the 'gormandizing' wisdom is of the highest class. The notice of 'Sir Morgan O'Doherty' (the name of one of Maginn's early aliases, and the book an interesting picture of manners bygone even in Thackeray's days) and the dinner at the widow's are among the brightest of Thackeray's minor gems.

There is no very obvious reason why the Essays collected under the title of *The Proser* and assigned to Dr. Solomon 'Pacifico' should not have been composed by Mr. Brown himself; but Thackeray had got so into the habit of changing his parts that he probably could not help it. And it has almost always been an idea with editors of newspapers that you should not keep up the same series too long. Except the greater Titmarsh—almost

> First made and latest left of [all these] knights,

in fact admittedly Thackeray's alter ego—they did their work and passed. The lesser Titmarsh and the Wagstaffs, Théophile and Lancelot; Gahagan the Invincible; the brace of Plushes that stand behind the Thackerayan chariot; Mr. Snob, Mr. Spec, Mr. Fitz-Boodle, Mr. Brown; shadows they are and shadows they depart, Dr. Solomon himself not quite bringing up the rear, for there were others down to 'Our own Bashi-Bozouk'. Only Titmarsh remained; indeed Titmarsh and Thackeray

were by this time inseparable: 'soul might divide from
body but not they One from another.' *The Proser* is by
no means too prosy and he is very fairly Solomonic:
though not always peacemaking. He does not, for
instance, seem to have forgiven 'Mrs. Trotter Walker'.
This curious paper—the personal quality of which is
quite unmistakable, though as usual it must not be
exaggerated or tied down too much to detail—is one of
the most characteristic instances of that intense *intimacy*
which there always was between Thackeray's life and
his writings. It is no doubt also an instance of the
equally intense and somewhat excessive sensitiveness
which, though it need not quite necessarily accompany
such intimacy, very generally does. He is quite aware
that it is excessive—he always is; it is that actual self-
consciousness, and the self-ridicule resulting from it,
which attract some people so much to him, and which
evidently annoy others so much. I do not believe that
men are really annoyed, as they say they are, by his
'drawing the moral' as he actually does here and often
elsewhere. That is only a blind to disguise the sting of
the *de te fabula*. After all, the 'Moralitas', the *envoi*, the
'conclusion of the matter'—is an excellent old thing and
was popular in days which, to put it mildly, were not so
very much less wide awake than ours. But it *is* unpleasant, perhaps, to some people to have the weaknesses
of which they are conscious rubbed into them by somebody who is quite conscious of them likewise in his own
case; who shams no stoicism, but who can laugh at himself and so at others likewise. If he would do it in a way
that would make us think 'Oh! I could do that better',
it might be a relief, but only the very stupidest can think
that. If he would pretend to be superior to it all—that
would be a relief, for it would be a sort of invitation to

us to share his superiority. There is in fact nothing to
do but to pretend that the correction is really too obvious
—a pretension which, in the slang that has grown up
since his day, is 'really too thin'. It is not wonderful
that Thackeray is intolerable to some folk.

Others may find him not much less delectable here
than elsewhere. It may be said that his 'Fogy' papers
are exaltations of tail-lessness or denunciations of sour
grapes; but as the stage comes to all who live long
enough, it is not quite superfluous to be prepared for it
—or to have it comfortably furnished and agreeably
decorated for us. 'On a good-looking young lady' is less
in his usual manner, though it contains one of his
characteristic name fantasias (Erminia-Victorina-*Boa*-
Chinchilla), but is a remarkable example of his pervading spirit. It may be a little too patronizing to his
subjects—but he has made that up elsewhere (in the
famous anticlimax—'and oh! my dear, what a fool you
are!') by excess in the other direction. After all, Elissa
and Perissa are more natural than Medina. The
'Interesting French Exile' should be read in connexion
with 'Crinoline' on his good-natured side, and with the
remarkable review of Michiel's which we mentioned
among the *Foreign Quarterly* doubtfuls on the more
serious. And the companion 'American Traveller' at
last 'tells his fact' to the egregious N. P. Willis, whom
either Thackeray himself or Macvey Napier had let off
pretty easily in the *Edinburgh*, two or three years earlier.
Lastly 'The Press and the Public' exhibits him in quite
a different light. It is probably the last thing ever
written on that still vext Bermoothe—the question of
signed and unsigned articles. It is the work of a man
who had had plentiful experience of both; and who
at last could be sure that his name would give solid

pecuniary value to any trifle that he chose to write, while for years he had received inadequate pay for a great deal of unsigned work that we more or less know and probably a great deal more that we do not. Yet he declares unhesitatingly against the signing system; and he supports his opinion by arguments as sound as arguments can well be—arguments thoroughly borne out by the experience of the last fifty or sixty years, during which signing has become more and more common. It was one of the latest of his semi-serious contributions to *Punch*, appearing in August, 1850; and though he certainly sent in a score or so of articles in 1851 and a very few later, it may almost be said to have coincided with his own farewell to unsigned writing. A large proportion of these *Punch* articles are mere scraps and *entrefilets*, sometimes evidently put in to introduce a drawing, sometimes without even that excuse. One or two pieces I feel absolutely certain that Thackeray himself never would have reprinted; others do seem to me worth reprinting from any point of view; many because they were mere 'balaam' as the then still existing word went —padding of various kinds on ephemeral subjects. Nearly all the early bickering with 'Jenkins' to which I have referred above may well be left unreprinted; much of the rather tasteless and overdone *fronde* against the Prince Consort (who in his earlier years certainly sometimes failed in tact but never so much as his assailants in taste) and a very great deal of the angry babel on Irish politics, Papal Aggression, Puseyism and other matters whereon God's great gift of speech was abused about the middle of the nineteenth century. In fairness, and as touching on that attitude to Ireland which concerns parts of his real literary work, I printed two O'Connell articles which illustrate the inconsistency or

at least the variation of Thackeray's position. And it
seemed to me that it might interest not a few readers to
have the 'Bashi-Bozouk' papers, which were about his
last contributions and which, by an odd coincidence,
'turned full East' as had *Jawbrahim-Heraudee*, the first,
though on a more serious occasion and with more than
literary cause.

There is not perhaps a very great deal of the absolutely
first class in this part of the collection; we could not, for
reasons already exposed, expect that there should be.
All of it is second, some third or fourth 'skimming'—in
fact, when the bulk and the goodness of the series which
have preceded it are considered, it is not a little remarkable that it should be as good as it is. The Paris articles
are nearly as good as ever—the touch of the *Pavé de
Paris* never failed to revive our author. There is the
force which comes from a subject being 'lived and felt'
in *The Great Squattleborough Soirée*, though I have always
wished that Thackeray had dealt more fully with
another grievance of men of letters—the way in which
large numbers of persons seem to think that they are
establishments at which you 'may inquire within upon
everything' without previous acquaintance, substantial
pretext, or the degrading preliminary or sequel of an
honorarium. *Hobson's Choice* is good 'second-growth'
Thackeray; and *The Lion-Huntress of Belgravia* very
nearly, if not quite, first: while I myself have always
been very fond of *The Sights of London* and *A strange man
just discovered in Germany*, and *M. Gobemouche* is all right.
The *Ingleez Family* gives a sort of foretaste of *The Newcomes* and *Our Own Bashi-Bozouk* more than an aftertaste
of Gahagan. In the series of *Authors' Miseries* and similar
things the letterpress is merely auxiliary though it is
often amusing. But on the whole the selection will

doubtless, even more than some things which have come before it, give occasion—not merely to the captious and petulant—to feel a certain relief at the thought that the author is going to settle to things more worthy of him—that the gad-fly of this perpetual demand for trifles is to be taken away.

Yet it may be permitted, in taking leave of at least the mass of these *articles de commande*, to remind the reader that there is another side of the matter: and that the ordinary complaints and lamentings over waste of genius and the like are somewhat hasty. In the first place it is a great question whether to a genius like Thackeray's—intense and individual, but impulsive, *primesautier*, irregular—a very considerable period of experiment is not absolutely necessary. In the second, it must be remembered that the peculiar discipline of miscellaneous journalism brings or should bring with it a certain knowledge of life as well as literature which is of the first importance. The journalist has many temptations, no doubt, and he sometimes succumbs to them: but at least he is kept (if he is not a mere home-worker) from that exclusive contact with books which is dangerous to weak brethren. He may breathe foul air; but even foul air is less deadly than an exhausted receiver. He may do clumsy work: but his work has at least to stand the rough test of achieving its appointed end whatever that end may be, instead of being put in a museum under a glass case to be admired, to be neglected, but to come into no positive action. For the novelist or dramatist at least such a preparation cannot but be of the greatest value: for the critic it is almost indispensable. Thackeray was not exactly born to be a critic, but we shall find that his criticism greatly improved with practice; he was not born to be a dramatist at all. But he was born to be a novelist, and in all his long apprenticeship and journeymanship he was perfecting himself for his achievements to come in practice of literature and in experience of life. Now the danger which was coming on in his time and has come on further since was that literature (or rather *literariness*, which is a different thing) should encroach on life and substitute itself therefor. At the present day a great deal of what is called and taken for knowledge of life is quite spurious—the result of 'the printed book', the citizenship and franchise not of the *civitas Dei* or even *Diaboli*, but of the city of Balzac, Ibsen, Tolstoy, Mr. Meredith, or somebody else. But Thackeray, in these fifteen years or so of preparation, had been pretty steadily and sometimes pretty uncomfortably in outside contact with the actual, while inside he had perfected his own vision and faculty. We may still not meet the completed results of this for a volume or two: but we shall see far less of the minor rubs of the time of fagging.

IX

A LEGEND OF THE RHINE—CORNHILL TO CAIRO—THE BOOK OF SNOBS

THE very delightful *Legend of the Rhine* was one of the first-fruits of Thackeray's repentance as to Dumas. It is true that *Othon l'Archer*, which Dumas certainly (see the end of the piece) did 'take from somebody else' (whether from Gottfried Kinkel I know not), is not indeed one of those greater works in which, about this time, the noble Alexander began to desert the theatre for literature. But it is a sign and token: and Thackeray burlesques it with that quaint mixture of sympathy and satire which makes these things so especially savoury. It appeared in George Cruikshank's *Table Book*, and the editor illustrated it in his own way—which was not exactly Thackeray's. The illustrations are vigorous and, in the Cruikshankian style, delectable: the river and its banks, and the oars, and the rocks, and the boat in the cut where Otto takes the water, could not be better. But there are the usual faces like gargoyles: Otto's countenance is that of an unusually hideous person about forty, and the Princess Helen, at the other end of the tale, is a plain female of perhaps the same age. This cannot be helped, and, in fact, the story needs no illustrations; while some of those that it has— such as the duel of Ludwig and Gottfried and the break- ing up of the unhallowed wedding-party—are beyond price. But, once more, it does not want them. It goes through with itself in the most admirable manner. 'Mistress MacWhirter'—who may have been suggested by the actual and most estimable Miss Emma Robinson, author, about this time, of divers Dumasian romances of no small merit—ought to have written several more herself. In the last words of the last chapter there had to be something of apology; there is no need of any here. Perhaps you must love Romance itself very much before you can be thoroughly enchanted with this parody of it, but whatever be the reason, there is hardly a book of Thackeray's that I find more invariably refreshing. Once again one notes that rarest combination of extravagance with moderation which distinguishes him in company with Swift and Fielding. He himself, little fond of Swift as he was, has expressed perfectly the admiration due to Swift's accomplishment in this way. But in the lighter vein, the touch where the repentant hermit, after his ungodly indulgence in watching the duel, springs down the edge of the rock 'uttering a hasty *matin*', is as good as anything in Swift. Not one humourist in a hundred but would have been ill at ease lest everybody should not see the point of the absurdity, and have gone back to it or emphasized it somehow by some fashion of finger-post or *nota bene*. Not so Thackeray.

On another point something should be said here, though we may have to return to it in connexion with the still more striking case of *Rebecca and Rowena*. It was all very well for the author, with that ironic humility which has been noticed, to class together various things as 'Burlesques' merely. But the list grew until, in the collected editions published after his death, the 'Prize Novels', Yellowplush and Gahagan, this present *Legend* and *Rebecca and Rowena*, *Cox's Diary* and *The Fatal Boots*, are more or less cemented together. That there is burlesque in them all is true: but otherwise the likeness is hardly closer than that between Macedon and Monmouth or between Thucydides and Tennyson. The 'Prize Novels' are, of course, burlesque pure and simple, ludicrous though sufficiently good-natured parody of more or less serious things in particular. At the other end, *Rebecca and Rowena*, as we shall see, retains, in its final form, little of actual burlesque except separable touches. This *Legend* has, of course, much more; it is a fantastic parody of serious modern followings of ancient romance. But there is nothing in it in the least offensive or even antagonistic to Romance itself. It stands, if not so glaringly and almost indignantly as *Rebecca and Rowena*, yet definitely enough, in contradistinction to the loathsome vulgarizings of romance— the attempts to sully and degrade it by ignoble modernizing and rationalizing—which we have seen since, and which are perhaps the most disgusting things in later literature. This kind of Yahoo business had begun in or near Thackeray's time. There is, as I have already pointed out, nothing of it in Barham, who was nearly as sound as Thackeray himself on the point, and has revealed his true sentiments in 'As I lay a thynkynge', and not a few other places. But I seem to remember a singularly offensive paper in *All the Year Round*, when Dickens was still alive, on some of the first issues of the 'Early English Text Society' in the sixties: and the kind of brute instinct to befoul and trample and tear is evident earlier in Robert Brough, and some of the lower Bohemians of the forties and fifties. In fact, one has regretfully to say that Mr. Punch, in his early days, did not invariably keep his acute-eared and sharp-hoofed satyrs from dancing where and how they should not. But it was impossible for Thackeray to commit this unpardonable offence, and he must be a very silly and weak-kneed devotee of Romance who finds relish of *A Legend of the Rhine* incompatible with relish, aye and reverence, for everything that is best of the kind from the *Morte d'Arthur* to *The Well at the World's End*. Not only is everything good-natured—I do not think the Canon Schidnischmidt (who died in the same year) could have had any difficulty in forgiving Thackeray on his death-bed if he knew of this mention of him— but, which is not quite the same thing, everything is in good taste. Nor shall we find many places where the priceless Thackerayan logic is more beautifully ex- emplified. 'A person who can offer oysters all the year round can live to no good purpose.' A mood of peace- ful adoration is the only one in which to receive such a sentence as that. And how many people could have left the description of Bertha's person, and the descrip- tion of Wolfgang's supper, so perfectly natural and so perfectly distinct, without a false step in either case in the direction of the other handling, and yet so as to preserve the keeping between both?

It is, however, necessary to remember that there are some persons (not utterly to be despised, though they may be deeply commiserated) to whom even the slight- est mixture of burlesque is a thing disagreeable and suspect; while there are yet others who, while neither disliking it, nor being shocked at it, think it in some undefined way inferior—not, as Aristotle says, 'to be taken seriously'. They have to be considered in speak- ing of such a thing as the *Legend*: they fortunately drop out of sight as we come to *From Cornhill to Cairo*. I have said before that the Eastern tour of which this very charming and almost perfect thing is a record, appears to me to have been in some senses the turning-point— a turning-point not passive and mechanical, but meta- physically active—in Thackeray's life. The character of the record itself, as part of his work, can not only be discerned but actually to some extent accounted for, in a fashion very unusually *not* futile. It was by no means his only occupation during the tour. He was at the same time sending, pretty regularly, the 'Fat Contributor's' articles to *Punch*, and finishing *Barry Lyndon*, while latterly he was sketching the delightful Christmas book of *Mrs. Perkins's Ball*. The 'Fat Contributor' provided him with a separate outlet for the most farcical incidents and aspects of the voyage, and gave him his own compensation for melancholy in high jinks; *Barry* with an equally copious one for the grimmer outpourings of his satire.[1] Thus the coarser and, if not baser (for there was nothing base in him), the less precious elements were (according to the old metaphor from smelting) skimmed off the silver of his style and thought, which was left to reflect his own nature. The style had never before reached such polished argent as in, for instance, the Telmessus passage: the thought had rarely united force and grace more happily. He could not, indeed, repress his old grudge at the classics (who nevertheless helped him as they have helped many a man, regardless of his ingratitude) at Athens; nor his crude theology and theodicy at Jerusalem. But there are very few such lapses in the book, and they can scarcely be said to be obtrusive.

These voyages to the East, after the pattern set by Chateaubriand, were in increasing favour during the first half of the nineteenth century, and the facilities of access given by steam at once fostered and hackneyed them towards the latter part of it. Thackeray has given a humorous list of the chief rivals to 'my own little book' elsewhere in *Our Street*. The special merit of the same 'little book' consists in the extraordinary variety

[1] 'The *mincing* pages of *Barry Lindon*' [*sic*] as I saw them happily described the other day.

of its appeals, and the way in which it 'goes trippingly off' with all of them. If it has not the brassy and insistent cleverness of *Eöthen*, its real wit is far greater; if it is less enthusiastic than *The Crescent and the Cross* (a book strangely missing in the innumerable reprints of a century which has, at least, the wisdom to prefer *réchauffés* of good to fresh dishes of doubtful food), that quality also is not wanting, though the shadow of Vanity is behind it, as was inevitable in the Preacher's own country. It produces the true and right panoramic and almost phantasmagoric effect of its class in travel-books. It does not instruct much or pretend to instruct at all; in fact, the writer's attitude of ignorance is evidently and not ineffectively exaggerated. But the vividness, without the least attempt at 'word-painting', of its description makes one really think that there may be something in the combined exercise of pen and pencil. Among a thousand or a myriad voyages and travels, I remember nothing like the lifelikeness of the run down the coasts of Spain and Portugal from Vigo to Cadiz. Gibraltar is spoilt a little by the tiresome anti-military obsession, as Athens is by that against 'classics'; but Constantinople, Smyrna, that simply magnificent Ionian passage referred to above, other things not a few—how good they all are and how strangely free from staleness even now! For the 'infinite variety' has its effect here as elsewhere, and is always the attraction and the salvation of Thackeray's work. The subject hardly matters, though here it happens to be of great interest. It is the writing that does it.

It was perhaps part of the good luck attending this journey that it should not be *all* good luck—that there should be a little *placebo* to Nemesis attending it. There was, of course, not the slightest real harm in Thackeray's accepting a free passage from or through a friend, and celebrating the journey in a very modestly-paid-for book. There seems to have been no connexion between the two facts except his own pleasure and profit, no stipulation or expectation of any kind on the part of the 'P. & O.' directors. He was not accepting, as perfectly honourable men of letters have since accepted, a regular commission; still less was he (as some persons of good repute have apparently found it satisfactory to themselves to be) a sort of 'paid guest' to millionaire or magnate of some kind, a 'led-chronicler' of landtravel or sea-faring. But the age was still not altogether discreditably punctilious about the status of the man of letters: and there undoubtedly was a kind of handle for real or pretended disapproval of the proceeding. Some, we are told, of his own friends expressed themselves rather strongly about it, and it was probably this which made him take up, as he did, an article in *Tait's Magazine* on the subject.

I do not remember whether the untiring industry of bibliographers has succeeded in rummaging out the authorship of this article which, though not goodnatured, is rather ingenious, and reminds one that De Quincey used at one time to write a good deal in *Tait*. But Thackeray thought it was worth answering. He was rather prone to neglect that golden maxim of Bacon's, *Qui replicat multiplicat*, and his impulsive sensitiveness probably prevented him from adopting that other counsel of the wise, 'Write your reply as stingingly as you possibly can; keep it a night, and put it in the fire next day'. In this particular instance, apparently, he did not think that he had done quite so well to be angry as in the case of 'Thunder and Small Beer', for he never himself reprinted the article 'Titmarsh *v.* Tait' in connexion with the Eastern Sketch Book. If it had not been regularly housed for many years in the standard editions of his works I do not think I should have given it at all. But as it has been thus adopted, I think it may come here better than elsewhere: and it may take its place as a footnote,[1] not being long. It is probable

---

[1] It runs as follows:

TITMARSH v. TAIT

[*Punch*, March 14, 1846.]

My dear *Mr. Punch*,

You are acknowledged to be the censor of the age, and the father and protector of the Press; in which character allow one of your warmest admirers to appeal to you for redress and protection. One of those good-natured friends, of whom every literary man can boast, has been criticizing a late work of mine in *Tait's Magazine*. What his opinion may be is neither here nor there. Every man has a right to his own; and whether the critic complains of want of purpose, or says (with great acuteness and ingenuity) that the book might have been much better, is not at all to the point. Against criticism of this nature no writer can cavil. It is cheerfully accepted by your subscriber.

But there is a passage in the *Tait* criticism which, although it may be actuated by the profoundest benevolence, a gentleman may be pardoned for protesting against politely. It is as follows:

'In the circumstance of a steamer being launched on a first voyage to Margate, or were it but to Greenwich, there is always an invited party, a band of music, a couple of *Times* and *Chronicle* reporters, also champagne and bottled porter, with cakes and jellies for the ladies. *Even* on the Firth of Forth or Clyde' (this 'even' is very *naïf* and fine), 'or the rivers Severn or Shannon, the same auspicious event is celebrated by the presence of a piper or blind fiddler, carried cost free, and permitted, on coming home, to send round his hat. On something like the same principle, the Peninsular and Oriental Company were so fortunate as to crimp Mr. Titmarsh. . . . We hope they have voted him a yachting service of plate, of at least five hundred ounces.'

This latter suggestion I complain of as being *too* friendly. Why should the critic insist on a collection? Who asked the gentleman for plack or bawbee? However, this again is a private matter.

It is that comparison of the blind fiddler who '*sends round his hat*', that ought to be devoted to the indignation of the press of these kingdoms. Your constant reader has never played on the English—or on the Scotch fiddle.

He leaves the sending round of hats to professors of the Caledonian Cremona. He was not 'crimped' by the Peninsular and Oriental Com-

that, as so often happens, the very possibility of his

pany, nor called upon to fiddle for their amusement, nor rewarded
with silver spoons by that excellent Company. A gentleman who takes
a vacant seat in a friend's carriage is not supposed to receive a degrading
obligation, or called upon to pay for his ride by extra joking, facetious-
ness, &c.; nor surely is the person who so gives you the use of his carriage
required to present you also with a guinea or to pay your tavern bill.
The critic, in fact, has shown uncommon keenness in observing the manners of his national violinist; but must know more of them than of the
customs of English gentlemen.

If the critic himself is a man of letters and fiddles professionally, why
should he abuse his Stradivarius? If he is some disguised nobleman

of lofty birth, superb breeding, and vast wealth, who only fiddles for
pleasure, he should spare those gentlefolks in whose company he con-
descends to perform. But I don't believe he 's a noble amateur—I think
he must be a professional man of letters. It is only literary men nowadays
who commit this suicidal sort of impertinence; who sneak through the
world ashamed of their calling, and show their independence by be-
fouling the trade by which they live.

That you will rebuke, amend, or (if need be) utterly smash all such
is, my dear *Mr. Punch*, the humble prayer of

Your constant reader and fellow-labourer,

MICHAEL ANGELO TITMARSH.

BLUE POSTS, March 10, 1846.

conduct being misrepresented had never occurred to Thackeray: and that his irritation was all the greater. Otherwise he could hardly have failed to see that the comparison of the hired minstrel, though mischievous and uncivil, was by no means destitute of that malicious appropriateness which constitutes a certain kind of wit. Nor was he by any means one of those people who can never see a joke against themselves. But the unexpectedness of this, as I take it, or the coincidence with private disapproval, seems to have had in this case the same effect as the 'unclubbableness' of Yates's conduct much later, and the owlish lecturing of Phillips midway between the two. Even in the *Roundabouts* this touchiness reappears, and it was no doubt an inseparable characteristic. In fact, it was almost a necessary consequence of the intense nature and impulse which have been so often assigned to him. Affectation of any kind was impossible in his case, and after all stoicism is only a kind of affectation.

The *Tait* reviewer seems to have thought badly, not merely of the ethics but of the literary quality of *From Cornhill to Cairo*, wherein not many good judges have agreed with him. With regard to the *Book of Snobs*, there has been a much greater dissonance of what should be competent opinion. That, from the first, it should have excited much smothered or open anger, and not a little distrust and fear, is natural enough—was, in fact, inevitable; and this had its recompense in the undoubted accession to Thackeray's reputation which it brought about as soon as he was known to be the author. If not admired he was henceforth at least redoubted, and people began to accept him as a formidable satirist before they accepted him as a delightful tale-teller. But this does not exactly bear upon the direct literary merits

of the collection. These have always been the subject
of a good deal of difference of opinion, while of late
years anti-Thackerayans have taken it as one of their
favourite grounds of attack. I think I have actually
seen it described as 'abominable' by a person who
certainly was neither fool nor Philistine, neither Radical
nor 'raff'. Its decriers base themselves, not unfrequently
on an alleged declaration of the author's to Motley,
years later, that he himself 'hated the book, and could
not read a word of it'—a declaration which, even if it
had his own endorsement, after all proves very little,
especially from a man of moods like Thackeray. On
the other hand, think what we may of it in whole or
in part, there is no doubt that at least one of the titles
which are indissolubly his, for better for worse, is
'Author of the *Book of Snobs*'. And it may, therefore,
be not so much desirable as necessary to make some
slight critical examination of it as it is—a process which
will enable us incidentally to show, much better than
desultory fisticuffs with its detractors, what it is not.

About one thing there should not be much controversy between reasonable opponents in any case: and
that is its astonishing inequality. The Goldmore-Gray
episode of 'Snobs and Marriage' is an unsurpassable
thing in its own light kind; and much of the chronicle
of the visit to 'The Evergreens' is on the same level.
On the other hand, some of the numbers are so questionable in taste and literary merit that Thackeray himself
omitted them, though for a good many years past they
have been readmitted by his representatives. Owing to
the great length of the series, to its extremely desultory
character, and to its author's usual want of system,
positive contradictions are by no means wanting. At
one time he, for instance, finds fault with people for

giving finer dinners than they habitually eat themselves, and at another expressly declares in favour of
the practice. That a great deal of it, including almost
all that he afterwards left out, is political, means in his
case (as has been often said) that it is worthless and
rather worse. For the greatest curse of politics is in-
coherence and absence of principle, and I suppose that
neither Tory nor Radical would dream of claiming
Thackeray as a consistent walker on either side. Whether
there is an actual breach of decorum in the direction
of personality is an undecided point. Yates's security
on the affirmative side is exceedingly Bardolphian, and
though few of Thackeray's originals of eighty years since
can be alive to-day, his personages are very much alive
in club and college, at kirk and market, on platform
and in Parliament, at this very moment.

But, to go higher, what are we to say of the attitude
and theory of the book as a whole? Thackeray was far
too intuitive and quintessential a critic of life not to
anticipate the certain charge of snobbishness in snob-
hunting, and far too much of a humourist not to admit
it—in a sense. As a matter of fact, the broom which
sweeps away uncleannesses will have some difficulty in
keeping itself clean, and it probably will be in some
danger of sweeping away things that are not unclean
at all. There is no doubt that the hunter here has
indulged too indiscriminately in the pleasures of the
chase—that his definition of 'admiring mean things
meanly' will not hold at all, and that in not a few cases
the things are not mean. There is nothing snobbish—
there may sometimes be something absurd—in liveries
and uniforms; and as to his famous instance of the gun
loaded by a keeper and handed through an equerry
to a prince, one may bet ten Newmans to a Kingsley,

using the terms in their logical currency only, that it will not survive five minutes' unsparing dialectic. That the book is full of faults of tact and taste must be admitted, and for my own part I have always, since I read that it was at first attributed to Douglas Jerrold, been inclined to attribute Thackeray's distaste for it to that fact. It is improbable that he would have liked his son's coat to be taken for the garment of an offspring of Jerrold. And he may have recognized the fact that, from some points of view, the coats were a little too much of a colour.

On the other hand, though I should be very far from attributing, as I did in another case, the dislike of all those who dislike this *Book* to a sense of *de te fabula*, I think there is nothing uncharitable or offensive in suggesting that the very success of Thackeray's crusade is in part the reason of their objections to it. He made snobbishness such an odious thing that it has become a point of honour to resent even the far-off suggestion of the possibility of its existence. That the crusade was wanted I fear nobody can doubt, however little he may think our times superior to our fathers': and that the evil was to a great extent only 'driven in' I fear no clear-sighted person can deny. There has for some time been room and verge for a *New Book of Snobs* which would exhibit some piquant variations. But this, taken rightly, is to the credit of the old one. And that old one has many other things to its credit of a more concrete and less disputable nature. I have specified what seem to me its *apices*. The dinner in Bittlestone Street appears to me flawless—the suspicion of a flaw can lurk only in the mind of a stern denouncer of practical jokes even of the most innocent kind, or of a sterner moralist who may suggest that Gray got his parliamentary business on false pretences. Such persons do exist, but we need hardly reason of them. Their virtue is doubtless its own reward.

The satire on the Pinto family and their circle is more mixed and dangerous, but the greater part of it is again perfect. There may be an overdose of burlesque in the opening papers for some tastes, though they must be very difficult ones not to be appeased by the blank verse—blank verse *is* argument in such a case and place. And is there any one who can resist: 'The most good-natured of women pardoned the error; and the butler removed the bird'? If such there be, no doubt he will not enjoy the history of the De Mogynses. I shall give anybody leave to remind Thackeray when he calls the Oxford title of 'servitor' 'very pretty and gentleman-like', that it is only snobbery which has attached any stigma to 'servant' and its fellows. And I own that I myself, greatly as I revere him, should rather have liked to examine him for half an hour or so on his knowledge of the 'brutal un-Christian blundering feudal system'. But with a very little patience and shuffling of the cards (especially omitting what the author wished to be omitted) we find plenty of trumps. For my part I do not in the least care whether Mr. Papworthy and Captain Shindy 'took off' any member of the Garrick or the Reform too closely or not. They are not *named*, and the actual names serve as indicators to two of the most precious of one's mental acquaintances. I would not be without the excellent Poppins's answer, when Mr. Papworthy demanded a specification of the club claret in pints, for a whole bookcase of the most respectable and improving literature. And I have *seen* Captain Shindy (long after Thackeray's death, and after he had first taken up another profession and then given that up and gone into Parliament) abusing a club waiter in his own inimitable style. It is well known that Thackeray's characters have this uncanny knack of turning up alive. *He*, as it was once observed, need not be afraid of the Mahommedan penalty on artists, that they will have to vivify their creations at the Day of Judgement or it will be the worse for them.

Those, then, who want high purpose and such things in a book ought to excuse the *Book of Snobs* for its sins (which are certainly not few), because it really did endeavour to quest and chain a loathsome beast, and to some not little extent did succeed in doing so, though the beast, after the manner of its kind, has broken loose again. Those who are not troubled with such lofty literary morals, but want to *enjoy*, ought to enjoy. There is certainly plenty of enjoyment for them, and they can leave what is not enjoyable alone.

X

CHRISTMAS BOOKS—REBECCA AND ROWENA—LATER MINOR PAPERS

OF the 'Christmas Books' proper, there has perhaps been less difference of general public opinion during the whole time of their existence, which is long—a full ' *eighty* years since' in the case of the first—than in regard to any other division of their author's works. That *Mrs. Perkins's Ball*, even more than *Vanity Fair* or the *Book of Snobs*, gave Thackeray popularity is one of the best known remarks upon him: and probably has at least as much truth about it as most such sayings. The egregious Mr. Phillips was very nearly alone in his disapproval of *The Kickleburys on the Rhine*, which was bought greedily for a book of its goodness: though of course the sale was nothing in comparison with that boasted, then and now, by mere rubbish. As for *The Rose and the Ring*, you must either be totally insensible or congenitally hostile to its whole kind of appeal if you do not feel it. *Our Street* and *Dr. Birch* have perhaps had fewer partisans: but there are still not a few who regard them as inferior, bulk and scope considered, to hardly anything that their author did. The 'Christmas-Book' fashion must of course be taken into account as far as their original balance-sheet goes, but this would have militated rather against than for the continuance of vogue. Thackeray, however, had been wise enough not to make them Christmas Books *only*, or even mainly. Dances of the cheerful Perkins kind were indeed usually given in the winter of old time; school naturally suggests Christmas holidays; and *The Rose and the Ring* was written to supply the want of Twelfth-night 'characters'.

But *Our Street* can only suggest Christmas rent, Christ
mas bills, and perhaps 'waits': and no imagination,
however fertile in resource, can suggest a real connexion
between Christmas and the Rhine, except perhaps that
Rhine salmon is then mainly available for persons who
will have things at the wrong time. Thackeray had no
superfine and superficial contempt of Christmas customs
—the *Roundabouts* show that. But he was, be it repeated,
too wise to *afficher* his title excessively.

On the other hand no kind of book, given its usual
fashions of appearance, could better suit his ambi-
dexterity with pen and pencil. In a sense *Cox's Diary*
and *The Fatal Boots* are Christmas Books—indeed in
more senses than one, for they actually appeared at the
time: but here the illustrations were not his as they are
in the Christmas Books proper. Nothing could better
suit him: and nothing has better suited him. He altered
his dealings slightly, from the pure succession of scenes,
sometimes wholly dramatic, of the *Ball* to the continuous romance of *The Rose and the Ring*: while in *The
Kickleburys* the pictures are perhaps more separable from
the text than in any other. But even there the connexion is fairly close: while the accepted licence of
'cawicachaw' exactly suits his style. He has not indeed
overcome, to any great extent, that singular inability
of his to draw a really pretty face which he has confessed immortally in 'Peg of Limavaddy'. Miss Joy is
tolerable, and Miss Martin not ugly: but the beautiful
Emma Trotter rather suggests that Lord Methuselah's
taste was not much better than his morals. Naughty
Mrs. Stafford Molyneux in *Our Street* is good-looking,
but then she is in profile and not difficult: while Anne
Raby and Rosa Birch are no more than comely, as is
Fanny Kicklebury. Rosalba is charming as a child—

Thackeray could always draw pretty children—but when she grew up one does not fear that, as an inhabitant of Paflagonia, one would be in danger of incurring the ban of that clause in the law of High Treason which forbids falling in love with the King's wife. On the other hand the men, and the women where beauty is not needful, can be thoroughly recommended to the most fastidious friend: and the quaint dumpy figure of Mr. Titmarsh pervades the whole like an atmosphere—in his likeness and his unlikeness to his original and creator suggesting the unique mixture of intimacy and aloofness as regards his characters, which is that original's secret.

The summary judgements of book-catalogue and other second- or tenth-hand criticism dub *Mrs. Perkins's Ball* as 'the first and best' of the books. 'First' is indisputable: 'best' very disputable indeed. For each is best in its way, and if one could get a common denominator for things so different, I think *The Rose and the Ring* would show the highest mark above the line. But the *Ball* is certainly charming; and there is more 'architectonic' than Thackeray is usually credited with in the beginning and ending of the story, not with Jove, but with The Mulligan. And the rapidity and variety of the cartoon succession, with the laconic sufficiency of the letterpress, at once rivet the attention of the reader and make comment rather absurd. Perhaps not everybody nowadays knows that the thing owed a little in suggestion to the 'Physiologies' which had appeared some years before in Paris and were being copied by Albert Smith and others in English. But the debt is small: and Thackeray, as always, centuples it with his own invention. And he has kept the shadows out completely, except in the last paragraph where indeed they were well enough in place: for when the skeleton is not at the feast it generally turns up just after. With regard to The Mulligan himself—greatest, though so slightly drawn, of all Thackeray's great Irishmen save the father of Emily Fotheringay—his relations to the actual world seem to have been curiously different from those of his compatriot. Costigan is said to have come alive (rather uncannily) *after* his presentation in the book, but quite unconsciously on his own part. The personality of The Mulligan is said to have been, if not exactly claimed by, identified with several existing human beings—and resented by some of them. The favourite has, I believe, been that famous and eccentric but very popular fire-eater and patriot The O'Gorman Mahon who, more than ten years Thackeray's senior, survived him for nearly thirty, had almost as much of Gahagan as of Mulligan about him, and was long afterwards better known than ever as an Irish M.P.—on the Home Rule side, but (as always) much of a free lance there.

Our Street was written when Thackeray had established himself in a neighbourhood very much the prey of the alterations which he describes. Young Street itself had few of the characteristics of the ci-devant Waddilove, actually Pocklington, thoroughfare. But the exact processes had begun in many places all round Kensington Gardens from Knightsbridge to Craven Hill: and they can hardly be said to have ceased yet, though it is terracotta rather than stucco that is now the devouring material. The humours of the book are naturally somewhat more complicated than those of the single *Ball*, and require more letterpress to work them out. Much greater assistance moreover is given towards working out that interesting but rather puzzling 'Autobiography

of Mr. Titmarsh' which I really wonder that no one
has written. Let it only be hoped that the episode or
catastrophe of suicide, at which Lady Ritchie darkly
hints as having once been in contemplation, was
not a result of one of the disappointments recorded in
these Christmas Books. But there is the comforting
reflection that Mr. Titmarsh was so constantly being
disappointed that he could not have committed suicide
on all the occasions, and therefore probably did not
on any.

His house-companions—the thievish landlady and the
acid if not exactly sour old maid—are rather more of
stock characters than is usual with Thackeray: but he
lived so much and so long in lodgings that he was
probably speaking with feeling. Clarence Bulbul has
strong resemblances to the late Lord Houghton, though
only in good-natured caricature. Thackeray did few
things more remarkable than the plate of 'Some of Our
Gentlemen', a wonderful group of character heads and
figures—better than 'from the life', but 'from the life'
also, fully in the right artistic sense. It may be feared
that Captain Bragg of the *Ram Chunder* is from the life
too; as (in one sense) everything in the piece is. But
it is in a quieter vein than most of its companions, and
has I believe been one of the least popular. Most commentators say very little about it: though it is full of
delectation for right readers and, in its direct connexion
with its successor, has a rather peculiar interest.

For *Dr. Birch and his Young Friends* is, in general
scheme, a sort of episode of *Our Street*, which semi-
metropolitan locality Mr. Titmarsh is induced to desert
for a time by one of his futile attacks of heart-disease.
In fact Thackeray, with the proverbial but by no means
universal carelessness of rich givers, threw away upon

this trifle the scantling of a very respectable novel of his own, and still more of the Trollopian, kind. The business-like author of *Framley Parsonage* (not that there is the slightest intention here to sneer at him) would have made three good volumes out of the society of Rodwell Regis and the Birch family, and the Davison-Raby romance and the Reverend Mr. Prince (a character susceptible of very great development), and the parenthetic tragedy of the heir to the Marquisate of Steyne. But Thackeray used it all up as the merest paper and string for wrapping and tying together a certain amount of his caustic melancholy and a much larger one of his favourite studies of school-life. Though there is nothing in the least surprising—to any one who can construe in human nature even as well as Mr. Titmarsh could construe in Ovid—there is something curious in his dealings with schools and schoolboys. On the one side we have his tirades against the school system, and his well-attested discomfort during his own experience thereof: on the other his constant, extraordinarily natural, and one would say distinctly loving sketches of school life. Of course there is *haec olim meminisse juvabit* and other tags to explain what hardly wants explaining. But the fact remains that his own letters, such explosions as that in the Eastern Sketch-Book, and divers other things, do contrast rather humorously with the pictures of 'Greyfriars' in nearly all the novels from *Vanity Fair* to *Philip*, and with the sketches of Archbishop Wigsby's resuscitated College here.

Putting this aside, the book is certainly not the least amusing of the group. Among the cuts—appropriate word to the alarming frontispiece of Jack Birch in panoply—there is hardly a weak one: and whether by accident or not, they are more carefully finished off and furnished with accessories than most of their designer's work. He has nearly got hold of the elusive beauty in one of the demure damsels (next to the ugly little one) who are entering church under the unhallowed gaze of Dr. Birch's young friends: and most of the boys are admirable. So are the situations, from that supreme one, dealt with by pen and pencil alike, where Mr. Tipper finds his nephews 'at their studies', downwards. Just as Thackeray could always draw prettier children than 'grown-ups', so he could impart truer and more various expression to boys than to men. The difference between the two sneaks, Lurcher and Bullock, is quite delectable. Also all these things are fitted with suitable letterpress in a wonderful way. Gavarni, they say, used to keep in his studio rows of stones with their faces turned to the wall, though he had actually drawn on them, because, as he said, they had not yet 'spoken to him'. There was never, I think, any of this unmannerly refusal to speak to each other and their master on the part of Thackeray's pen and pencil. The latter had not quite such perfection of expression as the former: but they always spoke in unison.

The piece is distinguished from its fellows by its curious and affecting epilogue in verse—which, I suppose, seems mawkish to Catiline the blood-drinker, who invariably uses gunpowder for salt, and thinks an allusion to Prayer-book or Bible quite sickening. Its exact reason has not, I think, been explained: for the death of Charles Buller which is referred to in it had taken place six years earlier, though about Christmas time. It is perhaps the most unaffectedly and unmixedly 'serious' of all Thackeray's work—certainly of all his verse: there is not a quirk or a gibe in it. In fact it was probably written after the serious illness which interrupted *Pendennis*, and when (as the Brookfield letters show), though the peril was passed, the saint was not by any means bilked of his due. I cannot help drawing attention to the effect produced here by the shortening (with no previous parallel) of the last line

To men of gentle will.

The Kickleburys on the Rhine is inseparably associated with that *Essay on Thunder and Small Beer* which, ever since its own second appearance less than a month after the first, has always accompanied it. I have already, in connexion with the not wholly dissimilar alliance of *From Cornhill to Cairo* and 'Titmarsh *v.* Tait', hinted a doubt whether Thackeray did altogether well to be angry. It may be doubted whether anybody ever does well to be angry in this particular way. The great line of a rather unequal poet

Mais le plus sage en rit, sachant qu'il doit mourir

remains the last word on the subject: and certainly Thackeray was the last man to deny it—in the abstract. In fact he might have written the very line just quoted. But the person who is always *le plus sage* is not quite human, and Thackeray was very human indeed. Moreover, there was a curious compound of absolute stupidity and apparent malevolence in the critique which provoked the essay. It would seem that Samuel Phillips, to whom *The Times* review has always been attributed, was *not* a malevolent person. But he was rather a stupid one—LL.D. of Göttingen as he was, and reviewer in chief to 'the Jupiter' as he was likewise—and he illustrates the curious mid-century degradation of English criticism from which Matthew Arnold and the *Saturday Review* in their different ways rescued it. Moreover, it was the time of that equally curious and rather

unhealthy 'Jupiter' attitude which, though Thackeray
never took notice of it as a whole, his disciple Trollope
has exposed so admirably in the 'Barsetshire' chronicles.
In order to show this attitude, people of distinction
'had to be *took* down': and apparently Thackeray was
selected for the particular taking. Very probably the
selection was that of Phillips's employers: but the blundering fustian of the article must have been his own,
and therefore he may in a sense have the credit of the
admirable retort which he provoked. Perhaps he was
actually stupid enough not to see the excellences of the
book. One of them, the record of the duel with 'the
horrid contrebanquists' even *he* saw.

There were plenty more for him to see if he had had
the eyes: for the fact is that none of the group is more
pleasantly and unerringly hit off. It is, if not 'small
beer', small wine compared to some of its author's work;
but it is a passing good creature. In the *Contrebanque*
episode, in that delightful one of Lady Kicklebury's
forcing herself on the society of the Princesse de Moga-
dor, and indeed in the general sketches of scene and
personage, it is something more than a 'little wine'—
it is certainly never less. Phillips, a very unlucky man
during the first part of his short life, was a lucky one
later. He died long before Thackeray; let us hope that
he had altered his opinion of *The Kickleburys on the
Rhine*. He certainly will have to do so before he gets
out of Purgatory.

As for *The Rose and the Ring* it is extremely difficult
to be equal to that occasion. There is really nothing
to do but once more to echo the famous combination
of orthodox theology and unerring aesthetics about
strawberries, and to say that it would undoubtedly be
in the power of Heaven to create a better book of the

kind, but that Heaven has never yet been pleased to
do so. The charm of the drawings, the astonishing
felicity of the poetical page-headings (the rhythm of
which suggests Milton come again and endowed with
a gift of humour, a stupendous and terrible idea), the
unity and convincingness of the story, and above all
the more than Ariostian heroi-comedy of the treatment
—simply defy eulogy. If you see them at all you see
them for yourself, and as no one else can see them for
you. The worst of it is that it suggests an impious
presumption—even greater than that of the man suggested by Thackeray himself who wanted 'a flounder
with two backs'. One wants *more* 'Fairy Blackstick' [1]—
a whole *Cabinet des Fées* of her performances, and more
about herself. For she is not only a fairy but a person,
a Morgana-Urganda-Abunde become more human and
diviner at once. One desires, like the more romantic
auditors of *The Princess*, a *serious* Fairy Blackstick—one
who should have lovers and everything suitable about
her.

But this, as has been said, is exorbitant and sinful;
and the thing is quite delightful enough as it is. I have
always thought Valoroso rather hardly treated; there
was something good in Valoroso, as there was even in
his prototype Claudius, and it must be remembered
that, while there is here no suspicion of fratricide, the
laws of succession as between brother and brother or
father and son were, in those early times and uncertain
longitudes, very uncertain themselves. But still there
had to be 'a Nemesis' as Trollope would say: and there
it is. It does not seem to have been shared by the Queen
(whose name by the way is never given), though she

---

[1] I know, of course, that she is elsewhere most worthily and rightfully
represented in literature, but not quite as I mean.

was very nearly as guilty. Otherwise everything goes
as it should: and it is difficult to decide between the
personages. I think Hedzoff is my own favourite,
though the unfortunate Bulbo himself has very great
merits. I am afraid the staunchest of legitimists cannot
exactly poohpooh the satire on his party; and to question
the propriety of the probation of Giglio were flagitious.
But next to the page-headings the scattered gems of
Thackerayan phrase are perhaps the great feature of
the piece. From the statement—so *simplex munditiis*—
that 'blank verse is not argument' to that final and un-
answerable question of Padella, 'If you ride a fairy
horse and wear fairy armour, what on earth is the use
of my hitting you?' it is unique and sublime.

Rebecca and Rowena was not, strictly speaking, a
'Christmas Book', but it has what may be called Christmas-book qualities, and it has been dignified of old by
what may be called special honorary membership of
the Christmas-book body in the later editions published
by its author's representatives; though earlier it went
with the burlesques. As was hinted before in speaking
of *A Legend of the Rhine*, it has much less of the burlesque
than of the romantic quality in it: and like *The Rose
and the Ring* itself, is much more a specimen of romance
with burlesque-affectionate touches than anything else;
while it is not in the very least a satire on romance itself.

In its original *Fraser* form—which is very little known,
and the omitted and altered portions of which will
probably be a surprise to many fairly diligent students
of Thackeray—it had much more of the burlesque in
it. And the attitude to Dumas, though improved from
that of the early miscellanies and reviews, is nearer to
this than to the perfect appreciation of the *Roundabouts*.
How wise Thackeray was in dropping the 'Arthur'

scene few people can need to be told: for it is out of keeping both with the lighter burlesque (it would have done well enough with the *Catherine* vein) and with the only partially mock-romantic sequel. As the piece first stood indeed (and this is one main reason for giving it in that habit), it was one of the Januses in the Thackeray Pantheon—looking before and after and evidencing the cruder and the less crude states of his development. As it stands in the later form it is one of his most mature and exquisite things—full of inset jewels of verse (the 'Canute' piece revived with singular appropriateness, and others of the first water added) and of casual flashes of happy phrase and thought. It must be a strangely 'heavy' soul (to borrow one of Dryden's pregnant epithets) which cannot adjust itself as well to the lighter touches of Athelstane's schoolboy slang and the 'stones, kettles, bootjacks, chest of drawers, crockery, umbrellas, Congreve rockets, and bombshells' discharged by the garrison of Chalus, as to the rather terribly true jests of Wamba's satire and the romance of Ivanhoe and Rebecca themselves. Perhaps Thackeray was a little hard on Rowena. It is curious that he was never quite just to ladies with fair hair—Becky, Blanche, Rowena herself, Lady Maria, are instances that occur at once. There are not much more than possibilities of priggishness and prudishness in her as she appears in Scott, though she certainly had been spoilt horribly by Cedric. But it was necessary for the story that she should not be here one of those women, who, as Aristotle graciously allows, 'are good *sometimes*'. And the whole is what it so lovingly laughs at.[1]

---

[1] Doyle is, of course, and as usual, beyond praise or pay here. But 'do look' (as Lamb says) at the expression of the lion on Richard's helmet!

The few scraps and oddments which Thackeray wrote for publication in the last decade, and a little more, of his life are now to be dealt with in chronological order. The chapters to come will be occupied by substantive work. Like many men who have written much 'for the papers' he was not greatly given to writing *to* them, and 'kept himself from beans' (in this new but, to those who possess understanding, easily understandable sense) when better sustenance was at hand. But there are some remarkable things in this batch, and in commenting on them the chronological order need not be observed rigidly. The most important is perhaps *Charity and Humour*, which he delivered several times but always with reference to the first word of the title, though he sometimes varied that title itself. The first occasion was in America for a charitable society; the second and third in England, for the benefit of the families, in the first case, of Angus Reach, in the second, of Douglas Jerrold. It was on the last occasion that he, as one of the best-known anecdotes about him tells, adjusted the opening words (which a lecturer often if not generally adds to something not quite novel) to his own circumstances by an allusion to the 'High Street of a certain ancient city', to wit, Oxford, where he had just stood for Parliament and been defeated. The lecture is a sort of coda to *The English Humourists*, but there is much else in it and it can stand very well by itself. *Mr. Thackeray in the United States* is one of his latest appearances as a Fraserian and has some of the old local colour, though *Fraser* was getting—not exactly staid but—the reverse of high-jinky. The paper on *Weimar and Goethe* was written for and to George Henry Lewes as a contribution to his well-known *Life of Goethe*: and the Preface to the American edition of his own minor works is one of the most sensible of all dealings with a rather burning subject. It contains some interesting remarks on his own early work, remarks the spirit of which the Oxford edition endeavours to carry out. But there can now be no reason for passing over the two 'Yellowplush' satires on Bulwer, even if they had not long taken up their abode with their fellows under authority. The Animosities (to use Wilson's great words)—and the *animosi infantes* who felt them—are long dead; there is Humanity in the pieces enough to make them live for ever.

But he had less and less need and less and less liking for things of this kind. The actually last I think—in the time of the *Roundabouts* and very nearly a 'Roundabout' in itself—was the piece entitled *A Leaf out of a Sketch Book*, contributed to Adelaide Anne Procter's *Victoria Regia*. It is, as the Schwellenberg in one of her rare moods of amiability observed of Fanny Burney, 'most *agribble*', and it suggests (with *The Orphan of Pimlico* and numerous other recovered things, some of which also appear here) an odd reflection. If Thackeray had taken all his sketches: all those that have been fished out since; all those that he left in the drawers at Larkbeare and the desks in the Temple; all the products of that divinely fertile and only humanly faulty pencil-pen—and had given them letterpress like this—what a book it would have been! But it was right that it should not exist: for had it existed, in the dozens and scores of volumes that it would have filled, the result might have been, to many respectable persons, fatal. 'What', to vary Mr. Weller, "ud have become of the *other* undertakers' of works of pastime then? As it is, there is some room for some of them.

XI

VANITY FAIR

IN this and the following chapters we have no longer to arrange, and comment upon, a mosaic of productions smaller and larger, better or worse, but heterogeneous, except as pervaded by the spirit of their author. Nor have we to contemplate any longer the spectacle of that good man struggling with adversity—a spectacle which may be legitimately attractive to gods, but which has very little legitimate attraction for fellow men. Each chapter will now consider either, as in the case of most, a single and substantial masterpiece, or, as in one or two, a group of pieces the worst of which could not have been written except by a master. And although *Vanity Fair*, the first of them, did not immediately receive the welcome it deserved—though it needed (or is said to have needed) a friendly shove from Hayward to clear it of the launching-ways, a sisterly haul from the 'little tug' *Mrs. Perkins's Ball* to get it out of the shallows—yet before long it had its share at last of triumph and of gale.

There are some odd chronological coincidences about it. Not only was Thackeray just at 'the middle of the career of our life' when the first number appeared on New Year's Day, 1847, but, still more curiously, he had reached almost the exact centre of his own much shorter career of literature. Between the *Snob* and *Vanity Fair* almost exactly the same space of years passed as between *Vanity Fair* and the last *Roundabout* or chapter of *Denis Duval*. His experiences were to be happier in the second period than in the first. The gods showed themselves at last *not* helpless in the fight with stupidity. But that fight never entirely ceased: and it was waged pretty sharply (and for some time, as has been noticed, even dubiously) in reference to *Vanity Fair* itself.

Stupidity was still not entirely without excuse, though certainly without justification. There is perhaps no book of Thackeray's which gains more than *Vanity Fair*, in respect of intelligent enjoyment, by being read in its proper chronological order. The later books gain in this way because there is a certain chronological order in their actual *matter*—if you read, for the first time, the *Esmond-Virginians* pair, or the *Pendennis-Newcomes-Philip* trio, out of order, you lose a good deal of appreciation of plot and character, and may even, at times, be somewhat puzzled materially. But in manner, though there is some development, there is little real difference between *Pendennis* and *Denis Duval*. The author is in almost every sense of the phrase 'at home'—he has conquered his own house and is living at ease in it. With *Vanity Fair* this is not quite the case—reasons and details may be given presently.

But the advances and advantages in respect of all his former work are immense and unmistakable. In the first place he has at last given himself—or has been given —proper scope and scale. In the second, he has at last discarded the conditioning limitations which (one hardly knows whether by choice or chance or compulsion) have affected his earlier work. The suspicious reader is no longer approached with a 'mere burlesque' as in *Yellowplush* and *Gahagan* and so many of their successors; with enigmatic transformations of the historical novel like *Catherine* and *Barry Lyndon*; with apparently wilful preference of more or less 'low' life as in the *Shabby Genteel Story* and *The Hoggarty Diamond*. Misspelling and other devices of the kind, if they do not disappear, are 'put in their proper place'. And instead of all this miscellaneous and incomplete work which, instinct with genius as much if not all of it was, presented itself with all the disadvantages of ephemeral and apparently hand-to-mouth circumstance, people had put before them almost exactly the Aristotelian prescription—a work 'serious, entire, and of a certain magnitude', dealing, if not with their own time and society, with a time and society which were hardly of yesterday to many of them—telling a connected and dramatically arranged story—vivid in manners and character—with incident moreover both of the lighter and the graver kind—distinguished too from the merely usual novel to the requirements of which it had so far condescended, by a coherent satiric purpose, of the fulfilment of which the author had already given proofs of being a master. 'The brew may have been too bitter' (as he said afterwards in his own way) for some: but none could call it mawkish, or merely sour, or merely 'small'. As for construction, *Vanity Fair* is nearly the best of all its author's works—in fact it is almost the only one in which any attention is paid to construction at all. In scheme, as apart from details, it is difficult to remember any other author, except perhaps Defoe, who, having written so long and so much, suddenly made such a new and such an ambitious 'entry' in literary competition, and not merely in the particular department of novel-writing.

In that department, however, the novelty, if not so absolute as that of *Robinson Crusoe*, was of a higher strain. A succession of great novelists from Richardson onwards had been endeavouring to bring the novel proper—the prose fiction which depends upon ordinary life and character only—into complete being. Fielding had very nearly done it: but what was ordinary life in his time had ceased to be ordinary. Miss Austen had quite done it:

but she had deliberately restricted her plan. In the thirty years between her death and the appearance of *Vanity Fair* attempts at it had multiplied enormously in number: but the magnificent success of Scott in another line had drawn off the main body of attention and attempt—to no great profit. The really distinguished novels since Scott had been sports of eccentric talent like Peacock's; specialist studies like Marryat's; medleys of genius and failure of genius like Bulwer's and Disraeli's; brilliant but fantastic, and not poetically fantastic, nondescripts like the work of Dickens.

After, or rather amid all this chase of rather wandering fires, there came forward once more, 'the proper study of mankind', unerringly conducted as such, but also serving as occasion for consummate work in art. The old, old contrast of substance and shadow is almost the only one for Thackeray's figures and those of his immediate predecessors and contemporaries. In comparison (though by no means always positively) they walk and act while the others flit and gesticulate; they speak with the voice μερόπων ἀνθρώπων while the others squeak and gibber; they live and move and have being while the others dance the dance of puppets and execute the manœuvres of *ombres chinoises*. It is almost impossible to estimate the solidity and reality of Thackeray's characters in the stage he had now reached, except by careful observation of chronology. As always—because a writer of this kind is rather the first articulate prophet of a new revelation than its monopolist—something of the same quality was soon diffused. But he was the first prophet: and to this day he is the greatest.

The book indeed is not faultless. It is said to have been begun as early as 1841, but it was interrupted, probably, by the trouble of his wife's illness. The interruption may have something to do with a certain drag at one place of the story: but it is pretty certain that Thackeray had not, five years earlier, attained to the art and craft he possessed in 1846. Of the spirit in which he wrote it we have a frank and informing confession to his mother. 'Don't you see how odious all the people are in the book with the exception of Dobbin? . . . What I want is to make a set of people without God in the world (only that is a cant phrase).' Now this confession—as probably most confessions are unintentionally as well as intentionally—is a self-accusation. No set of people—probably no person, though certainly there are some who give us pause—is wholly 'odious'. You can't 'leave out the sunshine'—fortunately—without making your world untrue. And *Vanity Fair* is (without any contradiction to what has been said above) a little untrue in places. Even Dobbin and Briggs (whom he elsewhere adds to this exception) are only allowed not to be odious at the price of being more than a little idiotic. Moreover Thackeray here fell into a mistake which only Shakespeare has avoided wholly—but which Fielding, who fell into it sometimes as in the case of Blifil, has avoided in that of Jonathan Wild and others. He took sides against his characters—and especially against Becky. Whether Becky really poisoned Jos (as is suggested more than once and almost affirmed in the grim and dreadful picture of her as 'Clytemnestra again', which is one of his best compositions in line) is not certain: and his explanatory letter to the Duke of Devonshire is rather against it.[1] One's impression is that Becky knew tricks a good deal better than that, and less

---

[1] One story is that somebody once asked him the question, and received after an interval the natural answer, given with a laugh and a puff of smoke, 'I don't know'.

dangerous. But putting this aside, he is certainly not fair on Becky—he does not even try to be fair as he did, later, on Barnes Newcome. Becky is very great, but she is ill-treated: the potter has made the pot too clearly to dishonour. Yet how great she is! Compare her with Valérie Marneffe, her sister certainly in a sense, her mother perhaps—and her true greatness will be seen. Valérie is not, and never could have been, anything but a courtesan of the worst but not the most distinguished kind. Becky has in her the makings not only, as she pathetically observes, of a quite respectable person— but of all manner of persons, bad and good. *Mulier est —nihil muliebre ab illa alienum est*: though her cruel creator has chosen to show her only, or mainly, in unpleasant relations. Even he has made one fond of her in certain situations—in her partial victory over the green chili, in her breaking-down after the failure with Jos and the too late offer of Sir Pitt, in her general way of being *bonne diablesse*, and even *bonne princesse*, so far as she has the chance. If Sultan Mourad after all his impalings, &c., was saved by the *écorché* pig which he moved into the shade, may not the communication of George Osborne's letter to Amelia and the making of two fools happy, outweigh some at least of Becky's little weaknesses? Say she did it partly from vanity: perhaps the Sultan saved himself partly from whim. Anyhow she is great and of the greatest—except her other sister Beatrix, there is no woman so great in English literature out of Shakespeare. And her creator *is* hard on her.

Whether he is also hard on Amelia is less easy to say. Amelia is a fool by the law of her nature: and a fool is capable of anything. But Dobbin need not have been made such a fool as he is. Parson Adams is as simple: but *he* is not a fool at all. It is evident that at this time

Thackeray had not finally got rid of the habit of *charge*—of exaggeration and caricature—which he had cherished so long. It appears least in Rawdon Crawley who, if not respectable, is *verisimilar* from beginning to end—a perfectly marvellous piece of verisimilitude, neither rouged nor blackened. Of the famous studies, or supposed studies, of real life in public or private characters one must say a little more. Of late the tendency has been rather to exaggerate their coincidence with their originals. One of the first published stories on the subject—and the first that the present writer ever read—a story adopted by Lady Ritchie—is Kingsley's in *Yeast* (published 1849). It asserts that Thackeray (who is not mentioned by name) being reproached with having made 'the baronet' (Sir Pitt Crawley) unnatural, laughed and said that he was 'almost the only exact portrait in the whole book'. (The original is sometimes said to have been Lord Rolle, the owner of Stevenstone and Bicton in Devonshire, of whose eccentricities Thackeray may have heard in his Larkbeare days.[1]) It will be observed that the limitation has an important bearing on the much more common identifications of Lord Steyne with Lord Hertford, of Wenham with Croker, &c., though no doubt there was a certain indebtedness, as in the case of Wagg to Theodore Hook. The model of Dobbin referred to is given as Archdeacon Allen, Thackeray's schoolfellow, while he himself assigned portions of Amelia to his mother, his wife, and Mrs. Brookfield. The foolishest parts certainly did not belong to the third lady: let us hope they did not to the two others. But it is well to say at once, in reference both

---

[1] Becky herself appears to have had a prosperous prototype. Lady Ritchie saw her once alive, fascinating, and, as one would expect, apparently not in the least angry with the author of her second being.

to this and to all the other books, that it is a great mistake to lay too much stress on these things. Sir Leslie Stephen has already given a caution on the subject: but it needs emphasizing, for the writer has read a German monograph on Thackeray in which almost the entire biography is laboriously, and with the utmost seriousness, built up out of the details of his novels. Now not merely is this unwarranted and unwarrantable, but it involves a complete and disastrous misapprehension of Thackeray's art and genius.[1] Only perhaps in his very earliest period and in his immature work is he guilty— if even there—of this 'lowest imitation',—this mere carrying off of whole figures from the pageant of life, and botching them into the tapestry of literature. That a very large number of his traits, incidents, individual details are taken from, or suggested by, actuality, there need be no doubt—it is in fact the secret and reason of his unsurpassed truth to life itself. But these things are all passed through the alembic or the loom of art— redistilled or rewoven into original and independent composition. The mere fact—if in any case it be a fact— that this or that point in the behaviour or history of a personage may have, as the children say, 'really happened' will suffice to suggest, in intelligent minds, a strong suspicion that the next did *not* happen. There are, let it be laid down, two classes of books that can be brought under this category. There are the books which depend for their interest on the fact that their characters *have been* live men and women; and those which depend

[1] He, who knew his *Spectator* by heart, must have read, and might have taken for motto, Addison's statement of his own practice in No. 262. 'When I draw any faulty character . . . I take care to dash it with such particular circumstances as may prevent all ill-natured applications.' Only he would have known very well, as doubtless did Addison, that you cannot 'prevent' them. You can only make them unjustifiable.

for it on the fact that they *are* live men and women. Thackeray's books belong to the second.

Those other vivifying arts of his which have been many times sketched in general, appear to the full in *Vanity Fair*. Thackeray does not 'set' his scenes and situations with the minute touches of detail as to furniture and the like, which Dickens borrowed from Smollett and from Scott, and made more specially his province. But he has a setting of his own which places things and persons quite firmly in the reader's conception: and he employs it here from the Academy for young ladies in Chiswick Mall to his final (or almost final) scenes at Pumpernickel. It is, however, perhaps not in actual description of any kind that his life-giving and individualizing touch most fully consists. It is in queer nondescript devices—though 'device' is a bad word for things that come so naturally—tricks of names, humorous or fantastic asides—indescribable confidences as it were between himself and his reader, which establish intimate relations. In particular his extraordinary 'science of names' has rightly attracted attention. Take for instance the quaint whimsy (arising probably from the old slang of 'quite the *cheese*') of the catalogue of Becky's guests 'the Duchess Dowager of Stilton, Duc de la Gruyère, Marchioness of Cheshire, Marchese Alessandro Strachino, Comte de Brie, Baron Schapsuger and [most whimsical of all] Chevalier *Tosti*'. And it is very important to notice that this is not done in burlesque fashion—even to the extent in which he himself would have done it earlier. There is no head-over-heels—no tongue-in-cheek even. The passage—or rather the clause—forms part of a perfectly serious paragraph; the author takes not the slightest trouble to draw attention to it; in fact he glides off into more quietly humorous nomenclature of the same kind, leaving this also un-advertised—unheralded by so much as a 'hem' or a wink to invite admiration. Moreover these names (compare the grimmer list of the Marquis of Steyne's titles) are in no respect grotesque or impossible. 'Baron Pitchley and Grillsby' Why not? Why not 'Pitchley' if 'Pytchley'? Why not 'Grillsby' if 'Grimsby'?

It is with these subtle condiments of humour and suggestion that the author seasons his whole book. Whether it has, or has not, 'the best story' as he himself thought, he was quite right as to the excellence of the title. In the steady maintenance of the point of view of that title—so admirably defined and described in the Preface—its greatest merit as a book, from the severe old critical standpoint, perhaps consists. Its greatest claim to admiration, with some at least, is in the lavish and masterly presentation of character—too uniformly sombre-tinted it may be, but faultlessly drawn—from the triumph of Becky downwards. But its greatest attraction of all is in the constant procession-pageant of scenes and incidents which serve to bring out these characters, and in the wonderful dexterity and variety of presentation and style—one or two only of the devices of which have just been pointed out. From the older review-point, perhaps, one objection, and not a light or easily removed one, may be brought against a certain stagnation in the narrative between Waterloo and Becky's last stage of triumph and fall. The author does not quite take the gap flying (as his business would have allowed him to do), nor does he fill it sufficiently: and though Becky's career is of the highest interest, its stages are neither very probably nor at all fully made out: while the sordid sufferings of the Sedleys and the dreary prosperity of the Osbornes are rather too like the class of situations which Mr. Arnold stigmatized, in a famous passage, at the expense of his own work. But even here the *manner* is great. So also the Devil's Advocate may say, with some truth, that in the opening or ante-Waterloo part, which occupies half the book, the action somewhat drags, and that, though the Amelia and Becky stories are ingeniously enough intertwisted, the transitions from one to the other, and even some of the scenes themselves, do not 'go off trippingly' as Captain Clutterbuck says. Still, once more, the manner saves everything: and so it does in the latest division of the book which succeeds the discovery of Becky's misdoings.

But there is another part where, though the manner is more triumphant than ever, the matter partakes the triumph and is fully worthy of its less unequal partner. From the beginning of chapter xliv, when Sir Pitt *fils* comes to stay in Curzon Street, to the great catastrophe itself, the artist is thoroughly inspired, the rider has settled to the race, and is getting every possible effort out of the horse. Not merely is it all good, but there is in it that steady *crescendo* of expectation and satisfaction which only occurs at the supreme moments of life and of literature. The catastrophe itself is simply beyond praise—it is one of the greatest things in English: but it is perfectly led up to. For, as in other uncertain and accidental matrimonies, when matter and manner do go thoroughly together, then all is indeed well. In these hundred pages—they come to about that in closely printed editions—there is not a line, not a phrase that is weak or wrong. There is nothing like them anywhere— one may know one's Balzac pretty well and look in vain for their equal in him, while anywhere else it is simply vain even to look. The variety, the intensity, the cool equal command, are not only unmatched, they are unmatchable in novel-literature: and the circumstances preclude their being matched in any other. Most novelists stray into fields where they are strangers, and get hedged or ditched: some keep to known but limited ground and are monotonous. Thackeray here is κῡδεϊ γαίων. He cannot go wrong. The very Sedley-Osborne scenes throw up what is now the main plot—the 'splendour and misery' of Becky—like the Porter scene in *Macbeth* or the Fool and Edgar in *Lear*. The visit to Queen's Crawley; the irruption of Becky into the 'highest circles'; her double management of Sir Pitt and Lord Steyne; the charade; the plot; its defeat by Lady Jane's innocent agency; the great catastrophe itself; the almost greater negotiations about the duel; the comic justice of the Coventry Island appointment—all these with minor things hardly less wonderful in their way, do the part of the matter. And the manner plays up in unfailing provision of style and atmosphere, of satire, and pathos, and humour, and 'criticism of life'.

Not that one would attempt to belittle a hundred things before—the departure from Minerva House;[1] Becky's residence with the Sedleys and the minor catastrophes (warnings too unheeded) of the curry and the Vauxhall punch; the mighty combat of Figs and Cuff; the introduction of Becky to Sir Pitt and the half chance, half machination, which leads to her union with Rawdon; the plots for Miss Crawley's inheritance; parts (though they are not so thoroughly *concocted*) of the Osborne and Sedley business; the Waterloo scenes. And the Hundred Pages are not ill followed. The restoration

---

[1] Anthony Trollope surely made an amazing blunder when he objected to Becky's return of the 'Dixonary' as unnatural. She would not have done it later: as she was then it is one of the most 'inevitable' touches in all fiction.

of Jos—too little satisfied with his felicity—to English society; the great opening of chapter lxi which some new and more intelligent Drelincourt will some day insert in a cento-book on Death; the Pumpernickel scenes—others might be mentioned. But the magnificence of the Hundred Pages rather puts out these lesser lights.

Vanity Fair then, is not perhaps Thackeray's best book: but it can hardly be denied that it contains his best long passage. And this is almost a book in itself in quantity as well as in quality, for you might print it so as to fill, and fill handsomely, one of the usual French volumes in yellow paper covers. When he had finished it, he had not finished his work or taken possession of all his property: but he had lodged his 'proofs', his titles, his diploma-piece—once for all.

XII

PENDENNIS

AFTER *Vanity Fair* Thackeray must have felt like Prometheus Unbound. There were still vultures; *they* do not abandon the *cor luctificabile* of man at any time, and in his case we see them at work through the medium of the letters to Mrs. Brookfield, which are plentiful at this date. But the great and master vulture—the gnawing sense of insufficient recognition of genius—had fled, as his assistants, the cramps and chains of inability to get that genius into free play, had fallen away, burst and broken. Thackeray was never a man to possess his soul wholly in peace; but from this time he, at least, possessed his powers in plenitude, and was recognized as possessing them.

This 'calmed and calming *mens adepta*'—a great phrase of Fulke Greville's which can hardly be quoted too often, especially as it is absolutely unhackneyed—displays itself to the full in *Pendennis*. The book has been considerably and variously abused by nearly all who do not like Thackeray, and even by some who do. This mainly takes the very uncritical form of abuse of Mr. Arthur Pendennis himself, who, they say, is something of a prig and something of a nincompoop. In particular, they get into a most 'igstrawrinary' rage (as Yellowplush says of his master) with Arthur because he does not actually seduce Fanny. Their torments on this supposition are only equalled by Helen's when she supposed that he *did*. When they think of the 'frankness' with which a French novelist would have treated this situation, they hardly know whether to weep or to testify. On the opposite side to these amusing persons are some others not much stronger in the head, though a little more decent, who insist that Warrington is the real hero, that you are not expected to think Pen heroic, and so on.

Brushing aside 'all this foolish people', tenderly or not tenderly at all, as the case may be, one finds a curious unanimity among qualified and well-affected judges that *Pendennis* is, perhaps, the most *delightful* of Thackeray's novels. It certainly does not owe this delight to artful construction, and nobody knew this better than the author. He has (with *his* frankness, which is of a different kind from that of the French novelist) told us how such plot as there was had been altered at the very last: and the piece is full of his usual 'loose ends'. It is true that one wonders how it ever got finished at all. Not to mention the nearly fatal illness which came upon him in its course, it seems to have been written in a manner almost impossible to understand. The references to it in the Brookfield letters, which tell us more about it than we know about any other novel, are the merest Sibylline leaves—you cannot piece them into any coherent account. One is told by several authorities that he received the story of it *after* it was begun, from one of Horace Smith's daughters. What is 'the story' of *Pendennis*? To Mrs. Brookfield he himself writes as if he had written it in some sense or other twice over—as if parts some way on had been written before any of it appeared, and other comparatively early parts were scarcely ready when the time for publication came. No real explanation of this imbroglio is to be found in the Biographical edition, and probably there is none.

Nor need any be wanted, unless it be by the fanatics of rule and by the hungry *coprophagi* who look up and are not fed. The book is a long one, but from first to last it is prodigal of delights, and the person who wants his delights explained deserves to become a one-eyed calender, and *not* thereafter to meet with anybody as agreeable as Zobeide and her sisters. Perhaps, indeed, it would be difficult to find another, not merely among its author's books, but among anybody else's, which contains such a 'God's plenty', as Dryden says of Chaucer. The beneficent influence which has been referred to at the beginning of this chapter seems to have set all sources of interest and attraction flowing, and to have tinged them all with sweetness and light. The old half-revengeful and more than half-grudging estimate of school-life has mellowed and sweetened itself. If his University career was none of the most successful, Mr. Pendennis would certainly not have said, as Mr. Thackeray had said, that *haec studia* were of no use to him. The club element has churned and foamed itself into an elderly but wonderfully attractive Venus of the other sex—Major Pendennis. The remnant of self-distrust which threw the action of *Vanity Fair* back for half a generation has vanished entirely, and the society is practically contemporary. Almost every kind of life comes in, and the parts in these kinds are played by almost every sort of character. Much more trouble is taken with scene and setting. There is hardly anything in *Vanity Fair* (except the grim arch between the two staircases) which gives us the *décor* as a hundred things do in *Pendennis*, from Fairoaks and the country about it to Shepherd's Inn. If, as has been admitted, the texture of the story is very loose—if it is a chronicle-play rather than a drama of the Unities—there is the consolation (very much more than a compensation for some folk) that the scenes of which it is combined or strung together never flag or drag for one moment. In exactly

how many tableaux *Pendennis* is arranged I should be
very sorry to say—the number, I should think, must be
not so close to seven as to seventy and seven. But I know
that there is not one that is not, to me, interesting, and
that I never feel (though I must have read it literally
scores of times) the slightest shock or jar in the transition
from one to another.

The fact is that you cannot do so, if Fate has made you
in the least 'gleg at the uptak'. The old tableau has not
lost its hold before the new fixes it; you have no time to
be hypercritical. The admirable opening—one of the
best, liveliest, and most original that I can think of in
any novel—introduces one of those explanation-retro-
spects which are sometimes dangerous, but which certainly do no harm here. And the abrupt leaving of
school (again one of the most vivid of things) enlivens
the narrative once more till it has to settle down for
a moment, and only a moment, into history, and so
brings you round to the subject of the Major's sudden
journey and the Fotheringay episode. Then you have
fourteen chapters of such stuff as it will be hard to beat
from any novel before or after—of such stuff as even
great novelists might have been thankful to work up into
a whole book. But Thackeray leaves it with perfect non-
chalance, and passes on to his University act—a shorter
one, but even more marvellous. How he has 'caught the
blossom of the flying terms' most people have seen—
'those who were there, and those who were not'. But,
once more, he makes no stay. I suppose some readers, if
they do not exactly skip, hurry from this to the London
initiation; but if they do so, they make a most woful mistake. Not only do the chapters from xxii to xxvii give
us the blessed Blanche (for she is blessed, though, perhaps, her benediction was given her with a Black Pater-

noster), but it shows us the new manipulation of social reality as nothing had yet done. On the initiation itself —the dubbing of the knight of press-industry—almost everybody comes together again. The delinquent Yates has left a frank and glowing account of the effect it had upon him: and it is difficult to imagine any one but the dullest of insensibles or the silliest of cheap paradoxers who can fail, or pretend to fail, to see its force, freshness, and fixed artistic value.

The book is now half over, and I suppose persons of the temper which was once attributed to a child at the Zoological Gardens—who 'always look at the next beast'—may think that it goes off. But it does not. The success with *Walter Lorraine* and the throwing together of Blanche and Foker ought to do pretty well, and even those who cannot forgive Fanny's escape might, one would think, be pacified by the fresh introduction (through the Shepherd's Inn scenes) of Costigan. Nor is the German visit dull, while the most implacable anti-sentimentalists might surely be at least half placated by the death and removal of their enemy, Helen. Perhaps, however, it may be admitted that just about this period —which is, indeed, just about the beginning of 'the straight'—the pace is a little slower than usual. It recovers itself, however, for the 'run in' with that admirable scene between Morgan and his master, the scarcely less admirable one where Arthur breaks his uncle's plot, and that, even better than either, with Blanche in pursuance thereof. Nor is the close in any way objectionable, though closes in novels, as in life, are rarely quite satisfactory unless they are tragic. In fact, it is *not* a close, and does not pretend to be, as, indeed, it need not in this chronicle sort of work. The author simply cuts you off your most bountiful pennyworth, and keeps the rest for the next time—which next time in this case was happily no longer in coming than the beginning of *The Newcomes*. Indeed, *Esmond* itself is an Irish kind of sequel, for is not its hero an ancestor of George Warrington's? It would be possible, and, indeed, very easy, to guess without rashness at the reason of Thackeray's fancy for the curious intercommunication which he established between the *personae* of almost all his work, and which made him even bring *Vanity Fair*, though by slight and casual connecting-links, into the family. But it is unnecessary. It is enough to have indicated the unfailing interest which is provided in this central meeting-place of the various stories. We must pay a little more attention to the characters by which it is worked out.

The extraordinary wealth of these is scarcely matter of argument, though the disappointed controversialist may, and generally does, endeavour to recover himself by attacking the principals. Pen, they say, besides his uppishness and pertness, and that unpardonable absence of sin as regards Fanny, is 'essentially unheroic'—a statement, by the way, which I think Thackeray would have most cordially accepted. Warrington is rather spoken of than made to speak himself. Helen is not only mawkish, but a she-Pharisee. Laura, with touches of mawkishness, too, loses her last chance of even sentimental attraction by being in a way unfaithful to Warrington, and marrying a man whom she nearly half despises, and hardly more than half loves. Perhaps there is a certain amount of truth in all this, though Heaven help the man who 'sins his mercies' by objecting to have women like Helen and Laura about him! But is it not all beside the point? I should not myself in the least mind carrying the controversy out into the open field, and (as Athelstan would say) 'giving it over the face and eyes' to the stupid old 'great, uncommon, and beautiful' conception of heroes and heroines in inventive fiction. These may be—I think they are—necessary in poetry; they are not necessary in prose. But put this aside. Pen, Warrington, Laura, Helen, are, and do, are not, and do not, this, that, and the other. Well, and is not 'this, that, and the other' exactly what human beings are, and are not, do not, and do? Will anybody lay hand on waistcoat, and say that any one of the four is not *alive*? If he does, I think we may disable his judgement of life. It is true that Laura and Warrington might have been more worked out—Laura is a little more in the subsequent books—but the author did not choose to do it, and it is his business, not ours. I doubt whether Helen is in the least improbable. You may say that you do not care for her kind, but that is not your business. As Victor Hugo pointed out long ago, in her time though not in reference to her, she is perfect *in her kind*, and that is enough. As for Pen, the author's comments on him in the Brookfield letters only fill in what he has said of him in the book, and what every intelligent reader ought to have realized from that book itself. Pen, if anybody in modern fiction, is *l'homme sensuel moyen*—a little cleverer in some ways, and a little better in others, than the average gentleman of the upper middle class who has received a liberal education and has been thrown into decent society, but not much. Thackeray gave him enough of himself to make him individual, but, as Addison (once more) puts it, dashed the mixture with a great deal that was not himself at all: and, having made him, he put him through the paces that he wished to show. He did not want to make him a pattern; he did not want to make him an awful example; he was to live the average life, undergo the average fates, experiences, temptations, luck, and ill-luck. Perhaps it may be said that these fates, &c., were more the subject of the book than Pen's own attitude to them or his dealings with them. I do not know why it should not be so.

Nor do I know why we should not turn to the other characters, who are hardly minor in some cases. Take Blanche—all but a heroine—and Major Pendennis—all but a hero—free, too, both of them, from any nasty bread-and-butterish virtue or scruples, as human as you can wish. Blanche, it seems, for whom I have not a sneaking, but a distinct and open, affection, was almost more of a real person than any one else in the gallery—a 'Miss G.' apparently, who openly (and very sensibly) claimed the identity, and had it allowed in a Brookfield letter to the extent of 'She says she is Blanche, *and I think she is.*' Blanche is extremely nice—one would not, I think, marry her, except in polygamous and cloistral countries, but that is about all that can be said against her. As for the Major, praise is superfluous. The Major, who had respect for all important institutions, included Shakespeare; but oh! how Shakespeare would have delighted in the Major! Then there is Foker. It is almost a pity that the enjoyment of this most excellent personage has been meddled with by the anecdotes about Mr. Andrew Arcedeckne. That there was a person of that name who was a schoolfellow of Thackeray's, and who had some of the externals of Foker's character, appears certain. That he called Thackeray 'Thack' is a legend; and there is nothing either shocking, or surprising, or amusing, or particularly interesting about it. School or college intimacy authorizes these things, though one knows what to think of persons who adopt them without the title to do so. It appears also that he suggested to 'Thack' that he should have a piano for his lectures, and that this was a rather brilliant revenge for Foker. I fear I must say that all this seems to me very trivial, and more than a little silly. The students of Mr. Arcedeckne's career have made it abundantly evident that he had nothing (except, perhaps, the insinuation that as a schoolboy he was not sufficiently fond of soap-and-water—'which many is not') to complain of in Foker. One may add that they have suggested at least that Foker has something to complain of in being identified with Mr. Arcedeckne; for Master Harry, except in the matter of the early soap-and-water, has a distinctly *beau rôle*. If he is not represented as very learned, or as having the manners of a Chesterfield, he *is* represented as being a thoroughly good fellow, shrewd, good-natured, with the feelings, if not the flourishes, of a gentleman. He is left with an ample fortune, and without Blanche as a wife—the one capacity in which one would, as it has been suggested, perhaps not desire that ingenious and agreeable young lady. Surely this is not exactly bad treatment!

Unluckily, there is no room for dwelling on the individual members of this most 'starry' company. Costigan and his daughter once more unite almost all suffrages—certainly all that are worth canvassing. As for 'the General', he is a nineteenth-century Falstaff—without the brains, of course; but then a nineteenth-century Falstaff with brains would be almost impossible. The divine Emily, on the other hand, is one of Thackeray's 'terrible' characters—so absolutely human, so blameless in all important aspects, so 'coted and signed', as it might seem, to be loved, and yet so hopeless and impossible as love's object. And who but Thackeray would have thrown in (as a kind of *remarque*) the satellite figure of Bows—a whole novel-centre in himself? And Captain-Chevalier Strong, and Mirobolant, and the Claverings themselves (Sir Francis, a mere super, has once more 'star' quality), and Altamont, and the minor Oxbridge and Fleet Street figures, and the publisher's dinner, and the ball at our old scene, Gaunt House, and Vauxhall, and the Derby, and a hundred things and persons more?

But there is a third point which, amid all this wealth of scene and character, must be noted as a fresh attraction for *Pendennis*, and which, to some at least, is not inferior to either of the others, while perhaps, here as elsewhere, it helps to constitute the perennial attraction of these books. Of scenes and incidents you may, they say, weary. I doubt it, but I think it possible. The play of character may become so familiar that the enjoyment of it is, at least, palled; but there is in *phrase*—in certain peculiar collocations of the written word—a charm like that of Cleopatra. It never wearies, because it is never quite the same. Imbedded as it is to a certain extent in its context, you may miss it wholly on one re-reading, and so it comes to you all the fresher at the next. Even if this does not happen, it has, if it is of the first water, a quality at once of the opal and of the diamond which is absolutely infinite and inexhaustible. Thackeray had always had correspondences with this Golconda, and a very few instances of his traffic with it have been cited. But now and from this time forward the gems seem to have dropped at pleasure from mouth and pen. Not a page—hardly a paragraph—is without them in *Pendennis*, and sometimes they are curious. Matthew Arnold, as we shall have to notice later, did not think Thackeray a great writer, yet Mr. Arnold's finest poem by far, the second *Isolation*, is simply an extension of a phrase in an early chapter of *Pendennis*: 'You and I are but a pair of infinite isolations with some fellow-islands more or less near to us.' It is true that both may have been suggested by 'Jacopo Ortis', but the exact coincidence of phrase and the nearness in date of *Pendennis* (1849, Mr. Arnold's *Poems* 1852) are suggestive, and there are thousands of others unborrowed and unborrowable. 'The evening was a great triumph for him: it ended. All triumphs and all evenings end.' That is what some people at the present day, I believe, call 'the obvious'. Pity that, in their own walks abroad, they seem to meet anything similar so seldom!

Independently of its extraordinary wealth of internal attraction, the external circumstances of *Pendennis* have unusual interest. As has been more than once observed, its composition entwines itself with that of the Brookfield letters after a fashion not paralleled, as far as published correspondence goes, in regard to any of the other books. It was in consequence of an allusion to the murderess, Catherine Hayes, in *Pendennis* that the ultra-farcical incident occurred which has been glanced at in a note to *Catherine* itself. A muscular son of Erin actually took lodgings in Young Street (with intent to avenge his wronged countrywoman *par voie de fait*) till Thackeray, tired of the nuisance and the absurdity, bearded the adventurer in his lurking-place, and succeeded in convincing him that there was no offence meant. The Cambridge and Temple reminiscences are unmistakable in general, though, as has been pointed out, they may easily be overforced in particular. Nor has any of the novels so definitely and elaborately described a *country* as this. But a careful student of this country will derive from the study some salutary warnings (which he may utilize in regard to matters other than topographical)

as to Thackeray's manner of incorporating the real and
the imaginary. That 'Chatteris' is Exeter, 'Clavering
St. Mary' Ottery of the same invocation, and 'Baymouth' Sidmouth, not only is said with regularity, but
may be said with perfect confidence. So, further, the
'Brawl' is the Otter, and so on. One need not be dis-
turbed by doubts in walking or driving along the very
roads that Rebecca and the Butcher Boy and poor
Smirke's pony travelled. It is no wonder that Rebecca
had enough of it on one occasion, for it is over a dozen
miles from Baymouth to Chatteris, even without the
detour by Clavering, and the ups and downs are not a
few. But when it is said that Fairoaks is Larkbeare, not
a few provisos have to be added. Fairoaks is spoken of
as close to Clavering—almost, in fact, in it. It has a
lodge-gate on the London road, and some of the few
fields attached to it run down to the Brawl, on the other
side of which is Clavering Park. In fact, one images
Clavering, Clavering Park, and Fairoaks as all close
together, with the Brawl, so to speak, in common. Now,
as a matter of fact, Larkbeare is some mile and a half
from Ottery, and not near the Brawl at all, but in
another valley—that of the Tale Water, a small tribu-
tary of the larger stream. And though there is a greater
country seat (that of the Kennaways at Escot) pretty
close to it, that also has nothing to do with the Otter.[1]
Of course, this is absolutely unimportant from one point
of view, but from another it is most important. It shows
how Thackeray, like all the greatest artists, took hints,
but did not brook dictation, from his sitters and his
scenes; how at any time you may find yourself sliding off
solid fact into pure fiction; how, in fact, you are dealing
with an artist and not with a reporter.

[1] In an essay Thackeray gives the real names of 'Fair *Mile*' and 'Escot'.

One more point, and we may have done, though the astonishing abundance of the book would lend itself to endless scholiastry. Thackeray is often accused—and it is not always easy to clear him from the charge—of careless preparation of his books. In regard to *Pendennis* in particular, we have his fullest confessions on the subject, and his illness would by itself have made them almost unnecessary; but if he was a careless 'putter forth', he was often a very shrewd reviser, and most certainly no indolent one. Hardly any alteration of more value has ever been made in a novel than the omission of a long passage about the Clavering gossip as to Mrs. Pendennis and Smirke. Still earlier, a short one about the ancestral portraits and Helen's attitude to them, though a lesser, is perhaps a more delicate instance of Thackeray's revising powers. This attitude is inconsistent with that of determined admiration of her husband's wisdom which is constantly attributed to her elsewhere—and he saw it, and it *went*. But the best instance of all comes later. Most people who have read *Pendennis* remember the Cambridge dinner (not unlike some that young Mr. Thackeray, as we know, used to give there) at which the Major takes the measure of Bloundell-Bloundell. They will find that in the earlier issues this scene takes a different form—the ex-cornet and actual undergraduate 'cheeking' the Major, hinting that he is an old fogey, and so forth. Now this, though it explains still further the Major's breakfast judgement, deprives him of nearly all merit and character in respect of it, and, what is more, is out of keeping; for it is certain that *at this time*, whatever may be the case in the *Newcomes* period, or even at the latter end of the present book, the Major is not in the least decadent or *passé*. He still 'lives in the fust society both at 'ome and foring'. He still 'rides with Lord John and the noble Whycount at the 'edd of Foring Affairs', and is 'consulted by the Marquis of Steyne in everythink'. It was therefore a mistake to make him overcrowed by a youthful bounder and plunger like Bloundell—and Thackeray corrected it. He did not immediately hit on the convenient hybrid 'Oxbridge', and left inconsistencies in the first version, correcting them later. And his care was so minute that he sometimes—and, indeed, pretty often—changed things like 'amusements and occupations' to 'occupations and amusements', in which case the principle above referred to was applied in the Oxford edition, and we gave the later and settled version in the text without loading the Appendix with the earlier. But where, as at p. 219, the stages of thought—'Dillon' (cf. 'Napper') and 'Dilley' Tandy—may interest the reader, the signpost to them was kept.

Other minor mistakes, of the kind more easily perceived by meticulous dullness, he perhaps did not correct, nor was it in the least necessary that he should do so. We do not want novels to be Dutch Paradises, with Euphrates and Gihon running at exactly the same angles in corresponding corners, and Behemoth vignetted on the right in precise balance of Leviathan on the left. We want the 'God's plenty', and we have it here. In fact, as one thinks over the book—over casual but priceless things like the watching of the lovers from the Dean's garden, or the delivery—non-delivery, rather —of the challenge by Mr. Garbetts; like the little scene between Colonel Altamont, the footman, and the constable, or the unfortunate afternoon tea at Fairoaks[1]—

---

[1] I do not know whether anybody has noticed a curious coincidence between this and a scene in Miss Austen's unfinished, and indeed hardly begun, *The Watsons*. Neither writer could by any possibility have seen

it seems idle and impertinent to say anything about such a book. It makes no difficulties about itself; it is not problematic; its gold requires no smelting. There is really no need to do much more than Warrington did with Pen's first review-parcel—which most assuredly contained nothing a hundredth part as good. Throw it to the lucky recipient with a 'Catch it!'—and he is foolish if he does anything that day but read.

the other's work, for Thackeray had been dead just about as many years when *The Watsons* was first published as he was old when Miss Austen died. But the coincidence in two such artists is curious, nor is it the only foreshadowing of 'snobography' in the lady. It may be just permissible to draw attention to the way in which the 'science of names' is shown at once by the selection of the real but, in reality, perfectly unrelated *Chatter*is and *Claver*ing for two country centres of gossip. A few readers may even pardon the reminder that 'Chatteris' is an actual place near *Cambridge*; and 'Clavering' a name famous in *Indian* history.

XIII

ESMOND—THE ENGLISH HUMOURISTS—
THE FOUR GEORGES

WE know exceedingly little of the genesis and progress of *Esmond*. 'It did not seem to be a part of
our lives as *Pendennis* was,' says Lady Ritchie, though
she wrote part of it to dictation. She 'only heard *Esmond*
spoken of very rarely'. Perhaps its state was not the
less gracious. The Milton girls found *Paradise Lost* a
very considerable part of their lives—and were not the
happier.

But its parallels are respectable. The greatest things
have a way of coming 'all so still' into the world. We
wrangle—that is, those of us who are not content simply
not to know—about the composition of Homer, the
purpose of the *Divina Commedia*, the probable plan of
the *Canterbury Tales*, the *Ur-Hamlet*. Nobody put preliminary advertisements in the papers, you see, about
these things: there was a discreditable neglect of the
first requirements of the public. So it is with *Esmond*.
There is, I thought, a reference to it in the Brookfield
letters; but in several searches I cannot find it. To his
mother he speaks of the book as 'grand and melancholy',
and to Lady Stanley as of 'cut-throat melancholy'. It
is said to have been sold for a thousand pounds—the
same sum that Master Shallow lent Falstaff on probably
inferior security. Those who knew thought well of it—
which is not wholly surprising.

It is still, perhaps, in possession of a success rather of
esteem than of affection. A company of young men
and maidens to whom it was not long ago submitted
pronounced it (with one or two exceptions) inferior as

a work of humour. The hitting of little Harry in the
eye with a potato was, they admitted, humorous, but
hardly anything else. As representing another generation and another point of view, the faithful Dr. John
Brown did not wholly like it—Esmond's marriage with
Rachel, after his love for Beatrix, being apparently 'the
fly in the ointment' to him. Even the author could
only plead 'there's a deal of pains in it that goes for
nothing', as he says in one of his rare published references to the subject: but he was wrong. Undoubtedly
the mere taking of pains will not do; but that is when
they are taken in not the right manner, by not the
right person, on not the right subject. Here everything
was right, and accordingly it 'went for' everything. A
greater novel than *Esmond* I do not know; and I do
not know many greater books. It may be 'melancholy',
and none the worse for that: it *is* 'grand'.

For though there may not be much humour of the
potato-throwing sort in *Esmond*, it will, perhaps, be
found that in no book of Thackeray's, or of any one
else's, is that deeper and higher humour which takes
all life for its province—which is the humour of humanity
—more absolutely pervading. And it may be found
likewise, at least by some, that in no book is there to
be found such a constant intertwist of the passion which,
in all humanity's higher representatives, goes with
humour hand in hand—a loving yet a mutually critical
pair. Of the extraordinarily difficult form of autobiography I do not know such another masterly presentment; nor is it very difficult to recognize the means
by which this mastery is attained, though Heaven
knows it is not easy to understand the skill with which
they are applied. The success is, in fact, the result of
that curious 'doubleness'—amounting, in fact, here to

something like *triplicity*—which distinguishes Thackeray's attitude and handling. Thus Henry Esmond, who is on the whole, I should say, the most like him of all his characters (though of course 'romanced' a little), is himself and 'the other fellow', and also, as it were, human criticism of both. At times we have a tolerably unsophisticated account of his actions, or it may be even his thoughts; at another his thoughts and actions as they present themselves, or might present themselves, to another mind: and yet at other times a reasoned view of them, as it were that of an impartial historian. The mixed form of narrative and mono-drama lends itself to this as nothing else could: and so does the author's well-known, much discussed, and sometimes heartily abused habit of *parabasis* or soliloquy to the audience. Of this nothing has yet been directly said, and anything that is said would have to be repeated as to every novel: so that we may as well keep it for the last or a late example, *The Virginians* or *Philip*. But its efficacy in this peculiar kind of double or treble handling is almost indisputable, even by those who may dispute its legitimacy as a constantly applied method.

One result, however, it has, as regards the hero-spokesman, which is curious. I believe thoroughly in Henry Esmond—he is to me one of the most real of illustrious Henrys as well of Thackeray's characters—but his reality is of a rather different kind from that of most of his fellows. It is somewhat more abstract, more typical, more generalized than the reality of English heroes usually is. He is not in the least shadowy or allegoric: but still he is somehow 'Esmondity' as well as Esmond—*the* melancholy rather than *a* melancholy, clear-sighted, aloof-minded man. His heart and his head act to each other as their governing powers, passion and humour, have been sketched as acting above. He is a man never likely to be very successful, famous, or fortunate in the world; not what is generally called a happy man; yet enjoying constant glows and glimmers of a cloudy happiness which he would hardly exchange for any other light. The late Professor Masson—himself no posture-monger or man of megrims, but one of genial temper and steady sense—described Thackeray as 'a man apart'; and so is the Marquis of Esmond. Yet Thackeray was a very real man; and so is the Marquis too.

The element of abstraction disappears, or rather retires into the background, when we pass to Beatrix. She also has the *Ewigweibliche* in her—as much of it as any, or almost any, of Shakespeare's women, and therefor more than anybody else's. But she is very much more than a type—she is Beatrix Esmond in flesh and blood, and damask and diamond, born 'for the destruction of mankind' and fortunately for the delight of them, or some of them, as well. Beatrix is beyond eulogy. 'Cease! cease to sing her praise!' is really the only motto, though perhaps something more may be said when we come to the terrible pendant which only Thackeray has had the courage and the skill to draw, with truth and without a disgusting result. If she had died when *Esmond* closes I doubt whether, in the Wood of Fair Ladies, even Cleopatra would have dared to summon her to her side, lest the comparison should not be favourable enough to herself, and the throne have to be shared.

But, as usual with Thackeray, you must not look to the hero and heroine too exclusively, even when there is such a heroine as this. For is there not here another heroine—cause of the dubieties of the *Doctor Fidelis* as

above cited? As to that it may perhaps be pointed out
to the extreme sentimentalists that, after all, Harry had
been in love with the mother, as well as with the
daughter, all along. If they consider this an aggrava-
tion, it cannot be helped: but, except from the extreme
point of view of Miss Marianne Dashwood in her earlier
stage, it ought rather to be considered a palliative.
And if they say further that the thing is made worse
still by the fact that Harry was himself Rachel's *second*
love, and that she did not exactly wait to be a widow
before she fell in love with him; why, there is, again,
nothing for it but to confess that it is very shocking—
and excessively human. Indeed, the fact is that Rachel
is as human as Beatrix, though in a different way. You
may not only *love* her less, but—in a different sense of
contrast from that of the Roman poet—*like* her a little
less. But you cannot, if you have any knowledge of
human nature, call her unnatural. And really I do
not know that the third lady of the family, Isabel
Marchioness of Esmond, though there is less written
about her, is not as real and almost as wonderful as
the other two. She is not so fairly treated, however,
poor thing! for we have her Bernstein period without
her Beatrix one.

As for my Lords Castlewood—Thomas, and Francis
père et fils—their creator has not taken so much trouble
with them; but they are never 'out'. The least of a
piece, I think, is Rachel's too fortunate or too unfortunate husband. The people who regard Ibsen's
great triumph in the *Doll's House* as consisting in the
conduct of the husband as to the incriminating documents, ought to admire Thackeray's management of
the temporary loss of Rachel's beauty. They are certainly both touches of the baser side of human nature

ingeniously worked in. But the question is, What, in this wonderful book, is *not* ingeniously worked in—character or incident, description or speech?

If the champions of 'Unity' were wise, they would take *Esmond* as a battle-horse, for it is certain that, great as are its parts, the whole is greater than almost any one of them—which is certainly not the case with *Pendennis*. And it is further certain that, of these parts, the personages of the hero and the heroine stand out commandingly, which is certainly not the case with *Pendennis*, again. The unity, however, is of a peculiar kind, and differs from the ordinary non-classical 'Unity of Interest' which Thackeray almost invariably exhibits. It is rather a Unity of *Temper*, which is also present (as the all-pervading motto *Vanitas Vanitatum* almost necessitates) in all the books, but here reaches a transcendence not elsewhere attained. The brooding spirit of *Ecclesiastes* here covers, as it were, with the shadow of one of its wings, the joys and sorrows, the failures and successes of a private family and their friends, with the other fates of England and Europe; the fortunes of Marlborough and of Swift on their way from dictatorship, in each case, to dotage and death; the big wars and the notable literary triumphs as well as the hopeless passions or acquiescent losses. It is thus an instance—and the greatest—of that revival of the historical novel which was taking place, and in which the novel of Scott[1]—simpler, though not so very simple as is sometimes thought—is being dashed with a far heavier dose

---

[1] The influence of Scott on Thackeray is undoubted and freely confessed. But I cannot fall in with 'certain persons of distinction' in making *Esmond* very specially indebted to *Woodstock*. *Woodstock* is a very great book in itself and amazing when one knows its circumstances: but it is, even for Scott, very specially and exclusively *objective*. *Esmond* is subjective also in the highest degree.

of the novel-element as opposed to the romance, yet without abandonment of the romance-quality proper. Of these novel-romance scenes, as they may be called, the famous mock-duel at the end is of course the greatest. But that where the Duke of Hamilton has to acknowledge the Marquis of Esmond, and where Beatrix gives the kiss of Beatrix, is almost as great: and there are many others. It is possible that this very transcendence accounts to some extent for the somewhat lukewarm admiration which it has received. The usual devotee of the novel of analysis dislikes the historic, and has taught himself to consider it childish; the common lover of romance (not the better kind) feels himself hampered by the character-study, as Émile de Girardin's subscribers felt themselves hampered by Gautier's style. All the happier those who can make the best of both dispensations!

Nothing, however, has yet been said of one of the most salient characteristics of *Esmond*—one, perhaps, which has had as much to do with the love of its lovers, and the qualified esteem of those who do not quite love it, as anything else. This is, of course, the attempt, certainly a very audacious one, at once to give the very form and pressure of the time of the story—sometimes in actual diction—and yet to suffuse it with a modern thought and colour which most certainly were *not* of the time. The boldness and the peril of this attempt are both quite indisputable; and the peril itself is, in a way, double. There is the malcontent who will say 'This may be all very fine: but I don't like it. It bothers and teases me. I do not want to be talked to in the language of Addison and Steele'. And there will be the possibly less ingenuous but more obtrusive malcontent who will say that it ought never to have been

done, or that it is not, as it is, done well. With the
first, who probably exists 'in squadrons and gross bands',
argument is, of course, impossible. He may be taught
better if he is caught young, but that is all: and certainly
the last thing that any honest lover of literature would
wish would be to make him say that he likes a thing
when he does not. That may be left to those who
preach and follow the fashions of the moment. Nor,
perhaps, is there very much to do with those who say
that the double attempt is not successful—except to
disable their judgement. But as for the doctrine that
this attempt *deserves* to fail, and must fail—that it is
wrong in itself—there one may take up the cudgels with
some confidence.

So far from there being anything illegitimate in this
attempt to bring one period before the eyes of another
in its habit as it lived, and speaking as it spoke, but
to allow those eyes themselves to move as they move
and see as they see—it is merely the triumph and the
justification of the whole method of prose fiction in
general, and of the historical novel in particular. For
that historical novel is itself the result of the growth
of the historic sense acting upon the demand for fiction.
So long as people made no attempt to understand
things and thoughts different from those around and
within them; so long as, like the men of the Middle
Ages, they blandly threw everything into their own
image, or, like those of the Renaissance to some extent
and the Augustan period still more, regarded other
ages at worst with contempt, and at best with indulgence
as childish, the historical novel could not come into
being, and did not. It only became possible when
history began to be seriously studied as something more
than a chronicle of external events. When it had thus

been made possible, it was a perfectly legitimate experiment to carry the process still further; not merely to discuss or moralize, but to represent the period as it was, without forfeiting the privilege of regarding it from a point of view which it had not itself reached. The process of Thackeray is really only an unfolding, and carrying further into application, of the method of Shakespeare. Partly his date, partly his genius, partly his dramatic necessities, obliged Shakespeare to combine his treatment—to make his godlike Romans at once Roman and Elizabethan, and men of all time, and men of no time at all. Thackeray, with the conveniences of the novel and the demands of his audience, *dichotomizes* the presentation while observing a certain unity in the fictitious person, now of Henry Esmond, now of William Makepeace Thackeray himself. If anybody does not like the result, there is nothing to be said. But there are those who regard it as one of the furthest explorations that we yet possess of human genius—one of the most extraordinary achievements of that higher imagination which Coleridge liked to call *esenoplastic.*[1] That a man should have the faculty of reproducing contemporary or general life is wonderful; that he should have the faculty of reproducing past life is wonderful still more. But that he should thus revive the past and preserve the present—command and provide at once theatre and company, audience and performance—this is the highest wizardry of all. And this, as it seems to me, is what Thackeray had attempted, and more, what he has done, in the *History of Henry Esmond.*[2]

---

[1] This form, which he used elsewhere than in the *Biographia Literaria*, is better than *esemplastic* which he employed there.

[2] The justice or accuracy of his individual presentments and even of his general view of the time is quite another matter. We may touch

He could not have done it without the 'pains' to which he refers in the saying quoted above; but these pains, as usual, bore fruit more than once. The two main after-crops were *The English Humourists*[1] and *The Four Georges*. Exactly *how* early Thackeray's attention was drawn to the eighteenth century it would, in the necessarily incomplete state of our biographical information about him, be very difficult to say. We have pointed out that the connexion was pretty well established as early as *Catherine*. But it was evidently founded upon that peculiar congeniality, freshened and enlivened with a proper dose of difference, which is the most certain source and the purest maintainer of love in life and literature.

At the same time, the two sets of lectures are differentiated from the novel not so much by their form—for Thackeray as a lecturer had very little that smacked of the platform, and as a novelist he had a great deal that smacked of the satiric conversation-scene—as by their purport. *Esmond*, though partly critical, is mainly and in far the greater part creative. The Lectures, though partly creative—*resurrective*, at any rate—are professedly and substantially critical. Now, a good deal has been said already of Thackeray's qualities and defects as a critic: and it has been pointed out that, in consequence of his peculiar impulsiveness, his strong likes and dislikes, his satiric-romantic temperament, and perhaps certain deficiencies in all-round literary and historical learning, his critical light was apt to be rather uncertain, and his critical deductions by no means

on part of it presently. But the real point is that the whole is of a piece at least *in potentia*: that it gives a world that might have existed.

[1] The lectures on the *Humourists* were, of course, delivered before *Esmond* was published; but, in another sense, they are only after-crops or by-products.

things from which there should be no appeal. But *The English Humourists* is by far the most important 'place' for this criticism in the literary department; and *The Four Georges* (with *The Book of Snobs* to some extent supplementing it) is the chief place for his criticism of society, personality, and the like. Moreover, both have been, and are, violently attacked by those who do not like him. So that, for more reasons than one or two, both works deserve faithful critical handling themselves.

It is always best to disperse Maleger and his myrmidons before exploring the beauties of the House of Alma: so we may take the objections to the *Humourists* first. They are chiefly concerned with the handling of Swift and (in a less degree) of Sterne. Now, it is quite certain that we have here, in the first case at any rate, to confess, though by no means to avoid. It is an instance of that excessive 'taking sides' with or against his characters which has been noticed, and will be noticed, again and again. Nor is the reason of this in the least difficult to perceive. It is very doubtful whether Thackeray's own estimate of average humanity was much higher than Swift's: nor is it quite certain that the affection which Swift professed and (from more than one instance) seems to have really felt for Dick, Tom, and Harry, in particular, as opposed to mankind at large, was very much less sincere than Thackeray's own for individuals. But the temperament of the one deepened and aggravated his general understanding of mankind into a furious misanthropy; while the temperament of the other softened *his* into a general pardon. In the same way, Swift's very love and friendship were dangerous and harsh-faced, while Thackeray's were sunny and caressing. But there can be very little doubt that Thackeray himself, when the 'Shadow of Vanity' was heaviest on him, felt the danger of actual misanthropy, and thus revolted from its victim with a kind of terror; while his nature could not help feeling a similar revulsion from Swift's harsh ways. That to all this revulsion he gives undue force of expression need not be denied: but then, it must be remembered that he does not allow it to affect his *literary* judgement. I do not believe that any one now living has a greater admiration for Swift than I have: and I know no estimate of his genius anywhere more adequate than Thackeray's. As for Sterne, I do not intend to say much. If you will thrust your personality into your literature, as Sterne constantly does, you must take the chances of your personality as well as of your literature. You practically expose both to the judgement of the public. And if anybody chooses to take up the cudgels for Sterne's personality I shall hand them over to him and take no part on one side or another in that bout. To his *genius*, once more, I do not think Thackeray at all unjust.

The fact is, however, that as is usual with persons of genius, but even more than as usual, the defects and the qualities are so intimately connected that you cannot have one without the other—you must pay the price of the other for the one. All I can say is that such another *live* piece of English criticism of English literature as this I do not know anywhere. What is alive is very seldom perfect: to get perfection you must go to epitaphs. But, once more, though I could pick plenty of small holes in the details of the actual critical dicta, I know no picture of the division of literature here concerned from which a fairly intelligent person will derive a better impression of the facts than from this. Addison may be a

little depressed, and Steele a little exalted: but it is
necessary to remember that by Macaulay, whose
estimate then practically held the field, Steele had been
most unduly depressed and Addison rather unduly
exalted. You may go about among our critics on the
brightest day with the largest lantern and find nothing
more brilliant itself than the 'Congreve' article, where
the spice of injustice will, again, deceive nobody but
a fool. The vividness of the 'Addison and Steele' presentation is miraculous. He redresses Johnson on Prior
as he had redressed Macaulay on Steele; and he is not
unjust, as we might have feared that he would be, to
Pope. 'Hogarth, Smollett, and Fielding' is another
miracle of appreciation: and I should like to ask the
objectors to 'sentimentality' by what other means than
an intense *sympathy* (from which it is impossible to
exclude something that may be called sentimental) such
a study as that of Goldsmith could have been produced?
Now Goldsmith is one of the most difficult persons in
the whole range of literature to treat, from the motley
of his merits and his weaknesses. Yet Thackeray has
achieved the adventure here. In short, throughout the
book, he is invaluable as a critic, if not impeccable in
criticism. His faults, and the causes of them, are
obvious, separable, negligible: his merits (the chief of
them, as usual, the constant shower of happy and
illuminative phrase) as rare in quality as they are
abundant in quantity.

The lectures on *The English Humourists* must have been
composed very much *pari passu* with *Esmond*; they were
being delivered while it was being finished, and it was
published just as the author was setting off to re-deliver
them in America. *The Four Georges* were not regularly
taken in hand till some years later, when *The Newcomes*

was finished or finishing, and when fresh material was wanted for the second American trip. But there exists a very remarkable *scenario* of them—as it may be almost called—a full decade older, in the shape of a *satura* of verse and prose contributed to *Punch* on October 11, 1845. All things considered, it gives the lines which are followed in the later lectures with remarkable precision: and it is not at all improbable that Thackeray actually, though not of necessity consciously, took it for head-notes.

No book of his has been so violently attacked both at the time of its appearance and since. Nor—for, as the reader must have seen long ago, the present writer, though proud to be called a Thackerayan stalwart, is not a Thackerayan 'know-nothing', a 'Thackeray-right-or-wrong' man—is there any that exposes itself more to attack. From the strictly literary side, indeed, it has the advantage of *The Book of Snobs*: for it is nowhere unequal, and exhibits its author's unmatched power of historical-artistic imagination or reconstruction in almost the highest degree possible. But in other respects it certainly does show the omission 'to erect a sconce on Drumsnab'. There was (it has already been hinted at in connexion with the Eastern Journey) a curious innocence about Thackeray. It may be that, like the Hind,

> He feared no danger for he knew no sin;

but the absence of fear with him implied an apparent ignoring of danger, which is a danger in itself. Nobody who has even passed Responsions in the study of his literary and moral character will suspect him for one moment of having pandered to American prejudice by prating to it, as a tit-bit and *primeur*, scandal about this or that King George. But it was quite evident from the first, and ought to have been evident to the author long beforehand, that the enemy *might* think, and *would* say so. In fact, putting considerations of mere expediency aside, I think myself that he had much better not have done it. As for the justice of the general verdict, it is no doubt affected throughout by Thackeray's political incapacity, whatever side he might have taken, and by that quaint theoretical republicanism, with a good deal of pure Toryism mixed, which he attributes to some of his characters, and no doubt, in a kind of rather confused speculative way, held himself. He certainly puts George III's ability too low, and as certainly he indulges in the case of George IV in one of these curious outbursts— a *Hetze* of unreasoning, frantic, 'stop-thief!' and 'mad-dog!' persecution—to which he was liable. 'Gorgius' may not have been a hero or a proper moral man: he was certainly 'a most expensive *Herr*', and by no means a pattern husband. But recent and by no means Phari-saical expositions have exhibited his wife as almost infinitely *not* better than she should be; the allegations of treachery to private friends are, on the whole, Not Proven: if he deserted the Whigs, it was no more than some of these very Whigs very shortly afterwards did to their country: he played the difficult part of Regent and the not very easy one of King by no means ill; he was, by common and even reluctant consent, an extremely pleasant host and companion; and he liked Jane Austen's novels. There have been a good many princes—and a good many demagogues too—of whom as much good could not be said.

Admitting excess in these details, and 'inconvenience' in the circumstances of the original representation, there remains, as it seems to me, a more than sufficient balance to credit. That social-historic sense, accompanied with literary power of bodying forth its results, which we noticed as early as the opening of *Catherine* has, in the seventeen years' interval, fully and marvellously matured itself. The picture is not a mere mob of details: it is an orderly pageant of artistically composed material. It is possible; it is life-like; the only question (and that is rather a minor one) is, 'Is it true?'

Minor, I say, because the artistic value would remain if the historical were impaired. But I do not think it is. I shall bow to the authority of persons better acquainted with the eighteenth century than I am: but if some decades of familiarity with essayists and novelists and diarists and letter-writers may give one a scanty *locus standi*, I shall certainly give my testimony in favour of 'Thackeray's Extract'. The true essence of the life that exhibits itself in fiction from *Pamela* and *Joseph Andrews* down to *Pompey the Little* and the *Spiritual Quixote*; in essay from the *Tatler* to the *Mirror*; in Lord Chesterfield and Lady Mary and Horace Walpole; in Pope and Young and Green and Churchill and Cowper, in Boswell and Wraxall, in Mrs. Delany and Madame d'Arblay, seems to me to deserve warrant of excise and guarantee of analysis as it lies in these four little flaskets.

And, as has been done before, let me finish with an almost silent indication of the wonderful variety of this group also. In one sense the subject of its constituents is the same. Yet in another it is treated with the widest and most infinite difference. Any one of the three treatments would be a masterpiece of single achievement; while the first of the three is, as it seems to me, *the* masterpiece of its entire class.

XIV

THE NEWCOMES

FOR the sensible and rational lover of contrasts, that between the circumstances of *Esmond* and those of its successor has some attraction. As was pointed out in the last volume, we know almost nothing of the origin, conduct, or surroundings of the greatest of historical novels; not only its 'buth' but all the rest is 'wrapped in mistry'. It did not come out in numbers, but was the only one of the fleet to make its first appearance as a fully launched 'three-decker'. It had no illustrations, and except that it was written, so to speak, 'on the spot,' i.e. in Young Street, close to part of its own scene in Kensington Square, we know hardly anything about it. About *The Newcomes*, on the other hand, we have, if not so much external light as is thrown upon *Pendennis* by the Brookfield letters, much more internal. The author himself has told us when, where, and how it was that the general idea of the story struck him; and his daughter has told us a great deal more. It was written in many places, abroad and at home: in the latter case mainly in the new house at Onslow Square, a more commodious but also more commonplace residence than the Young Street one. It appeared once more in numbers, like *Vanity Fair* and *Pendennis*; and, like *Pendennis*, was interrupted by an illness—the Roman fever—which perhaps was the first reading of the bill of attainder on Thackeray's life. Moreover, it is once more full of personal touches. Clive mainly resembles Thackeray, as far as one can make out, in his love for drawing, in his limited success therein, and perhaps in some of his later hardships and misfortunes; but he too is at 'Grey Friars', the later and more filial equivalent of 'Slaughterhouse'. Colonel Newcome is an admitted free study of various relations and connexions—Major Carmichael Smyth first of all, Sir Richmond Shakespear and others. The author, while disclaiming any such faculty of drawing North-, as he had shown in reference to West-Britons, told Professor Masson that he had taken James Binnie directly from the life. In his own uncanny way he anticipated reality in the election scenes. There is possibly not a little of it in Rosey; and there is, to a terrible though unproven certainty, a great deal in the Campaigner. The Colonel's end enchanted and enchants everybody who is susceptible to the sentimental, and appears to have disarmed most of the anti-sentimentalists by the intensity of its humanity. Nobody is bothered here by antique language or manners.

The consequence has been that, so far as I can estimate, and admitting that positive statements of preference may not be at hand, *The Newcomes* has probably been Thackeray's most popular book on the whole. I feel pretty confident that, if a succession of plebiscites could be taken for the successive generations of his readers, this would be established statistically. I am sure that it would be the result of striking a balance (if, again, such a thing could be done) between unpopular and popular, critical and uncritical, opinion. There is something to please everybody, and little to displease any one. Even the irreconcilables on the matter of Arthur and Fanny should be appeased by the relations of Mrs. Delacy and Barnes.

And assuredly no partisan of *The Newcomes* will find advocacy difficult. Once more we have the abounding wealth and ease—the *copia*—of *Pendennis* without that certain disorderliness which has been admitted in the case of the elder masterpiece. That the catastrophe—in fact that the general tone is sadder can hardly be regarded as against it—the moderately unhappy ending has never been seriously unpopular, and here there are 'condolences and vails' enough. In a certain sense, too, the story is not merely more definite and coherent than that of *Pendennis*, but it is of a higher strain—the strands are not only more deftly twisted, but they are more various and of choicer quality. If there are no such unique presentations of special sides of life as those of the Oxbridge and Fleet Street parts of *Pendennis*, life itself at large is treated much more fully, freely, and variously. The higher society which had been partly anticipated in *Vanity Fair*, wholly so in *Esmond*, and slightly touched in *Pendennis*, is here grappled with and subdued to the purposes of art in the most fearless and triumphant fashion. It is infinitely more real in handling than Balzac's, and superior in artistic powers to any one else's attempts in the same kind. The mere variety, subordinated as it is to a fairly general scheme, is a wonderful thing, as is the way in which the great length of the book permits itself absolutely no *longueurs* of episode or padding. Above all, perhaps, there is no book in which Thackeray has attained to such a Shakespearian pitch of pure tragicomedy: that is to say, not tragedy with a happy ending, not comedy turned to tragic conclusions, but both blended and contrasted, grave and gay mixed, in the special English fashion of dramatic presentation. *Vanity Fair* had had the mixture, but there the Shadow is always brooding. And one cares so little for Amelia or for Dobbin, that their 'bringing it off' at last (especially as Dobbin has his eyes partly opened) is not a very great solatium at the end. *Pendennis* has but one really tragic passage—the death of Helen—and that is not much. In *Esmond* there are numerous lighter touches, but on the whole 'there is a Nemesis'; the piece, in fact, is half Greek in its evolution of the natural consequences of a saturnine temperament and destiny in the individual, and of great qualities and charming ones going to wreck and ruin in the House. But in *The Newcomes* grave and gay are welded, 'rainbowed' together in real English fashion. The career, triumph, and fall of the Colonel; the unsmooth course of the loves of Clive and Ethel; the tragedy of Lady Clara; other things besides; are arranged with extraordinary skill for the keeping up of the interest, which is also subserved by the revival and inclusion of the story of old friends from *Pendennis* itself. The glimpses of the married life of Arthur and Laura, the end of the Major, even the passing appearance of Dobbin, and the very admirable figure of Sir George Tufto, not from *Pendennis* but from *Vanity Fair*, should add to the attraction for most people, though I believe there are some martinets who regard them as impertinent. Let these see to their principles, and we will see to our pastime. Revolutions and discoveries are provided in the most lavish manner. It would be indeed interesting to feel the bumps of any one who found *The Newcomes* 'dull'.

As always with Thackeray, however, though perhaps to an extent below the average, it is not so much to the general run of the story as to the several, if not exactly separate, tableaux of which it is composed, and still more to the characters by which it and those are worked out, that the reader owes his enjoyment and his admiration. Here, again, no book is quite so rich as *The Newcomes*. What other novelist is there, in any literature, who has projected on his scene such a family as 'the Newcomes' themselves? The Colonel and Sir Brian and

Hobson in one generation, Clive and Barnes in the next, are not indeed connected with each other in the elaborately ostentatious fashion of Zola, or even of Dickens; but they have a subtle and impalpable kinship which is really far truer to nature, and a far greater triumph of art, than the preposterous heredity of the Rougon-Macquarts and the caricatured typicalness of the Dedlocks. And the same is the case with the nobler branch of the connexion—Lord Kew and his brother (for the sketch of George Barnes, slight as it is, is masterly), Lady Ann, Ethel (for she is much more of a Barnes than of a Newcome, except for the touch of the Colonel in her), and above all Her Unserene Magnificence Lady Kew herself, with her further ramification into the fatal house of the Gaunts. The way in which all these kindreds, from the extremes of the Honeymans and the old pensioner at Newcome to Lady Kew and the Pulleyns, are mapped and reliefed out—with no cumbrous genealogical insistence, but in such fashion that the reader feels as if, on the humbler or less humble side, he too were of the company, and all the persons and their affairs were naturally known to him—is simply marvellous. The way in which every one of them is made actual is more marvellous still. Observe, for instance, the three brothers, Thomas, Brian, and Hobson, sketched with decreasing minuteness from one to the other, and yet all alive, and each 'finally settled' for artistic purposes. Observe the way in which the sisters-in-law, Lady Ann and Mrs. Newcome, are contrasted, not in the clumsy way of constant holding up side by side which the ordinary novelist would have adopted—for they are seldom brought into actual company, and I think never made to hold conversation of any length. And then come to individuals.

The Colonel himself, Clive and Ethel, I shall postpone for a purpose; and not much more need be said of the younger Newcome brothers and their wives, except to give the heartiest applause to the latter. But not in such comparative silence can we pass over Barnes.

Barnes is not only one of the most artistically splendid and delightful, but also one of the most critically instructive, of Thackeray's characters. There is no doubt that Thackeray disliked him; indeed, the human race at large appears (and quite properly) to have been similarly affected towards the second baronet of the house of Newcome. But he knew he disliked him, and he struggled vigorously not to let the dislike interfere with the justice of the presentment. This virtue has been to a great extent rewarded in kind, because in consequence of it *we* can dislike Barnes to our hearts' content while enjoying him, and without feeling any qualms of partisanship such as are aroused in the cases of Becky and of Blanche. The true, the genuine, the unsophisticated pleasures of the gallery are ours when he has the claret thrown in his face; when he is in terror of Jack Belsize and the thundering big stick; when Sir George Tufto (vice Sir Thomas de Boots exchanged) requests to know why the dash he sends for *him*, dash him, and suggests A 22; when Highgate strikes him down; when the 'Poetry of the Affections' is interrupted by the introduction of the supposititious infants. And at the same time we have the most refined delights of the stalls when he enunciates that great maxim about the impossibility of mending broken glass; when he 'does the civil' to (and at the same time acquires valuable information about) Rummun Loll; when he appears at breakfast; when he conducts that little negotiation about his sister's hand, and 'lies *at home*' for the good of his family with an aplomb really deserving that success which it is not in the power of mortals to command; when he is for once unfeigned and natural in his unfathomable surprise that the Prince de Montcontour should keep his principality —and its latent power—in abeyance. Very rarely—so rarely that out of Shakespeare it is difficult to think of another place—is this double rapture vouchsafed to us; and even Shakespeare, being a poet and having to deal with simpler and higher conditions, had not the opportunity of giving it quite in the same way. Fielding (who is often to be joined with Shakespeare and Thackeray as no one else, not even Cervantes, is) most distinctly failed to give it in Blifil. For Blifil is not *interesting* and Barnes is, while Jonathan Wild does not quite come in.

Something of the same magic in the same conditions is enjoyed with Lady Kew, though the grandmother is as much higher in nature as in rank than her grandson, and with her we can positively sympathize. She has to fail, but she manages after all to do a good deal of harm, and she is always 'great'. Thackeray has even, though gingerly, and perhaps not more than half consciously, brought out something between her and Ethel of the terrible parallel-parable of Age and Youth which he was to bring out later between Beatrix I and Beatrix II. When one thinks what a character she is; what infinity of delicately drawn life there is in her without any of the clumsy by-work and interleaved process of the more modern character-novelist; how in this vast book she, who is enough to give life and individuality to a whole novel, merely fills a part—an important one certainly, but only a part—one stands once more astonished at Thackeray's immoderation—at the prodigality of his givings. Such a scene, such a conversation, as that between Lady Kew, her two grandsons, and their mother during Kew's convalescence—if well and duly ravelled out and woven in—would make a volume for any one of our moderns, and one would wonder where he got it. Yet this is but one—is not perhaps the absolutely best—of half a hundred in which she appears from the time when she is instructed in the meaning of 'brick' and 'trump' to her death at Lady Pallgrave's, when she thinks her triumph is sure—the death itself killing the triumph, indirectly but inevitably, with her.

There may, however, be some who think long till we come to the inestimable Paul de Florac himself. It is quite certain that, if Thackeray had never drawn another character, he would have put in his proofs for the degree of Genius by this alone. And I do not think it much more contestable that Florac is unique. There is certainly no one who can touch him as a sketch of a foreigner in the enormous range of the English novel. I am as certain that there is no one in the equally enormous range of the French novel who can come within leagues of him as a picture of an Englishman. And though I do not pretend to know as much about the novels of other literatures, even German, as I do about French and English, I do not believe that in any of them there is a picture of a native of a country other than the author's own which can compare with him. Of course French—and, for the matter of that, English—critics may say that the comic features are, if not caricatured, thrown up. But then it is impossible that with a sitter foreign to the artist, and an artist foreign to the sitter, they should not be. The wisest and most philosophical of us may endeavour to check and allow for, but only the dullest and most unimaginative of us ever fail to feel, the absurdity of the human being who, with the same number of eyes, hands, &c., as we ourselves possess, followeth not us in ways and manners and speech. Florac, no doubt, is not Florac's Florac, or his mother's, or any of his countrymen's or countrywomen's Florac. But, on the other hand, he is not John Bull's Florac merely. He is the eternal Florac—the idea of Florac— presented through the best English glasses with all possible and no forced allowances and compensations. Moreover (to come down, like Benedick, from altitudes), he is the very best of good fellows and of good company. Thackeray has said hard things of the French: some people would have it that he has said unjust things of them. But if any Frenchman feels otherwise than com- plimented by this figure of Thackeray's gallery, why then it is to be feared that international jealousy has not been entirely in the wrong when it fastened to the French character a kind of vanity which is not Thackeray's Vanity at all, though it has connexions therewith.

But in this way there is no end. Pages would not suffice to do justice to the Honeymans and the Sherricks and to that Commodore of all Red Rovers whom Thackeray has thrown in after his own fashion. James Binnie (one very particularly regrets the loss of James's fortune after his death, though not so much as his depri- vation of cheroots in his life by his odious sister's tyranny) chiefly makes one think of that sister herself and of the quite extraordinary power with which she is drawn. Nobody but Thackeray could have evolved the worse side of her character so naturally, so inevit- ably, so unobtrusively. Her detestableness grips upon you exactly as it would in life, and with the same absence of warning. And the folk at the studios, and the company at the 'Haunt', and the Marquis of Farintosh's toad-eaters (the Marquis himself is not quite of Thacke- ray's greatest triumphs, perhaps), and Madame la

Duchesse (she would certainly have owed one a grudge for leaving her so long unnoticed), and Victor Cabasse de Castillonnes (whom she might have got to execute it), and the pale and gracious shadow of Léonore de Florac with her matchless and not overdone appearance at the catastrophe, and Kew and Highgate—better figures, I think, as well as better fellows, than Farintosh—and the reappearance of the Pendennis people— all these and many more crowd the memory. And, as always with Thackeray, they combine themselves into the most amazing number of scenes—complete in themselves, and yet furthering the story—leaves of the folding panorama which opens itself out as that story proceeds. There are eighty chapter headings; it is hardly rash to say that there are eight times eighty of these separate and yet not separate situations, conversations, sudden presentments of real though fictitious life. And yet, once more, there is the ambient ether of phrase—surrounding, uniting, pervading all:—enough of itself to give the book hold, if it had neither character nor incident; certain to enhance the incident and the character that it has.

It may be observed—the observation taking something of the form of an objection—that little or nothing has yet been said of the three chief characters—Clive, Ethel, and the Colonel. It is true; and the reservation is due to a cause easily to be anticipated—that the writer has never been able to bring himself into a perfectly homogeneous and decided frame of mind about them. To take the lady first, I think I like her a good deal more than I used to do many years ago, and more, even, than I did comparatively recently. But I have never thought her, and I do not think her now, either positively charming or definitely 'brought off'. I must be excused for repeating, yet once more, that it was usually necessary for Thackeray either to like or to dislike his characters in order to be quite successful with them, unless they were more or less 'supers', where liking and disliking did not come in. I know that he meant to like Ethel, and that he thought he ought to like her; but I am not so sure that he thoroughly did. And so he has left her a little 'betwixt and between'. Sometimes, when she appears with the green sale-ticket in her dress, when she goes to Brighton, in the confession-sacrifice scene at Madame de Florac's, once or twice at other times, she is all right. Elsewhere I am not so sure of her. For anybody else, '*Pass!*' but for Thackeray, '*Query?*' She, more than all the Amelias and Helens and Lauras, makes me feel how really nice it was of Beatrix to be naughty. She may have lost herself: but we have gained her. Ethel seems to me never to find herself, and therefore nobody can have found her—not even Clive.

As for that young gentleman, one is obliged to him for being the centre of so much good society and the occasion of so much good talk and writing. But somehow, I not only do not take very much interest in him, but I have even no very clear idea of him. He seems to have been good-looking, amiable after a fashion, rather *gauche*, fairly clever with his hands, not much good with his head. These elements will make up a very possible person: but he is not, to me, here quite made up. I see Pendennis perfectly; I see Philip pretty well. I don't quite see Clive. But I feel sure that if Ethel regarded him (as she seems to have done) with sufficient affection, she must have mingled with it a certain amount of contempt. They say the mixture is not uncommon.

The best criticism on the Colonel himself is contained in what is also one of the best anecdotes of Thackeray. It is that when Mrs. Bray (George Eliot's friend and his hostess at the time) asked him the usual question one morning as to his having had a good night, he replied, 'How could I, with Colonel Newcome making such a fool of himself?' Whereto she, 'But why did you let him?' And he, 'Oh! it was in him to do it. He must.' This is equally Balzacian and believable, though I doubt whether another saying in the context—that he 'made his women either without character or bad, because that was as he knew them', is equally exact. It looks as if the card was passed to him, and he did not explicitly reject it. But as for the Colonel, no doubt it *was* 'in his nature': and the only question is whether it is a blot on that nature or not. The answer must depend very much upon individual taste and fancy. There are some tastes and fancies to which it is rather hard to forgive a man who makes a fool of himself *without knowing it*. The very reason why it is perfectly easy to forgive men for making fools of themselves about women is that, unless they are the merest oafs, they always *do* know it. Now Colonel Newcome was not a mere oaf, but it must be owned that in the matter of the Bundelcund Bank, and perhaps not in that only, he deserved the criticisms of that very odious person, but very capable critic, his nephew. His beginnings and his end are of course admirable, the latter admirable beyond expression. Except Lear's, there is no death to surpass it in literature, for Cleopatra's is a triumph rather than a tragedy, and the great atonement in Othello's transcends mere pathos.

But when you have a book which ends with a scene like this, which begins with a scene like that in the Cave of Harmony, are you not in the presence of a novelist who has indeed 'fulfilled all numbers' in giving two such polar masterpieces? Yet the fact is that the globe between them is full of things almost as good in their different ways. Once more (it is permissible to say it once at least in respect of each of these achievements), there are the two unfailing provisions of Abundance and Life. *The Newcomes* is scarcely even a microcosm; it is almost the world itself, hardly reduced, as an ordinary member of 'a most respectable family' sees it, and hears it, and experiences it. To a sufficiently intelligent reader the scenes and the personages grow and body themselves out, as he reads them, to life-size at least. And for this very reason there is less to be said about them, unless one could spin out the saying after the fashion of Tennyson's spell-book, where each square inch of text had an atlas of margin filled with spider-written comment. Thus said they, and thus did they, at the times, on the occasions, in the circumstances: there can be no doubt of it. Only one thing may be added—that perhaps in no book is Thackeray's peculiar fashion of 'address to the reader' more happily managed. The abundance of incident, character, and conversation possibly carries this off better than is the case in books where the story is less skilfully managed, or, at any rate, rather less abundantly provided. Those who dislike it in itself, who are worried by it and cannot believe it to be justified by the Rules, or who are in other ways under what Mr. Toobad calls the temporary supremacy of the Devil, may not be more reconciled to it here than elsewhere. Those who are, as some excellent and happy persons are, always ready for it, may even ask for 'more'. But those who regard it critically as a method like another, capable of application with more and with less felicity, should surely be agreed in regarding this as one of the occasions where its application is uninterruptedly felicitous, from the Fable before the beginning to the disposition of the characters after the end.

XV

THE VIRGINIANS

IT would be idle to deny that, in leaving *The Newcomes*, we leave the 'Quadrilateral'—the great and practically impregnable central stronghold of Thackeray's work. People may, of course, take exception to this or that real or supposed defect of *Vanity Fair*, *Pendennis*, *Esmond*, and *The Newcomes* itself. They may urge the excessive pessimism and the sometimes languid flow of story in the first, the desultory character of the second, the somewhat artificial and complicated appeal of the third, while we have ourselves admitted spots in the sun of the fourth. They may, in a fashion not quite critically preposterous, though it may seem to us mistaken, object to the entire system of the novelist's procedure, to his loose order, to his constant 'ten minutes for' the discourse, which is not to them 'refreshment', and so forth. Nay, they may, if they have frankness and boldness enough, take the ground, not so uncritical as it is sometimes held to be, that whether the things be good or bad, they are not good *to them*—that they don't like them heartily. But I cannot conceive any one, save a very idle paradoxer of the mixed race of quack and crank, which is not unknown, or a man hopelessly deficient in literary judgement, denying that these four books constitute an extraordinary literary achievement, or that, whether they entitle the author to stand among the very first two or three of prose fiction or not, they establish him in the first division of that department to all time. If there is to be found such a denier, and if one could not rank him in either of the two classes just defined, it would be necessary to constitute a sort of species by itself for him, and suppose him to be congenitally insensible to one particular kind of literary perfection—colour-blind to one streak of the spectrum, and in fact to more than one.

But with most of the books to which we are now coming it is different: and *The Virginians* is the first as well as the most considerable[1] of the works which lie outside the impregnable zone. I have not the slightest doubt as to the place being tenable against any foes: but it requires some fighting to maintain it. To the mere parrot-cry about sequels not much attention need be paid. That is a rule (if it is a rule at all) with so many exceptions that one may simply regard it as a dead-letter. The *Odyssey* is not a failure. I do not think that *Paradise Regained* is a failure, *qua* 'sequel' at least. *Vingt Ans Après* is most certainly not a failure: and if Dumas could only have prevailed on himself to cut out some of the quite unnecessary parts of *Le Vicomte de Bragelonne* it would have been almost less of a failure still. The worst that can critically be said of sequels, *as such*, is that in the cases where their forerunners are good they heighten their own standard of comparison —handicap themselves as naturally as a good racehorse is handicapped artificially. But that's not much.

Nor is the other parrot-cry about 'writing out' much more—especially in the case of writers who come, as Thackeray came, rather late to perfection. There is not much sign of being written-out in the Dryden of the *Fables* or the Tennyson of the *Ballads*—each about his seventieth year, or a quarter of a century older than Thackeray. And if it be said that these were poets

[1] It is, owing to the system of publication, almost exactly the same length as *Pendennis* and *The Newcomes*, and with them makes up the three longest of Thackeray's books.

(though there is another popular idea that poetry and youth cease together), look at Scott and Smollett. The former, until he set himself to fight a hopeless combat of romance with the triplebodied giant of ill-health, misfortune, and crushing over-work, showed, at an age much beyond Thackeray's, no such sign in *Quentin Durward* or in *Redgauntlet*; while Smollett, a hard worker, a harder liver, and an older man by five years than the author of *The Virginians*, did his very best work in fiction, and his last, with *Humphry Clinker*.

No; these are no *verae causae*: but one must remember that they were causes sure to be alleged sooner or later, and that they were alleged here. And the book might seem to be vulnerable on less general and question-begging grounds. No attempt has been made to conceal the fact that the scheme of *Esmond*, which *The Virginians* directly continues, is an artificial one, though to the present writer the art seems quite triumphant over the artifice. It follows necessarily that the difficulties of continuation, whatever they are in ordinary cases, must be considerably aggravated; and that those who did not like, or only half-liked, the first book would be even less likely to like the second. Moreover, the advance of time complicated the difficulty, again automatically. The time of Queen Anne, though itself a very great advance in modernity even upon the time of Charles the Second, is still separated from us by very distinct manners of phrase and otherwise. You cannot read a page of Addison without remembering the gulf: though it may be a *tour de force* to talk as if you were on the other side of it, when the *tour* is once mastered there is no further difficulty. And you have, in the problem of combining the points of view of the times of Anne and of Victoria, the advantage, if you know how to avail yourself of it, that you can 'change rapiers', use modern dialect when you intend to be definitely modern, and not when you do not. But the third quarter of the eighteenth century is much more treacherous. Even at its beginning, and before its beginning, you will find—say in Horace Walpole— fragments and even blocks of diction that are perfectly modern. About the latter part of it or a little later— say in Fanny Burney—you will find things more modern still. Yet dress, habits, politics, other things, were still, as it were, of another world from ours. In applying the plan to such a time you have to walk on moving sands; to lay hold of supports which give no steady handle; to speak in dialect which is changing every day.

Nor does this consideration exhaust the apparently weak places. In no book of Thackeray's is that neglect of constructive unity, which has been freely admitted, and which is to some people,[1] it would seem, an un-pardonable sin, so prominent. If the sight of the two swords in Prescott's study really gave him his original idea for the book he allowed it to be almost entirely displaced. For, though George and Harry do actually serve on the Loyalist and the rebellious side respectively, it is only in a sort of appendix to the book; nothing really turns on it; and there are not even any separate scenes of a touching, thrilling, or amusing nature con-nected with the fact. *Pendennis* may in a way be even more of a succession as distinguished from a develop-ment; and *Philip* may come to an end with a more accidental and promiscuous Realms-of-Bliss transforma-

[1] Others, it is to be feared, are apt to regard the ingenious tesselations of plot rather as my Lord Verulam regarded those of the 'artificial bedding-out' in gardens of his time. 'They be but toys; you may see as good sights many times in tarts.'

tion-scene; but these have both, in another way, the unity of the single hero. *The Virginians* is practically two books, the hero of the first of which is Harry, with a few, though not unimportant, appearances of George; while the hero of the second is George, with a few, and very unimportant, appearances of Harry. Nor need one, however little one may care for abstract and preceptist Unities, or however much one may admit that, in the particular instance, Thackeray does not violate his almost inviolable sense of congruity and of life, refuse a certain sympathy to those who slightly resent, or at any rate feel chagrined at, the utter dethronement of the younger brother. No doubt his early brilliancy had been accidental and factitious, nor is he ever represented as being much of a genius, while he is evidently from the first the destined prey of any woman from whom Fortune or his friends will not be so kind as to rescue him. But the Fortunate Youth, and what is more, the generous youth, and the fine gentleman, tied to the apron-string of Fanny Mountain, and sinking not merely into a rebel but into a kind of half-loutish country farmer—without form, and void of breeding— may be permitted to go a little against the grain, to be 'not in accordance with the feelings of the commons of Bradwardine'. As he was really not wanted any more he might have been made a respectable victim at St. Cast or somewhere else, and so spared his later degradations. They are not indeed unnatural; but they are unnecessary.

Lastly—for if the list of admissions were to go on much longer it might be thought that the place was going to be wholly betrayed to the enemy—it may perhaps be allowed that in no book of Thackeray's is the digressive and address-to-the-reader habit so freely indulged. It would perhaps have been better if he had cut out the Garbage and Grub-street ebullition into which he was led by the coincidence of the Yates affair; and I am by no means so sure that he would not have done so if he had lived a few years longer.[1] At any rate, the objectors to the system have a right, if they like, to point out that it gives dangerous temptation to a writer to afford himself such indulgence.

But enough of this, and more than enough; for a great deal of it derives whatever validity it possesses from a source which really ought to be sealed to a good critic, at any rate until he has formed his judgement without recourse to it. The proper question to ask one-self—it is true that it requires both some wits and a good deal of critical practice to secure even the possibility of an answer—is 'What should I have thought of this book supposing that I did not know the author, or even supposing that it was the first book that author had ever published?' If any one will do me the honour of glacing back over the last page or two, he will see that the objections are all mainly, if not wholly, *comparative*, and in some cases almost certainly, in others most prob-ably, would not arise in readers who were not more or less familiar with the author's work already. Let us for a moment (certainly not otherwise) abolish *Esmond*; let all the work we have seen perish *ex hypothesi*. Let us consider *The Virginians* in itself and by itself. One of its own greatest and most shining virtues we shall indeed lose in part; but we can return to that. The others, or most of them, we shall see in a fashion which will put a fresh edge on our appreciation of the work generally, and purge the eyesight dulled by use.

It would depend, probably, on individual tempera-

[1] See note at end of this chapter.

ment and education whether a reader, approaching *The Virginians* under the supposed conditions, would be most struck by the reproduction of past scenes, manners, and language, or by the breath of the life of all time which meets him at once. That scene of the ship entering Bristol, and the captain, and the merchant part-owner, and the heir-apparent (or rather presumptive)—is there anything like it out of Thackeray in its combination of the two appeals? There is no pedantry in the antiquarianism, but there is an astonishing verisimilitude. The fact is that, owing partly to circumstances glanced at but much more to others not yet mentioned, the middle of the eighteenth century is about the first time when the materials for complete resurrection are at hand. Everything on the other side of the Restoration is on the other side of a great gulf— a gulf the existence of which is not very easy to explain, but quite impossible to mistake. Mr. Froude, in one of the finest passages of English prose, expressed the sense of such a gulf as regards the Middle Ages; but neither he nor any one else has really bridged it as regards periods far more recent. Neither his brilliant rhetoric and his acute if sometimes hasty historic sense, with all the assistance of Elizabethan literature for the sixteenth century, nor the art-neglecting and matter-preparing labour of Mr. Gardiner for the rest, with an even greater literary assistance from letters there, have made the men from 1500 to 1650 absolutely real to us. If I meet any one who tells me that he really understands even Charles or Cromwell I shall politely congratulate him aloud on his cleverness and good fortune—and devoutly congratulate myself in silence that I am not under any similar delusion. I may be enabled, by sympathy in the one case, by repulsion in the other, to form no bad conjectural estimate—but that is all.

The later seventeenth century becomes much easier, and the first half of the eighteenth easier still: but at first there is a great deficiency of the lighter literature to give us atmosphere, scene, colour. Even for the Queen Anne men we want more easy private letters, more diaries and memoirs, above all, more (it would be almost accurate to say *some*) novels. All this begins to be provided plentifully as the eighteenth century draws towards its middle: and of all of it Thackeray has made consummate use. One hesitates between the Castlewood, Tunbridge, and London scenes—or rather acts—of Harry's Prodigal's Progress for liveliness, for convincingness, for delight. And if the later divisions of the book are less lively in one sense they certainly are not in another. One sometimes feels in a pleasant quandary as to whether Fielding imitated Thackeray or Thackeray Fielding.

But the correctness and freshness of the *décor* sink into insignificance beside the truth to life, the vigour, the felicity of the characters in front, among, sometimes behind, the scenes themselves. It has been hinted that George Esmond Warrington perhaps has not fair play. He is kept very long out of the scene in person; his early recounted appearances are dashed by Thackeray's whimsical determination to make a saint, sage, and hero at once of George Washington; and the long *récit* of his Indian adventures in the middle, though perfectly suitable to eighteenth-century habits, has been less agreeable to nineteenth- and twentieth-century tastes. The same wilfulness is, perhaps, shown in the abundance of touches likely to make him unpopular; and perhaps to enjoy him thoroughly you must compare him with his grandfather Henry and his grandson George Warrington the younger: a trio worth contemplating, and a wonderful example of Thackeray's power over life in different times. But he is a very desirable young man in a novel, though there might have been drawbacks to him in the flesh. He strikes me as possessing more of the *serious* characteristics of Thackeray himself than almost any other personage in the book (except his grandfather aforesaid). Perhaps, indeed, he possesses a little too much, so that the artist has lost freedom and completeness in taking too much from one sitter only, and that a sitter whom no artist ever thoroughly realizes, while his greater modernity deprives him of one of the advantages of Henry Esmond. But still he is great.

Of the minor characters—and they are only minor for Thackeray—it may be said more confidently than ever that no one reading of them for the first time would be likely to stint his admiration. The standard is set at once by the passing sketch of the Bristol merchant above referred to; and it is maintained till the last. Gumbo, and still more Sampson, can hardly be called minor characters: they are too constantly with us, and they are too finely worked out. As for Gumbo, his re-transference from Harry to George—a symbolical one—is one of the rather harsh exertions of the right of primogeniture which we have noted. It is to be observed that Thackeray, like Marryat, obviously had a considerable partiality for the 'images of God cut out in ebony'; and that in this as in other things he was much of his beloved eighteenth century. For there seems to have been no dislike of 'the Nigger' in England until the fuss and fiddle-faddle of the Abolitionists created a reaction in personal disfavour, corresponding to the political favour which they worried the nation into giving. But Sampson has higher claims. Whether Thackeray deliberately set him against Parson Adams I do not very clearly make out: but there is no doubt that he is in the first place a most careful study of the English eighteenth-century cleric of the looser kind, transformed subsequently into a live man and a free work of art. The contrast with Honeyman on one side and Tom Tusher on the other is one which our supposed reader-for-the-first-time would miss—but which would strike him very forcibly later. All middling novelists, and some great ones, are wont to run characters in moulds: but this is generally rather a fault than a virtue. It is Thackeray's almost unique merit that while he keeps the class, he utterly discards the mould, and turns out individuals of the most undeniable individuality. The Castlewoods and the Lamberts and the other War-ringtons all share this individualizing faculty: but for some reason or other Thackeray has stinted his exhibi-tion of it in the case of that fair invader Lydia. She is individually, in separate points, quite *true*: and as the American girl was then little known and indeed not fully developed, it shows the master's extraordinary realizing genius that in two short visits to the country he should have attained to such a power of recreation. But as a whole she wants the last projection to be as thoroughly real as, for instance, poor Lady Maria is. In particular it must be thought somewhat of a *rifiuto* on Thackeray's part that he gives us no details of the scene in which, aided, it is true, by Time and Age, she conquered the unconquerable Beatrix.

But in the last sentence we have come to a reserved point and figure, the greatness of which, though it might not wholly escape our imaginary novice, could not be wholly revealed to him till he had read *Esmond*. The greatest achievement of art in *The Virginians*—one of the greatest achievements of art in prose fiction—is the completion of the character of Miss Esmond by the delineation of the Baroness Bernstein. That it is the most delightful, as well as the greatest, can only be said with a certain reserve. It is the most delightful to those who can really and at once enjoy art for art's sake and nature for nature's sake: and it is one of its great points that, even for others, Thackeray has kept it from being ever disgusting. The immeasurable scene in which stupid Harry does *not* recognize the portrait sets the treatment throughout. For my own part I set this scene beside the *Esmond* mock-duel, and the Steyne-Becky *éclaircissement*, though I dare say I am in a minority. At any rate, the presentation is complete. I suppose that, artistically, one ought not even to desiderate the *middle* stage—the sinking of Beatrix, *not* Beata, through her rivalry with Miss Oglethorpe (I speak in a Thackerayan sense, and apologize to my friend Andrew Lang and to the lady), and through that with Lady Suffolk, her declension upon Tom Tusher (who, remember, had been a far-off worshipper of old), and her very dubious ascension to Baronesshood by the aid of the ambiguous Bernstein. I doubt whether even Thackeray could have done this successfully—whether any art could do in a few strokes what Nature with *mille carinae*, ploughing wrinkles bodily and moral, takes thirty or forty years to effect. But it was difficult enough to give us the beginning and the end: and he has done it.

Hardly less skilful, though less delightful in many ways, is the extraordinarily skilful representation—this time not, indeed, a later stage of the same person—

of Beatrix's half-sister, Madam Esmond Warrington.
The one is not less of a very woman than the other:
but the way in which she has blended her mother's
faults of affectionate jealousy and virtuous injustice with
a little of the bad blood of the Esmonds (there was no
'bad blood' in poor Lady Castlewood), and few, but
the less engaging, of their good qualities, is masterly.
And indeed who, or what, is not?

The vividness of the pictures of life, which, again,
do not yield to Fielding's, has been noted. It ought to
be visible intrinsically to all, whether they are acquainted with eighteenth-century life and literature or
not; and it is hardly enhanced as nature, though it is
very much so as art, by knowledge of that literature
and that life. In the way of more deliberate and *tour
de force* following, the letter assigned to Horace Walpole
is, to my thinking, the superior, not merely of the sham
Spectator in *Esmond*, but of most other things of the kind.
You may go from it to the sixteen volumes of 'Horry's'
correspondence, or from them to it without finding a
note false or forced; though it is certainly a *pastiche* of
the original at his very best. And in like manner the
introduction of the realities or quasi-realities of the
story is unerring and, out of Scott, unmatched, while
it is more elaborate than Sir Walter's. In particular
the Johnson passages have a verisimilitude which is
almost diabolical. The author seems to have the uncanny advantages of his own creation in *The Notch in
the Axe*, and to have been the person that he personates.
Now, this is where almost everybody breaks down. It
is, in fact, the Loadstone Rock of the sea of the Historical
Novel: you cannot help being drawn to it, and it almost
always wrecks you. Even Dumas chiefly escapes it by
refusing it—by neglecting, with the audacity of genius,

to assimilate or reproduce the real at all save by direct, though unacknowledged, quotation. I know that d'Artagnan's adventures are in many cases, if not real, all but contemporary fiction; but I don't think that Madame de Sévigné's actual acquaintance talked at all like his very delightful representative. I have been in love with La Reine Margot ever since I was a school-boy; but I doubt whether the girl who spoke Latin with the ambassadors, and the middle-aged lady who carried dried lovers' hearts about in her many-pocketed farthingale, was really much like the Alexandrine one. But here the Johnson *is* Johnson—the very same Johnson who is in Boswell and in Mrs. Thrale, and in Miss Burney, and in his own writings.

Yet, after all, I am not sure that the greatest charm of the book—except the *Mort Béatrix*, as the *Chanson*-writers would have put it—is not to be found in the much-abused and not absolutely impeccant *parabases* or digression-addresses. They may be rather excessive [1]— a clear-sighted and candid critic may admit that it was almost time to break them off from their parasitic attachment to the novel, and let them take independent form as 'Roundabouts'. But they are so agreeable! I cannot be very angry even with the Tom Garbage out-break; for, after all, Tom, who during the past half-century, has been

> Blest with issue of a large increase,

is the very vermin of the literary fauna, and deserves neither law nor grace. I am not sure that the three pages torn out of Sir George Warrington's notebook are quite legitimate or artistic; but certainly I would not part with their context as it stands. Yet perhaps Sir

[1] See note at end of this chapter.

George, when he gets the narration finally into his own hands, does a little threaten us with the sensations of gloom which he so frankly admits as having been experienced occasionally by his guests in Norfolk. Perhaps too, though it was following the order of life, it was a slight mistake to set these 'skull things in order grim' at the end of a book. The run-in—there is ample authority both profane and sacred for the comparison —should be accomplished at a somewhat livelier pace. But at least it finishes, undoubtedly by intentional correspondence with *Esmond*, in a very lively scene at Castlewood itself.

Yet the practice of 'lying-to in order to discourse the ship's company' is abundantly justified earlier, and indeed throughout. The most perfect justification is in the noble panegyric on Bordeaux wine contained in chapter xxxi—the magnificence and truth of which may indeed be maintained 'in the face of all the pumps that ever spouted'. But there are others which are its equals in goodness and its superiors in length. From the first departure from Castlewood for Tunbridge to the breakdown of Harry's success in Vanity Fair they are numerous and brilliant. Has anybody in this age of infinite reprinting, extracting, and what not, ever taken the best of these parabases, not merely from *The Virginians* but from all the novels, and set them together, not as 'Beauties of Thackeray', but as 'Essays on Men and Manners and Things in General'? It so happens that, not so long ago, I was looking through again most of the more celebrated of such things in English literature from Bacon to the nineteenth century. I do not think that many would equal them. With such things as *hors-d'œuvre* and side-dishes, with the solid interest of life-story and manners-painting for centre, with the

'various vine' of character flowing unstintedly for us,
and an endless dessert of phrase and style, how shall
we quarrel with such a banquet as this?

NOTE

When I originally wrote the words to which attention has been
drawn above, I had no idea of the extent to which a full collation of
the text, in part and volume form, would confirm them, by showing
that Thackeray *actually* discarded not a few passages of this kind. One
or two of the discards may have been necessitated by the dropping of
initial letters, &c. (it may be fancy, but I think Thackeray, always
charming in these things, has never been more charming in them
than here).

XVI

PHILIP

IT has been admitted by the most partial, and yet certainly not the least competent of judges, that the last of Thackeray's major novels had not the success it deserved. Whether it is easier to deserve or to command success is a problem which has often presented itself, seriously or otherwise, since Mr. Addison made an antithesis of the two in the *style noble*. But whether Thackeray deserved success or not, it is quite certain that he did not, in this particular book, take in every respect, or even in most respects, the way to command it. Many things in it are of his absolutely best: it has a sort of *bonus* of autobiographic interest—not intruded, but generously offered for those who like to take or leave—which is not equalled by any of the books except *Pendennis*. It is full of delightful scene, character, incident, talk. But still the warrior has gone into battle with his armour rather carelessly laced and braced; the builder has not looked in all cases to the tempering of his mortar.

The faults which have to be admitted in *Philip* are not limited to the fact that it is not very *conséquioutive*, as the American said to Baudelaire about Poe; for this it shares with others, and with *Pendennis* in particular. Nor does the story, such as it is, break into two in the middle like that of *The Virginians*, or like the deca-syllables of the Pope school. It is true that *Philip* avails itself of the 'chronicle' licence to the uttermost. The author spins the life of Mr. Philip Firmin, barrister-at-law, till he is tired, or thinks we are, and then with a decidedly amusing but absolutely 'promiscuous' *coup de théâtre*, applies the shears. But this is not—to some of us—at all fatal; nor are the long gaps in the chronicle itself (Shakespeare allows himself ten years between two scenes of *Antony and Cleopatra*), nor the failure to join some of the ends together, nor the very doubtful, but for that reason very Thackerayan chronology. If, for instance, Mr. Firmin actually was an admirer of Mr. Anthony Trollope about 1840 or even later, he must have been very much more of a wizard than he has any appearance of being. This, again, is mere 'sea-coast of Bohemia', and troubles no sensible man. Even if it did, he would be very far from a sensible man if he did not allow his trouble to be swept away by the abundance of good things. I believe some people resent —even more than in *The Newcomes*—the reappearance of Pendennis and Laura. But for my part, without any extraordinary feeling of friendship for the gentleman or any designs on his conjugal happiness as regards the lady, I am ready to meet both until the end of time in the blessed Wood of Good Novels, and hold them excellent company. The fault, if fault it be, lies elsewhere, deeper set and more widely spread.

It has, I think, been said already that Thackeray was always inclined to take the importance of having a hero and a heroine, or at least one of them, rather too lightly. But he had hitherto, in his major novels at least, contrived to provide some *succedaneum* for them when they were lacking in interest, and not seldom to practice an ingenious system of *escamotage* on them, and keep them in the background to look in when wanted. Here he does just the contrary. No one of his heroes, with the single and most dangerously contrasted exception of Henry Esmond, is so constantly kept before us as Philip is. He is always with us—as no doubt he ought to be, according to the title. But the worst of it is that we take little pleasure in his company, except on rare occasions, such as that on which he projects Ringwood Twysden into the fountain and the lamps. Even when at other times he is tolerable, it is too often because we like his scenes, his friends, his circumstances—because we have sunned ourselves at Boulogne; and have been prepared to make such escorts as Mr. Pendennis's unnecessary after nightfall; and have earned the easy yet precarious penny by short or long day's work at the press; and have consumed Larose (though the vineyard has rather gone off of late years, the first growth had, at its best, very little advantage over the 'Lady of Clarets') in *mousseline* beakers of capacious construction. Personally, it would require much 'comradeship of college', as Florac puts it, much loyal gratitude for his father's early tips and dinners, much generous compassion for later misfortunes—even to tolerate Mr. Philip Firmin.

That he is unnatural is quite false. Thackeray, be it once more said, could not by this time, if he could at any time, draw anybody who was not natural. One has known Philips—better, worse, or pretty nearly identical in their Philippitude—and if one had not, one could see that he has all the vital marks. But then there are many persons who are alive and whom one does not want at all; and, unluckily, one does not want Philip, at least so much of him, so constantly. He has to be taken to get the good things of the book, but one resents him all the more for that, or at least feels him as much a burden as the 'paving-stones and rocking-horses' which his near contemporary, Mr. Bertie Stanhope in *Barchester Towers*, had to take as part consideration of his bill. He is not a scoundrel; one rather

wishes he were. He is not merely passively uninteresting and good. He is not—or not often—amusing in his
blunders. He is sometimes almost a lout and sometimes
almost a fool. His creator himself expresses an ingenuous
wonder that Philip was not kicked; and it may be
feared, to the dishonour of mankind, that the fact that
he was not was chiefly due to the other fact that he
was big and strong. All this Thackeray knew perfectly
well; and I suppose he would have said as he did of
Colonel Newcome, 'It was in him to do it'. To which
one can only reply, 'But it would have been so much
kinder of you to let him do it in some other universe!'

Nor is Mrs. Firmin sufficient to make up for the
defects of her husband. Charlotte Baynes is a nice and
natural girl, and Charlotte Firmin a natural and by no
means nasty woman. Even her cruelty to the Little
Sister is perfectly probable; in fact, rather inevitable.
The love-agonies of chapter xxv and its successors will
be contemned only by the contemptible. But she is
elsewhere something of a nonentity, and again her
creator knows this fact and confesses it with a non-
chalance which, though it increases one's respect for
him (if that were possible), is from another point of
view exasperating rather than disarming. One remembers some words of his own in reference to a dinner of
superior artistic qualities. 'Dear Sir, *do* ask us again.'
Certainly there is no temptation in putting down
Philip to say, 'Dear Sir, do *not* ask us again'. But one
is perhaps tempted to be very bold, and to say, 'Dear
Sir, do ask us again, and give us only as good a dinner
as this; but please ask some people to meet us different
from Philip and Charlotte'. To which he would probably have replied, almost in his own words again, and
as folk might say often in real life—that these people

had to be asked, that they asked themselves, and he could not refuse them any more than if they had been Costigan or Beatrix, to take the opposite poles of their own opposites.

For, after all, the dinner *is* an admirable one, and such as only Thackeray could provide. I have said elsewhere, in reference to the *Shabby Genteèl Story* itself, that I do not think *Philip* gains very much from close juxtaposition with its unquestioned 'Introduction'. The main, if not the only circumstance of importance—the irregular marriage—could have been intimated in any of a dozen different ways, familiar to the least skilled novelist. 'Missafis' is, alas, gone—gone from the con-solations of his Hart and the molestation of his Mari-anne, with his good deed to Caroline following and safeguarding him—not, one imagines, unaccompanied by other good deeds of the same kind. That polished corner of the temple, the Rev. Tufton Hunt, had made very slight appearance earlier. Mr.-Dr. Brandon-Firmin, and the earlier and later Carolines, are separated not merely from each other but from their earlier selves, not only by the years of change, and suffering, and guilt on one side, but, I think, by something a little more gulf-like—a difference of conception and attitude to them on the part of their maker. In particular, it has been said before, that Dr. Firmin might have been provided with more remainders of his old scholarship than tags from the grammar and Horace. Nobody else of importance reappears except old Gann.

But the later novel requires no 'send-off' of interest from its long-ago and fragmentary study. Perhaps it does not start very happily—clings and sticks a little to the launching-ways, and indulges rather too much in digressions and zig-zags. In fact the only sign of real weariness that I can see in Thackeray's latest novel-work is that his beginnings, formerly so brilliant, are a little apt to hang fire, not of course, in details. The actual opening scene is of the best: and in the very first sheet I could point out, if it were not impertinent, half a dozen or a dozen of those wonderful phrases and clauses which, as it were, *sting* you with literary delight. And with the introduction of the Twysdens, and specially Talbot, we know that once more 'there is no mistake about *our* fellow'. There are relapses, but the further introduction of Woolcomb and the reappearance of Hunt wake things up; and the negotiations about the bigamy raise the interest further still. Lord Ringwood is admirable: and there is the true Thackeray in the fact that he is not in the least Lord Steyne vamped up again. But it is not till Philip is jilted and ruined that the full zest of the book begins. If Charlotte Baynes be a little bread-and-buttery, the Baynes family, as a whole, though it may have consumed much of those commodities, is very far from having a flavour of them. And the touch of the 'pavement of Paris', even the sight of the French coast, has its inevitable effect on Thackeray. From the landing at Boulogne to the marriage—which is not very much less than half the book—there is no cessation of general interest, and a profusion of special scenes and character-pieces. If the rest falls back a little, what shall we say? The fact is that, laugh as people may at ending with marriage-bells, Fate and metaphysical aid too frequently are slow to help the rash artist who will not take these as a signal to close his book. It may be as easy to show that this is absurd as the scientific people find it to show that the sun cannot possibly put out a fire, or a poker inclined to that fire wake it up. Let us accept all the demonstrations with becoming respect. But let us, if we are wise, finish the novel, and adjust the screen, and put up the poker, all the same and *securi*.

Of course there are still plenty of condolences. I like the Transformation Scene itself very much. I can stand (it is true that the trial is quite different from Philip's) the Mugfords very gladly. The great act of unjust justice executed by the Little Sister on the Bearer of the Bowstring is one of the best things in novelry. But still the haunting fact remains that, except as Christians, we have no particular affection for our neighbour Philip—that indeed, except as Christians, we find it rather difficult to forgive him for his chuckleheadedness, his *outrecuidance*, his blundering, blustering blue-bottle omnipresence and obtrusiveness. The present writer is not ashamed to confess that he reads *Philip* as often as any of the books—that his objections as a critic do not interfere in the least with his enjoyment as a reader. But that is probably an unnatural state of things, begotten of long practice in separating personal likes from artistic appreciation. As a critic, though he certainly will not throw *Philip* to the wolves, he is bound to say that it is not the prettiest nor the best behaved of the children of its family.

One may go even further and question whether its defects, though blemishes on the particular work of art, are exactly blemishes on the artistry of the worker in general. They appear to me rather to be results of two legitimate but unfortunate experiments—the acceptance of the extreme doctrine that any real life will make a novel, and the attempt to adjust presentation of reality to the changes of time and manners.

I have acknowledged that Philip and Charlotte are quite real persons—that they exist, and behave themselves as they ought to do in accordance with the laws of their existence. But, in this one instance, Thackeray's experiments in the true realism may be thought to have brought him near that false realism of which we have since seen and are still seeing so much. It is true that, in the novel, to secure the highest artistic effect, and at the same time the greatest satisfaction to the reader, the characters must be real, and their actions must be probable in themselves, or made so. But it is not true that this is sufficient. They must be made in some way or other *agreeable*; and if they are made disagreeable they will not and ought not to succeed. Nor let the misguided anti-sentimentalist think that he has got a handle, and ejaculate, 'Oh, yes! you *do* want nothing but rose-pink and sky-blue'. Once more the handle has escaped him. Becky Sharp is not exactly a study in these two much-abused tints: yet she is in the highest degree agreeable. Barnes Newcome can scarcely be said to be drawn in them: yet, much as one would like personally to kick him, he is, in his presentment, not disagreeable at all. So, to take a different writer and a different class of subject, Miss Bates in the flesh would suggest murder or suicide: Miss Bates in *Emma* is a joy for ever. But Philip—Charlotte is rather null than anything else, she does not hinder, if she does not help—is not agreeable in any way. One does not grudge him his windfall; for, after all, he has a boorish and loutish sort of goodness and good-fellowship about him; he has no bad blood, though horribly bad manners; and he has been both very unlucky and not a little ill-treated. But one takes no interest in him; does not even passively enjoy his company; does not want to see him again. With the vast majority of Thackeray's characters you want to see them again very much.

I ventured some years ago to hint that there may be subsidiary causes for his ill-success. Thackeray is in this respect inferior to Shakespeare—that he either cannot, or does not choose to, leave his characters with the universal humanity which is of no special age at all; though he ransoms this to some extent by his unmatched faculty of giving them the character of their own age. Now, at the time he wrote *Philip* a change, slight but actual, was passing over the ways and language of society. He really need not have troubled about this; for Philip is, after all, though slightly younger, of the same generation as Arthur Pendennis and Clive Newcome; that is to say, of Thackeray's own. But with his oddly mixed indifference to chronology and sense of actuality he has striven to give the newer *nuance* to Philip, to make him a young man not of the late 'thirties but of the early 'sixties. And I think the effect is rather one of 'confusion of kinds'. But this may be a fancy; and, at any rate, it is needless to attempt to work it out here.

The wiser mind, without going back on the admissions of defect that have been made, will prefer to go back to the counter-allegations of excellence. There is really in *Philip* no lack whatever of the old plenty: in the central block, which has been marked off above, it is even more plentiful than ever. No stronger proof of Thackeray's extraordinary power as a novelist could be given than the way in which the vicissitudes of the contest for Charlotte's hand (an inoffensive but, as has been said, not ravishingly desirable little hand), and the fluctuating chances of her blundering good fellow of a lover seize on the reader in spite of himself. Madame de Smolensk by herself would save a novel. The vicissitudes of that famous evening where duels are averted are quite consummate: and the *bolgia* of mothers-in-law would be incomplete without Mrs. Baynes. I am not sure that I would not consent to read a hundred more of the dull hundreds that I used to review years ago, if I were promised in only one page of one of them such a thing as the youthful Baynes's comment on the *orgeat*: 'I say, Mother! what 's this beastly thing?' or that mother's summary of Mrs. Boldero's crimes: 'Prommy, pas payy.' This is the true manna; this is what you can recommend to a friend, and, whether he enjoys it or not, enjoy yourself.

As one looks back on the half-dozen novels now complete (for *Lovel the Widower* is of a different class, and *Denis Duval* is a fragment), it may be permissible to make a few general remarks on their quality to lighten the final chapter, which will necessarily contain a still more general survey. Their merits have, I hope, been set forth not unfairly as the inadequacy of the setter could perform it, and I am sure that their demerits have been honestly allowed for. But the merits themselves deserve grouping in this summary under two heads, after a fashion which will, I think, give some support to the very high general view of Thackeray's position as a novelist and a man of letters which has been taken throughout. The first of these heads is that *abundance* which has been constantly glanced at, and sometimes insisted on, in an interim fashion. I have even known it, by honest persons who were not fools, confessed as a reason why they do not quite like him. He 'puts too much in', they say: they cannot swallow and digest him quickly enough to suit their taste. All honour to them for their frankness which, it may be suspected, might be imitated by other objectors with advantage. But there are yet others who receive this abundance differently. To them, whether it be of what some call small things like the jets of wit and humour referred to at the close of the last paragraph, or of things subordinate, but in a more or less real sense substantive in incident, scene, and character, that 'God's plenty', which we have cited before, is still the only satisfactory phrase for Thackeray. Although there are few writers whose general attitude or 'humour' is more constant, there are, I think, still fewer who, in the common phrase, repeat themselves so seldom. In some very great novelists, and in almost all novelists of the second class, character, incident, thought, and phrase seem to be turned out *à la douzaine*, as the French satirical description had it as long ago as Rabelais. Now, this is never the case with Thackeray. Even his most colourless characters, as they are sometimes thought, have their own colour. Charlotte is not like Laura, and Laura is certainly not like Amelia; nor in the ascending scale have Philip, Clive, and Arthur anything real in common, except their schoolfellowship and the fact that each of them went through some of Thackeray's own experiences. Of his greater and lesser creations of more strongly coloured character this is even truer. Becky, Blanche, and Beatrix are all coquettes, all false, all rather under the malediction of Eve than under the benediction of Mary; but they are as different persons— as different girls—as they could possibly be. Mulligan and Costigan are both comic Irishmen; but there is as little of the mere 'Teague' about either as, again, is possible. Attention has just been invited to the fact that Lord Ringwood and Lord Steyne are not in the least cut off the same piece of 'wicked nobleman' cloth. The very footmen have their diversities; and when you remember that Paul de Florac and Madame de Smolensk are both friendly caricatures of French character, the more abysmal is the wonder at the difference and the independence of handling in the two cases.

Perhaps, although it is less uncommon, the inexhaustible abundance of still slighter traits and phrases is more wonderful still; and, at any rate to some readers, is even a greater source of the unfailing enjoyment which they find in Thackeray. It is sometimes laid down that the more trouble the artist takes the more lasting will be the delight he provides. It is a worthy sentiment; and, with certain provisos and considerations, a true one. But in the cases where it is true the delight in question is rather a recognition of the art itself than a pure unsophisticated joy in its result. Thackeray, though by no means a mere *improvisatore*, appears to have been a writer who did not, *as a rule*, labour particular scenes and phrases. That he could not dictate when the *awen*—the inspiration—came upon him seems of itself decisive on this point. But the fount of humour and quaint inventiveness was so perennial with him that he simply could not help pouring out its water without hesitation, without distillation, literally as water from the rock. Like that water it sometimes runs over and away almost before you can catch and drink it; though the metaphor is in this happy respect faulty, that it does *not* run away. I do not know how many times I have read these novels—if I were to venture at anything like the true number, readers would probably be unpolite enough not to believe me. Yet I never find any staleness and I do not even yet fail to find things actually new—things I have not noticed, or have not fully noticed, before.

But the other head is the greater, and that is the astonishing and unfailing life and nature which is

diffused through these novels. There is only one thing
more astonishing, and that is that some folk should miss
it. Few businesses can be so likely to bring the mind
into the state of not being astonished at anything as
the study and practice of criticism. It is half a lifetime
since I was pretty well broken to this by the discovery
that some people thought *Religious Musings* Coleridge's
finest poem. But one is never *quite* broken to these
things; and I own that a more astonishing judgement
still is that Thackeray is 'artificial', the judgement being,
moreover, passed not as a final condemnation, but, on
the contrary, as a prelude to praise, that 'artificial as
he is', &c. Of course the point of view from which this
judgement is delivered is obvious enough. Thackeray,
in his later books, at any rate, deals mainly with ladies
and gentlemen; ladies and gentlemen are artificial;
therefore, &c. And as the premisses are hopelessly inadequate it is unnecessary to discuss the conclusion.

But it is not unnecessary to lay down the opposite of
that conclusion politely but peremptorily. By the time
at which Thackeray wrote great part of *Vanity Fair*, and
the whole of its successors, it was impossible for him to
draw, in words, a character out of nature or unfurnished
with life. He is in this respect almost unique; certainly,
I think, unique among novelists. It may be that there
are classes or types which he does not attempt; there
might be some argument on that point, but it is unnecessary. In no class and in no individual from peer
to policemen that he attempts does he fail. You may not
think his good heroines good, in the sense that you think
them uninteresting, and to that there is nothing to say;
if you think Helen or Laura or Amelia or Charlotte
unnatural, I think your judgement must be politely
disabled. I have admitted that I do not enjoy Philip

as a person, but I not only admit, I positively assert, that Philip is not merely possible, but actual; that he might turn up any day, as Costigan did. In temperament, in action, in speech, Thackeray simply cannot set his puppets to dance to unnatural tunes; they will go right, because their nature is nature.

FitzGerald—whose intense personal affections by no means made him a partial or undiscriminating critic, as is well known in the case not merely of Tennyson but of Thackeray himself—called this lifelikeness, this verisimilitude, this *naturaleza*, 'terrible'; and it has its terrible side—one far more really soul-shaking than all the gloom and grime of the later Realists. But it probably struck the author-translator of *Omar Khayyam* in this way because it was almost wholly *new*. It had existed in Fielding, but the old-fashioned externals cloaked and masked it there. It really does exist in Miss Austen, though it is there studiously anodyned and palliated by the choice of situation and the provision of atmosphere. It is in Scott, but may be said almost to take trouble, if not exactly to conceal itself, to shift attention to something else: to be the life of Romance, not of Novels proper. Otherwise it is nowhere in the novel before Thackeray. The attempt at it has been common since—of the measure of success with which that attempt has met it is quite unnecessary to speak here. But what is fitting to say and to repeat here is that Thackeray attempted it, and that Thackeray achieved it. Life and Abundance—these are the two things that are to be found in him, to be found in him everywhere; and to be found out of him, in the same degree and to the same extent, nowhere, as I believe, in the English or in any novel.

XVII

THE WOLVES AND THE LAMB—LOVEL THE WIDOWER—DENIS DUVAL—THE ROUND-ABOUT PAPERS

T{HE} subjects[1] of our last chapter are of unusual though varying interest, and of excellence more various almost than their interest itself.

The Wolves and the Lamb is a curious comparative study. I suppose that, as the knowing ones say so, it is 'not a *play*'; yet, speaking as a babe and suckling in that matter, I should say it was much more like the plays of later days than those of its own. But no doubt it is still rather a novel thrown into dialogue than an actual drama. And it has distinct advantages over its *remaniement*. Julia is certainly rather more human than Elizabeth: though the objection taken by some to Elizabeth herself, that she is almost engaged to three people at once, and marries a fourth, will not hold for a moment. There is ample warrant for *that*. Touchit, less ambitious, is certainly more satisfactory than Batchelor: and if Bedford is pruned to some advantage in the novel, his presentation in the play has the interest of connecting more closely with his great elder brethren the Plushes or

[1] *Denis Duval*, though a posthumous work and left unfinished, is taken before the *Roundabout Papers* for two reasons: first because it completes, and naturally goes with, the Novel-series to which *Lovel the Widower* also belongs; but secondly, and still more, because it *is* unfinished and cannot (even in the part that we have) be considered to represent Thackeray's final judgement and intentions, as these are represented by the last 'Roundabout' which he sent to press. *The Wolves and the Lamb*, though earlier even than *The Newcomes* as a whole, necessarily shows the way to *Lovel*, the connexion being much closer than that of the *Shabby Genteel Story* and *Philip*.

Pluches. Undoubtedly, however, the double presentation has a peculiar interest of its own: and it is a great advantage to be able to set it before the reader.

Lovel the Widower itself has, I think, very few thoroughgoing partisans, except such as simply point to the things in it which, being Thackeray's, are indispensable. They exist, and in fair measure: but there is certainly not much to be said for it as a whole performance by such a performer. It was probably knocked together in some haste to supply a necessary contribution to the newly designed *Cornhill Magazine*: and, on a not unthrifty variation of the well-known French proverb, he made his arrow out of wood that had been wasted. Although some good plays have been made out of novels, the contrary process has seldom succeeded: and indeed it is not very common for complete rehandlings of any kind to be great successes. Thackeray, who had handicapped himself rather heavily in the play, more than doubled the handicap in the novel. His hero (who, though the names are changed, had first appeared in *The Kickleburys on the Rhine*) is very much the same in both, but his amiable nincompoopery is better suited to the stage than to the page. His heroine has great capabilities, but is insufficiently developed—which is rather hard on her. If Bessy had had the scope of Becky, Blanche, and Beatrix, she might have completed the rubber not unworthily.

But perhaps Thackeray's greatest mistake (though one sees the temptation to it, and it has engulfed others) is the transformation he effected of the personage of Captain Touchit into that of Mr. Batchelor. The onlooker in *The Wolves and the Lamb* naturally does not tell the story—seeing that it is not a story but a drama; and he has merely to act his own part in it. Moreover he is

—if not a hero or the player of a specially *beau rôle*—at any rate a personage who has to support none that is essentially not *beau*. To Mr. Batchelor Thackeray— probably not least because he put a certain portion of himself into him, and more, perhaps, than the mere succumbing to the temptation of buying a paper—has been whimsically unkind. He is represented as an elderly and vacillating philanderer; as something very like a coward; as something very much more like a fogy, with a tendency to twaddle greater than his forerunner by many years, Dr. Solomon 'Pacifico' (who boldly assumed the title), had ever shown. In fact, though in a different way, he doubles the attempt in *Philip* to keep constantly in front a figure which is not acceptable.

In parts, however, his creator can never go wrong; and he does not here. If the principals 'leave to desire', the supporters are inimitable and inestimable. Who but Thackeray could have created, or would have set to work in one almost trifling book, such a *triumfeminate* as Lady Baker, Mrs. Bonnington, and Mrs. Prior? Clarence Baker (as indeed they all are more or less) is of an old Thackeray house: but he is absolutely individual and differentiated from his elders. When Lady Kicklebury changed her title, and had a second son, she certainly did not improve matters. *This* little wretch would never have walked a hundred miles, or drunk a hundred pints of strong beer, in as many hours. But he is a perfectly live little wretch for all that. Bedford the Butler is, as has been said, an improvement on his original in the *Wolves*; and, as always, the scattered gems of trait and phrase are inexhaustible. One is indeed bound to differ with Thackeray as to the virtues of second sleep— lie as long as you like, awake or half-awake, 'cooking yourself for the day', as some famous physician is said to have said: but don't go to sleep again after it is light. This, however, is controversial and not literary. The sketch of the lieutenant of the Bom-Retiro Caçadores; the scene with the Master of Boniface; the semi-dramatized conversation in the schoolroom; the admirable utilization of Cecilia's harp, which is almost a *dramatis persona*; the apostrophe (referred to in the first of these chapters) to the comet of Fifty-eight; and the conclusion where the Harp asserts itself, are all, in the familiar words, 'good enough for anything' and too good for almost anything but something of Thackeray's. If the adversary insists on the last word, and says that they are too good for the something itself—why, there is nothing to do with a person who will have the last word but to let him have it.

It has been usual, even with no extreme admirers of Thackeray, to compound for dispraise of *Lovel the Widower* and *Philip* by expressing the highest anticipations of what *Denis Duval* might have been, and all but the highest approbation of that part of it which exists. Nor is this by any means to be set down to mere *respect humain*, or to the natural, laudable, and almost irresistible interest of a tale half-told in such circumstances. In many ways its advent was to be welcomed, and its death ere prime to be lamented. In the first place, it would have given—has actually given—scope for yet further utilizing of that marvellous acquaintanceship with the tones and manners of the eighteenth century; and would thus have helped to complete *Esmond* and *The Virginians*, still leaving room for another to fill the space between 1715 and 1755. Moreover, as has been more fully revealed later, but as appears to some extent in the book itself, and in the valuable 'Notes' on the book which Mr. Greenwood published in the *Cornhill*

Magazine after the author's death, there would have been something in it from that private stock of experience and reminiscence on which Thackeray knew how to draw so effectively. But it does not want 'considerations' of this kind to validate its claims. Denis is a person already, and a very vivid person for an autobiographer and biographer of others; with a promise of tone and attitude quite different from the melancholy moralizing of Henry Esmond and of his grandson, the half-impersonal or only now and then personal detachedness of Mr. Pendennis as a narrator, and the more than Montaignesque self-abasement of Mr. Batchelor. The escapades and the plots of the early scenes are capital: one scene, where Denny's pistol foils the rascal Weston, is almost of the best.

Still, there is not quite enough of it to criticize with great positiveness: and I have sometimes thought that it might, if continued, have shown a defect which certainly is apparent in the fragment, but which also might have been got over—a certain too great proneness to *récit*—to telling us what has happened instead of showing it to us in the happening. This, if it had appeared, would have been no necessary sign of senility or of decadence. Master as he was both of action and conversation, Thackeray had always been under a slight temptation to this less excellent way. There is something of it even in *Catherine*; much in *Barry Lyndon*; not a little even in *Vanity Fair*; and it would have been nothing strange had it recurred. But it is right, in the case of a mere fragment like this, to dwell mainly on its promise: and beyond all doubt or controversy the promise of *Denis Duval* is very considerable. One especially desiderates the sea scenes. Thackeray, it is not superfluous to observe, was a staunch and wise admirer of Marryat: and he had hardly his equal for 'getting up a brief' in the right novel way, and avoiding the dangers of that process to which Reade and Zola succumbed too often.

And so we come to the last, the real last, of Thackeray's books—to an end which certainly crowns the work. The Essay, if not exactly an English invention—it is indeed an invention of that *magister artis ingenique largitor*, Nobody—is to a great extent an English development. Putting aside its classical forerunners, if Bacon borrowed from Montaigne in its first modern flight, Marivaux was a direct follower of Addison in starting the second. Indeed, for the last three hundred years, the volume of English essay-writing has been greater than that of any other nation, and the proportion of that volume which has been of the highest quality has been larger still. Especially since Cowley, more than anybody else, refashioned the following of Montaigne himself; and since Dryden initiated a kind of literary essay which nobody—not even Corneille—had exactly hit before him; still more since Steele and Addison bettered his instruction in the literary and Defoe's in the business-like way, the thing has been ours. The long succession of English attempt and achievement in it would require a small literary history to do it justice. But it is not impertinent to say that the praise of giving the last special turn to the Essay is due, more than to any one else, to Leigh Hunt. As Keats took hints from this unequal writer in verse, so did Lamb and Hazlitt in prose: and from these three came all the essayists and all the Essays of the English nineteenth century. Among these essayists I do not know a greater than Thackeray: among the collections of these essays I do not know one so great as the *Roundabout Papers*. Nay, with a little less quintessence, it has far greater range and variety than *Elia* itself; with less *diable au corps*, and far less critical power, it is in the same qualities superior to any *collection* of Hazlitt's.

Some direct remarks, and more hints, have been scattered through earlier chapters as to the way in which these papers are, as it were, the Rome of their author's country, to which all its roads lead, and which represents its capital and chief achievement. That he was unable to compose a long work is not true: the single word *Esmond* disproves that sufficiently and at once. But that he had a greater tendency and aptitude towards work, small in individual bulk and fable, but interconnected by thought, manner, and handling, is true. To me the *Roundabout Papers* are almost as much a whole, a microcosm, as many celebrated books of great writers composed nominally on a single theme: but of course they are individual wholes as well. And their individuality and, so to speak, 'promiscuousness' prevented that appearance of the desultory which, though it far exceeds the reality, is charged against his larger single works. There is no doubt that though the old argument of Dryden (and of Tirso de Molina before him), 'Why should the soul of man be more sluggish than his senses?' is a notable and a sound one, the common run of readers do experience a certain discomfort at quick and unexpected changes of theme, subject, attitude. It took three centuries to reconcile critics to the English tragi-comedy, and I doubt whether all of them are reconciled yet. There is no more unpopular figure of Rhetoric than parenthesis.

But quick changes and many-faceted presentations of thought had always been natural to Thackeray; and now at last he was at liberty to indulge them as he liked, and yet under the control of his own judgement. I have never doubted that, whether his editorship of the *Cornhill* was on the whole successful or not, it practically gave us the *Roundabout Papers* in their perfection. For he was indocile to others' correction: and yet he was far too conscientious to take advantage of his position to ride hobbies, cut capers, or merely pass off inferior work to save himself trouble. There are some people who always ought to be their own editors, and some who never ought to be: and, curiously enough, the first are by no means always good editors of others, nor the second bad ones.

It is not uninteresting to turn for a moment to the originals of all such things—the periodical Essays of the eighteenth century, and to note how (no doubt quite unconsciously) good points of the conception are retained and developed, and bad ones evaded and eliminated, in the *Roundabouts*. In reading the originals, from the *Tatler* to that at first sight impossible *Looker-On* (which does actually contain some not unamusing parodies of the then contemporary mannerisms of Gibbon, Boswell, and Mrs. Radcliffe), one perceives that all the writers (again, whether consciously or not) were distracted between two sets of desires, one affecting handling, the other subject. They wanted to infuse a personal tone—to bring things under a more or less uniform survey: and yet they were half-afraid and half-ashamed to be boldly personal. Therefore they excogitated phantoms who exhibit different degrees of cleverness—from 'Mr. Spectator', the most shadowy and therefore the best of all, through his predecessor Bickerstaff, the rag-and-sawdust personages of the *Guardian*, that leather-and-prunella man of fashion Mr. Adam FitzAdam, and the rest, down to the aged Mr. Simon Olive-Branch and his more aged mother. They wanted

variety of subject, and did not know how to attain it
except by clumsy machinery of clubs, perpetual in-
serted stories without detail or character enough to be
really interesting, and the like. Hardly one of them,
except Cumberland, whose egotism was not vigorous
enough, and Shaftesbury (who stood outside of, and indeed anticipated, the periodical development) dared to
throw a strong personal element into their work. But
'Sir Fretful' was too much of a peevish and pedantic
weakling: 'My Lord' was too much of a coxcomb in
manner, and (to do him justice, more pleasant though
not more just) too full of serious purpose in fact, to make
a good essayist. Even when the trammels of the *Spectator* tradition had been thrown off, hardly anybody succeeded in combining the two things—variety of actual
subject and strong personality and individuality of
handling—which make the charm of the Essay. Even
Steele, even Addison, even Goldsmith sacrifice too much
of the latter.

Thackeray did not. 'His own sauce' is everywhere,
or rather his own array of sauces—for it is very little
that he takes out of the same bottle of ready-made con-
diment. But it is applied to an infinite range of material,
never forced either in the direction of connexion or in
the direction of desultoriness. It is fresh and of the day,
without being merely of the day; capable of serving as
an indicator, in the future, of manners and customs, of
ways and speech, yet incapable of becoming out of
fashion except to those to whom fashion is everything.
When one looks at the various headings, it might appear
as if some one of unusual genius had planned them all
beforehand for a miscellany: just as the gentleman sat
up all night to write his impromptu, but probably with
much more success. Yet we know that it never was

Thackeray's way to plan anything much beforehand: and that these things came to him, one after another, with little premeditation in the individual cases, and none in any general scheme. The titles of course are not always—in fact are rather seldom—indicative: the greatest lesson that Montaigne taught his family was perhaps this very apparent disrespect to titles. Sometimes they may deliberately 'conceal thought'. It is the actual contents which exhibit this uniformity in diversity and profusion in unity itself.

The variety of kind is almost as remarkable as that of individual matter. 'The Notch in the Axe' is at once a reversion to the old favourite line of burlesque story, and a great advance in it. 'The Notch' may be as burlesque as you like: and it is not unamusing to notice that, though Thackeray was long past any contempt of Bulwer-Lytton, it was still the author of *A Strange Story* who gave him his objective, just as the author of *The Captain* had done twenty years and more earlier. But it is much more than burlesque. Like the celebrated sonnet which was well worth an epic, it is well worth a book in three volumes. 'Here's richness!' you may say with justice. In fact Mr. Pinto, whatever his exact earthly title may have been, is a paladin and peer of Novel-land.

No subject recurs more frequently in the *Roundabouts*, and none is more happily treated, than that travel which, as has been often noticed, scarcely ever failed to inspire Thackeray. They start with it: and if, in all the travel-writing of the last two centuries or thereabouts, there are two better pages in 'the middle style' than those that give the description of Chur, this critic does not know them. 'Two Children in Black' recur to it; it makes a delightful scene (if only one of *home* travel) in 'Tunbridge

Toys'—a picture never to be forgotten as one stands at the end of the Pantiles, and looks up to Mount Ephraim across whatever objects may be in the way. Than 'Notes of a Week's Holiday' it is difficult even to imagine anything better—the unforced plenty, the unpremeditated art, the dream-reality of the panorama. You have it again at a greater distance of place and time in 'A Mississippi Bubble': and it forms at least part of the motive of 'Dessein's'. Perhaps nothing had, in the simple old phrase, done Thackeray so much good as travel; he certainly takes care not to be ungrateful and not to monopolize the benefit.

Partly mingled with these, partly separate from them, are the touches of autobiography which, having formed not the least attractive parts of the novels, recur here. In fact few of the papers are without them. 'De Juventute,' for instance, proclaims the fact, and 'Tunbridge Toys' (already mentioned) very soon makes no secret of it. But it is in almost all, from first to last, and supplies not their least charming parts. Even when, as seems to have been the case with the Sayers and Heenan fight, his presence in the flesh was a thing devised by the enemy (though certainly it would have been no discredit to him), this touch comes after a fashion. And I can very well remember the 'gorilla' photograph of him —it was a trick of the time in the first popularity of Du Chaillu's book—being brought by a schoolfellow to amuse us. Indeed, long enough ago as these papers may seem to have been written, their links with the actual present day are numerous. The 'wee solemn Highlander' at the royal wedding is the present German ex-Emperor; and the survivor of that mysterious business in Northumberland Street died but a few years ago.

One very remarkable feature of this crop of 'the last of

life for which the first was made' is to be found in the
large number of passages which it contains directly consisting of, or indirectly conveying, literary criticism. We
have seen that in earlier days this was Thackeray's very
weakest point (except politics which here hardly figure
at all); that, with occasional *aperçus* of surprising acuteness and truth, he was at the mercy of all sorts of gusts,
not exactly of caprice, but of irrelevant and extraneous
influence. Here the 'calmed and calming *mens adepta*'
remedies all this in the most satisfactory fashion.[1] The
papers almost open with a magnificent apologia or
palinode—extended and strengthened afterwards, and
all the better that it cunningly avoids any reference to
the older offences—to Dumas. This passes into praise of
others, and especially of his old foe Bulwer's 'The
Haunted and the Haunters', which certainly may be
said to be one of the best ghost-stories in the world. 'Nil
nisi bonum' follows with special reference to Washington
Irving, but spreading itself more widely. The delectable
'On Two Children in Black' opens with praise of Montaigne and Howell. Half (and the larger half) of 'The
Last Sketch' is devoted to Charlotte Brontë. 'On
Ribbons' is almost wholly occupied with literature, and
the tracing of the initials is amusing (there are one or
two about which I am still not wholly certain). Some of
the papers which follow deal rather with journalism than
with literature; and rather with journalists than with
journalism. But 'De Juventute' is full of the subject, and

[1] There is also another point which may be worth notice. In *The
English Humourists* he had been irresistibly tempted, dealing as he was
with whole-figure presentation, to 'make up' those figures as he did
the personages of his novels. These 'makes-up'—the Fielding is a capital
example—are wonderfully life-like and possible, but not completely and
historically exact. Here, in casual glances, there was no such temptation,
and the *aperçu* could be left alone.

even the 'Week's Holiday' admits it; while 'A Joke from the late Thomas Hood' naturally could not keep it out. The very 'Notch on the Axe' contains as well as implies it, and 'De Finibus' is *auto*-critical 'in the best sense of the term'—*not* as the ingenious testimonial-writer said when he wished to be decently unintelligible. 'On a Peal of Bells,' one of the most delightful of the whole, is nothing else; and it enters into 'Dessein's' and 'On Alexandrines'.

And in all this comment there is perceptible, not a mere acceptance of what had previously been rejected or questioned, because the critic's powers of discrimination are blunted and his interests cloyed, but a true mellowing of perception and a determination to hold fast to that which is good. Generous Thackeray had always been, even in the partly haphazard judgements of his youth, and the galls and jars of his yet unsuccessful early middle age. But his generosity never took, and it did not take now, the somewhat indiscriminate form of toleration and even eulogy, to which Scott at all times, and Goethe latterly, were rather prone. You will not find Thackeray praising rubbish anywhere, and in these *Roundabouts* least of all. But you will find him no longer inclined to harp and carp on trifles; and not in the least ready to be blown away by some gust of doctrine (or ignorance) in regard of his subjects. In fact, these *Roundabout Papers* exhibit their author in a state only to be described by one of the stock adjectives of criticism, and one which has been even more abused than most of these hardly treated vocables. They are thoroughly *ripe*. It is not exactly that the good wine has been kept till now, for there was plenty of it before—but that there is nothing but the best wine. The abundance of matter and the perfection of handling match each other constantly: and over all and above all and through all there is perpetual suffusion of that unforced and inimitable style and phrase which makes subject almost indifferent and constitutes treatment of itself. Over all too there rules the true *Phantasus*—the principle of that part or side of the poetic quality which belongs equally to poetry and to prose, which Thackeray shows in both, and which goes hand in hand with his unerring truth to nature and reality.

'Fantastic' has a good many senses in English, and they differ from each other pretty widely. There is the fantastic which is simply not real; and the fantastic which is reality sublimated, or at least adorned and partly transformed by that higher Fancy which need not be distinguished from Imagination. The first, though it need not necessarily be so, is very frequently prosaic only; the second can hardly be other than poetic. And it is this fantasy (though one would, in consequence of the ambiguity just referred to, hardly call him 'fantastic') that was always with Thackeray. There was a good deal in him, though it found no affected or apparently obscure expression, of the quality which, whether fully recognizing it or not, Johnson, when he borrowed the term from Dryden, called 'metaphysical' in the seventeenth-century writers. His subject, his handling of it, his very phrase, always suggested something else to him —and is often, if not always, made to suggest something else to the reader. Perhaps this is the reason or one of the reasons why he has never been really popular. You can obtain no credit for profundity by admiring him: he looks so like a simple matter-of-fact John Bull. You cannot, on the other hand, really enjoy him without possessing some not inconsiderable familiarity with literature, the old liberal education and associations, a pretty wide range of sympathies, and a sufficiently alert intelligence which is not disconcerted and 'put off' by being required to glance after his zigzags of associated suggestion.[1] Nowhere, perhaps, are these qualities of his shown better than in the *Roundabout Papers*; but they are shown in a form which, in a way, prepares the reader for something of the kind, and therefore they are less likely to puzzle or annoy than in the novels, where they are less expected, or the early works, where they are more mixed and less consummate. If a person, having by happy or unhappy accident read no Thackeray, wished to decide at once whether he should like him or not, I should recommend the *Roundabouts*; and if the result was favourable, then I should send him to the beginning of the Oxford edition.

I was reproached, more or less mildly, for not saying more about Thackeray's *drawings* in these chapters, on their first appearance. The reason was given in the second—that I cannot here boast of any technical knowledge of the matter. But I do not think that many people can have taken greater delight in them than I take. In the earliest examples the want of teaching is visible even to me. The *Snob* drawings and even those in the *National Standard* are of the curious 'blocky' kind that we know in Hood, whose work very likely did influence Thackeray. Then the effect of the Paris *atelier* begins to show itself, though always with the limitations noticed in the remarks above referred to. These appear least of course in designedly grotesque sketches of outline only: a letter-*croquis* of the artist, who

[1] It has been hinted above that this is probably a cause of dislike more common than usually admitted. Thackeray's expression looks very simple, but it has almost infinite depths in it; the expression of some writers looks fascinatingly complex, and has very little depth at all.

has slipped on a slide and is regarding the universe with the countenance natural to such an occasion, was once offered in a catalogue for eighteen guineas for which I would willingly give eighty—if I had them to give. Very many, too, of the small initial-drawings appear to me almost faultless—and the *humour* of the pencil is almost equal to that of the pen. It is when he attempts regular figure-compositions of some size and elaboration that the *numb* seems, and then not always, to come on his fingers. The actual drawing is not seldom 'out'; the composition itself is liable to be wooden and inappropriate; the faces lack not merely fashion-plate comeliness, but (what is much worse) individual and vivid expression. The numerous passages, both in his books and in his letters, where he expresses his full sense of this, have also been referred to. Yet it must be a rather peculiar taste which feels any satisfaction when the pencil is handed over to Millais or Walker. With Doyle or Leech it might be different. But the fact is that Thackeray's 'letterpress' (a word which always pleases me) does not really want illustration—it has (in his own words misused) 'its own candles' with it: and his drawings do not want letterpress—they speak for themselves. Yet in that speech there is something—not absolutely necessary for comprehension of the text, but still always in harmony with it, and adding immensely to the pleasure of the reader and to his comprehension of the writer. Prose, verse, and pictures—no one of the three could be spared from what the Greeks called the ἑρμη-νεία—rather insufficiently translated by some 'style'—the self-expression and self-interpretation of Thackeray.

No survey of the work of a great writer on the present scale—especially no survey of work so shot and mottled with personal colour as Thackeray's—would be complete without some remarks, fuller and rather wider-ranging than those in the first of these chapters, on his personality. I never knew him—I am not aware that I ever even saw him, though I was much in and about Kensington from 1850 to his death. But I have since known many people who did know him; and for the last thirty years the infallible searchlight of private letters, published by this person and that, has been more and more freely turned upon him. Now this is even of more value than the later spoken testimony of third parties.

It is well known that this last was not invariably favourable to Thackeray. Those who loved him loved him very much. But his daughter—and if, as Miss Rossetti says, 'There is no friend like a sister,' there certainly appears to be, despite the experience of Servius Tullius and Lear, no such loyal defender as a daughter —herself says, 'I suppose some people disliked my father'. They certainly did; and what is more, not a few of those who actually liked him, seem to have done so with grudging and 'by allowance'. It has even been said to a '*w*ash neophyte' who expressed sorrow that he had *not* known the object of his admiration, 'You are much better off as you are', or words to that effect. The 'rubs' seem to have been taken in various places. The 'bitterness' of which Mr. John Blackwood speaks in an excellent testimony after Thackeray's death, seems to have been one great occasion. His contemporaries (except intimate friends of more than usual wit, like Mr. Venables) do not seem to have detected the 'sentimentalism' which has been a later reproach. But even they appear to have been sometimes offended by his 'infatuations' (as they called them) for particular persons, and by his (as it seems to me) delightful interest in wine and dinners and harmless pleasures of various kinds. The fools of a certain type thought him not sober and serious enough—too fond of puns and misspellings and high jinks in life and literature. The fools of another were offended by his occasional severities of speech and outbreaks of temper. In fact, as he never suffered any kind of fool gladly, so neither did any kind of fool suffer him without a certain discomfort. Now, most of us contain something of some kind of fool.

Yet he has given a very sufficient key to his character in all his work, at least from the *Hoggarty Diamond* onwards, while his letters not merely supply the key, but open the lock, and display, with hardly its most secret drawers excepted, the whole cabinet. To expound Thackeray fully would be to write a *New Anatomy of Melancholy*. The causes of his melancholia were, no doubt, to some extent external. He was an instance of the not very uncommon combination of great capacity for work with a most profound loathing of compulsory work; and, partly by his own faults and follies, but much more, it would seem, by the faults and follies of others, he was at the very outset deprived of the income which would have made it possible for him to work or not, as he pleased. This was very likely our gain; but he would have been less than human if he had thought it his. He had singular ill-luck in his first attempts at making literature a profession—the branches broke under him, and the steps crumbled, as they do in a bad dream. He attained domestic happiness, only to lose it by a worse stroke than that of Death itself. For years even after this, he had not only the trial—how trying to an intensely nervous nature those who do not understand can never be made to understand—of picking up a livelihood from day to day, from hand to mouth, by bits and scraps and orts—but two great aggravations of this trial. He must have known that he was not doing himself full justice; he must have known that others were not doing him even the justice that he deserved. He was one of the greatest men of letters in Europe— with Tennyson and Carlyle he made up the trinity of greatest men of letters in England. And in 1845—on the eve of *Vanity Fair*, and after half a dozen things which, however imperfectly accomplished, were works of genius, if ever such works were—Macvey Napier, an official steward and inspector of literature, made quite sincere, polite, and respectable inquiries as to who Mr. Thackeray was? When he did achieve, he must have felt to the full Johnson's famous sentence to Chesterfield. It was late; he was alone; and he was weary. Nor, though nobody was ever further from Wertherism or Byronism or any other of the numerous cosmopolitan and polyglot synonyms for 'pose', does he ever seem to have recovered, save in fits and glimpses, the 'joy of living'. Though the last three or four years of his life, at least, were certainly passed in something like a Land of Beulah, he never seems to have clung to life, or shrunk from death, in the very slightest degree. Except in the case of actual saints and martyrs, and of sufferers from some great bodily or mental agony, I never remember reading about any one so little 'loath to depart' as Thackeray.

This could not come from, though it might be encouraged by, merely external causes of the kind mentioned—and it certainly did not. That Thackeray was, by nature, one of Aristotle's σφόδρα μελαγχολικοί there can be not the slightest doubt. The obviously autobiographical passages in *Pendennis* and *The Virginians* would be enough, if the whole context of the *Works* were not more than enough. And the conviction is driven home by all sorts of curious by-evidence. It is the sense of *proximus ardet*—the terror of the misanthropy into which melancholy so easily slips—which makes him such a hanging judge to Swift. The celebrated 'cynicism' is the harder, and the equally celebrated 'sentimentality' the more melting mood of this melancholy.[1] The puns and the cacographies, the little gastronomical diversions, and the flittings to Brighton and Paris, are its palliatives and its allopathic drugs. And in the higher ranges of humour it supplies exactly that tendency to 'feel in earnest while thinking in jest' which is perhaps the only approach to a satisfactory definition of humour itself and which is due to a friend and house-inmate of his own, Miss Anne Evans, who had the living embodiment of it often before her.

It is not mere paradox to say that this temperament is less difficult to live constantly with (though it may be that too if it lives with the wrong people) than to live with, or to meet, occasionally. For it is essentially a temperament of moods; and the Goddess of Chance cannot be trusted always or often to adjust these moods to other people's at the particular time. But assuredly it is not necessarily, or even probably, an unloving, and it should not be an unloved one. To Thackeray's good qualities almost every page of his works—certainly nine hundred and ninety-nine pages out of a thousand—will bear witness; and the witness is confirmed externally. 'Kind' is the adjective most frequently used of him by

[1] It is probably not worth while to say any more about these two silly 'tickets'. If, when the literary cant of the day on the whole turns to sentimentalism, a man is accused of being a cynic, and if, when it turns to anti-sentimentalism, he is accused of being a sentimentalist, it is pretty certain that *omne tulit punctum*.

those who knew him best. His generosity is unquestionable; and there is absolutely no trace of 'bad blood' in him, though he certainly did, at a bad time of journalism, acquire some of its bad habits, and was long before he got rid of them. His utterances on religion (at least ecclesiastical religion) and politics are something rather trying, not because of their purport, but because of a certain irresponsible and amateurish character about them which makes one wish that, knowing so little about these matters, he had held his tongue.[1] When you have, comparatively late in life, to borrow a Bible from the Carlyles in order to read (apparently for the first time) the Books of Joshua and Judges, it would surely be wise to let your opinions on theodicy mature a little.

But contrasts are of the essence of the melancholious temperament, and occasional irreverences—mostly ignorances likewise—of expression do not interfere with the fact of the immense reverence which was the citadel of Thackeray's mind, and the vantage-ground of his outlook on life. For here there was no ignorance, but, on the contrary, an astonishing and miraculous knowledge. And such reverence, with such knowledge, saves at once satire from being mere snarl or mere sniggle, and sentiment from being mere sentimentality. When they put some of our modern analysts above him, it makes me think of a story told in somebody's *Memoirs*—of an amateur in mechanics who used to carry some half-finished brass-work in his pocket, and take it out to file at odd moments, thereby setting his friends' teeth not a little on edge. Thackeray does not do this; he only gives

[1] 'It is very well known that religion and politics are perfectly understood by everybody; as they require neither study nor experience', says Chesterfield with admirable gravity—availing himself, it is true, of an earlier utterance of Swift's, but pointing and polishing it.

you the perfectly finished and infallible watch. When they say, 'Oh! but Balzac?' the answer is quite easy. Balzac's men and women are what Frenchmen and Frenchwomen would or would not like to be, or what they think they ought or ought not to be; Thackeray's men and women are what Englishmen and English-women are. Nor is there any mere insularity; for exceed-ingly cool admirers of his—or rather scarcely admirers of his at all—have admitted that if there is a perfect sketch of a 'foreigner' anywhere in the whole literature of Europe, that sketch is Paul de Florac. In fact, there is something uncanny in his perfect mastery of humanity.

The two most famous of the unfavourable judgements[1] passed on him by men who may count as his peers in the wide sense, are Carlyle's, that he was 'not a strong soul', and Matthew Arnold's, that he was not a great writer. They require somewhat different treatment. The first cannot be met with a simple contradiction. Carlyle's judgements, splenetic and one-sided as they often are, seldom or never can be so met. In a certain sense Thackeray was no more a strong man than the Sage of Chelsea himself—it may be even less. There was nothing still or stoical about him. But perhaps we are rather in need of a moral Longinus to point out that strength is not mere solidity or stolidity, not mere absence of weakness. And the concomitant allowance

[1] Of the accusation of another distinguished but exceedingly un-critical contemporary—that Thackeray is a 'meat-fly' who settled on and disgusts us with life—it can hardly be necessary to take serious notice. But I think I have seen a variant and probably a derivative of this complaint, which is even more curious if less extravagant—that the author of *Vanity Fair* 'makes us discontented with ourselves'. Now one had thought that to do this was to confer about the highest benefit possible. At any rate the person who wishes to be self-satisfied may be left to his desires, which are extremely likely to be granted, in spite of the teasing teeth of any troublesome Titmarsh.

'big, fierce, weeping', is remarkable, for it at least excludes littleness, and cowardice, and Voltairean snigger. Moreover, it has to be remembered that this character was written ten years before Thackeray's death; and when, though his fame was made, his fortune, such as it was to be, was still only beginning. Yet the chief demurrer to this judgement must always be that already advanced. Is mere absence of emotion, not merely a good thing, but *the* good thing? If it be, we must no doubt rule Thackeray out of the strengths of England. He will find himself in the company, for instance, of Swift, of Johnson, of Burke, of Nelson, not to mention his critic. It is just possible to imagine worse company.

As to the other complaint of his not being a great writer, I think we may, without any disrespect to its author, pass it by somewhat summarily. Mr. Arnold was in many ways different from Thackeray—in none, perhaps, more different than in his attitude to contemporaries, which was nearly always grudging, though I do not believe that this was due to any want of generosity. It is almost enough first to ask on what canon of greatness Thackeray is disqualified, and when the canon is produced to disqualify it at once as an inevitable consequence of its operation. It hardly matters whether we take 'writer' in its more limited sense as concerning 'style' or in its wider as extending to invention or choice of subject and to application of treatment. If fertility that is inexhaustible and variety that is infinite; if phrase that is at once utterly personal to the user and utterly suitable to the subject—if these things, and many others which have been pointed out, will not make a great writer, why, perhaps Thackeray is not one. But in that case one is driven to borrow from Miss Carolina Wilhelmina Amelia Skeggs, and ask where a great writer is to be found?

I remember having, some thirty years ago, delight of battle for at least an hour by, and not far from, Kensington clock, on the subject of Thackeray, with the late Mr. Henley. At last, apropos of exactly what I have forgotten, I happened to say, 'And this, you see, is because he was such a gentleman'. 'No', said Henley, 'it is because he was such a genius.' 'Well', I said, 'my dear Henley, suppose we put it, that it is because he was such a genius who was also such a gentleman.' So we laughed and shook hands and parted. And really I am inclined to think that these words were, and are, 'the conclusion of the whole matter' about Thackeray.